ArtScroll History Series®

Rabbi Nosson Scherman / Rabbi Meir Zlotowitz

General Editors

THE "FINAL SOLUTION"

A CHASSIDIC DYNASTY'S STORY

Published by

Mesorah Publications, ltd

IS LIFE

OF SURVIVAL AND REBUILDING

by **Laura Deckelman**
as told by **Rebbetzin Chana Rubin**

FIRST EDITION
First Impression … May 2000

Published and Distributed by
MESORAH PUBLICATIONS, LTD.
4401 Second Avenue / Brooklyn, N.Y 11232

Distributed in Europe by
LEHMANNS
Unit E, Viking Industrial Park
Rolling Mill Road NE32 3DP
Jarow, Tyne & Wear,
England

Distributed in Israel by
SIFRIATI / A. GITLER
10 Hashomer Street
Bnei Brak 51361

Distributed in Australia and New Zealand by
GOLDS BOOK & GIFT SHOP
36 William Street
Balaclava 3183, Vic., Australia

Distributed in South Africa by
KOLLEL BOOKSHOP
Shop 8A Norwood Hypermarket
Norwood 2196, Johannesburg, South Africa

ARTSCROLL HISTORY SERIES®
THE FINAL SOLUTION IS LIFE
© *Copyright 2000, by* MESORAH PUBLICATIONS, Ltd.
4401 Second Avenue / Brooklyn, N.Y. 11232 / (718) 921-9000 / www.artscroll.com

ALL RIGHTS RESERVED
The text, prefatory and associated textual contents and introductions
— including the typographic layout, cover artwork and ornamental graphics —
have been designed, edited and revised as to content, form and style.

No part of this book may be reproduced
IN ANY FORM, PHOTOCOPYING, OR COMPUTER RETRIEVAL SYSTEMS
— even for personal use without written permission from
the copyright holder, Mesorah Publications Ltd.
except by a reviewer who wishes to quote brief passages
in connection with a review written for inclusion in magazines or newspapers.

THE RIGHTS OF THE COPYRIGHT HOLDER WILL BE STRICTLY ENFORCED.

ISBN:
1-57819-519-5 (hard cover)
1-57819-520-9 (paperback)

Typography by CompuScribe at ArtScroll Studios, Ltd.

Printed in the United States of America by Noble Book Press Corp.
Bound by Sefercraft, Quality Bookbinders, Ltd., Brooklyn N.Y. 11232

*This book is dedicated to my dear
husband and children*

Table of Contents

Introduction

EBBETZIN CHANA AND HER HUSBAND, GRAND RABBI
Menachem Mendel Rubin, the Muzsayer Rebbe, *shlita*, are
among the unsung heroes of World War II. Their triumph
over Hitler and his evil collaborators, *yimach shemom* (may their
memory be erased) is a story of *miseras nefesh, yiras Shamayim* and
undying *bitachon* in our Creator.

The time my husband and I spent with the Rubins, compiling
information and looking at old pictures, was very precious. As the
Rebbetzin told me her life story, I listened intently to every word so
as not to miss a single detail. I painstakingly tried to empathize
with her sorrowful memories even though I knew it was impossible to do so. No one but the victims of the Holocaust could ever
understand what it was like or how it felt to be victimized by the
Nazis, who wanted to destroy their victims for no other reason
than their being Jewish.

When I began to write the book, I tried to put myself in the
Rebbetzin's place and to see the world from her eyes, starting with
her innocent childhood years in Selish, Czechoslovakia. The book
is written in first person, so in a sense, I had to "become" Rebbetzin

Chana and tell her story the way she would. I shared her tears when her revered father, Rabbi Chaim Horowitz, *ztk"l,* was taken away from her, and felt her bitter-sweet joy of standing under the *chuppah* with her *chassan.* I sensed the unbearable tension during the slow cattle car journey to Auschwitz-Birkenau, and her confusion as her husband and mother were separated from her at the Birkenau platform. Her struggle to survive in the death camps and to find her husband and other surviving relatives after liberation ran the gamut of emotions, from hope to despair to hope once again. Rebuilding her life took every ounce of strength and determination she could muster. The book, also tells the story of the miraculous survivalof her husband their closest family members. It should be read and reread to serve as an inspiration to all of *Klal Yisrael,* who, through the ages, have been the targets of those who want to destroy us.

Our memories of the Sunday afternoons at the Rubins' *heimishe* Brooklyn home, working on the book while enjoying the Rebbetzin's home-baked Hungarian cakes, will remain etched in our memory. Their stories of inner strength and *bitachon* were refreshing and enlightening. Throughout the years, the *kesher* between the Rubins and us grew, and we were *zoche* to partake in several family *simchas* together. I am grateful to Hashem for providing us with the opportunity to know them. Finally, I would like to express my gratitude *and hakoras hatov* to the siblings of Rabbi Rubin for their contribution and participation in this project.

Acknowledgments

I would first like to express my *hakoras hatov* and deep appreciation to *HaKadosh Baruch Hu,* the Holy One Blessed be He, for enabling me to complete this book. May this manuscript serve as a lasting tribute to the millions of Jewish victims who died *al kiddush Hashem* during the Holocaust, and to those who survived and had to rebuild their lives from the ashes of Nazi horror.

There are many wonderful people I would like to thank for helping me to see this work to completion.

Mr. Sender Schwartz introduced me to Rebbetzin Chana Rubin, the Muzsayer Rebbetzin. From that initial meeting, the seeds of this book were planted and have since blossomed beyond my expectations.

Rabbi Shimon Finkelman, a noted ArtScroll author, submitted our manuscript in its earlier draft to Rabbi Nosson Scherman and Rabbi Meir Zlotowitz, General Editors of ArtScroll/Mesorah Publications. I am grateful to Rabbi Scherman and Rabbi Zlotowitz for believing in this book and agreeing to publish it.

I would like to thank Rabbi Scherman for helping me to develop the format and style of the book. His understanding, patience and advice inspired me to persevere, even during the most challenging and trying moments of this project. May this work return substantial dividends on his investment.

Rabbi Avrohom Biderman, project coordinator, and his talented staff did a superb job in weaving together the diverse strands that go into the production of a beautiful ArtScroll book. The typesetting and layout was done by graphic artists, Avrohom Kay, Sholom Rosenson, Esti Weinberg and Hindy Goldner. Eli Kroen designed the book's evocative cover. Worthy of note is how esthetically unique the cover is because of its portrayal of the triumph of the Jewish spirit over Hitler's futile effort to obliterate any living remnant of *Klal Yisrael*. Eli's artistic talents enhance the visual power of this work.

My deepest, most heart-felt appreciation goes to my editor, Mrs. Nina Ackerman Indig, whose polished literary style shines in all of the books she has edited for ArtScroll. The job of an editor is often underrated. Editing is a grueling, tedious task which involves scrutinizing each page, or rather, each sentence of a manuscript, for accuracy and consistency in grammar, spelling and punctuation. Mrs. Indig also worked painstakingly to ensure the consistency of the story itself. Her keen insight and professionalism are to be commended.

The time I spent working with Mrs. Indig proved to be a profound educational experience. She taught me the intricate skills of editing which I will be able to apply in my future works. Personally, I found it a pleasure to work with her, and I hope we will be involved in future projects together.

Rabbi Yaakov Bender, Rosh Yeshiva of Yeshiva Darchei Torah/Mesivta Chaim Shlomo in Far Rockaway, has followed the progress of the book from its inception. As any author knows, writing a book can sometimes be an arduous task, with occasional setbacks and disappointments. Rabbi Bender's charisma and words of *chizuk* gave me the *koach* with which to continue, and complete a project which, at times, seemed as if it would never come to an end. I owe him a tremendous *hakoras hatov* for all of the support he has given me.

Since Rebbetzin Rubin and I live a considerable distance from one another, it was not always convenient for me to drop off and pick up revised manuscript material. Therefore, I thank Rabbi Daniel Szojchet, *z"l*, Rebbetzin Dicha Shapiro and Rabbi Yisroel Kleinman from the bottom of my heart for their untiring efforts in helping Rebbetzin Rubin and me to successfully complete our correspondence.

Mrs. Ethel Kosoff gave time out of her busy schedule to translate and explicate various Holocaust related documents written in Yiddish. Rabbi Chaim Weiser, a talented linguist, translated phrases in Yiddish and provided me with the correct spelling of pre-war Hungarian towns and cities. R' Michoel Weinstein, Rabbi Yisroel Kleinman and Rabbi Moshe Lubart were also instrumental in translating Hebrew and Yiddish material for the book.

A special note of appreciation goes to Mrs. Anne Ritholtz, Mrs. Zelda Volk, and Mrs. Judy Resnick for their interest in reading sections of the manuscript and critiquing the material.

Hakoras hatov to Rabbi Mordechai Finkelman for offering me his sage advice on various chapters of the manuscript and for editing and revising passages containing Hebrew and Yiddish.

My friend and colleague, Dr. Gerald David, took a special interest in the book and offered me support throughout the duration of the project. His input was very much appreciated.

Another friend and colleague, Mr. Richard Landres, offered constructive advice on a section of the manuscript's content and grammar. I wish to thank him for all of his help.

A close friend, Mrs. Miriam Bergos, lives 6,000 miles away in *Eretz Yisrael*, having made *aliyah* with her family, and yet, remains close in my heart. Before she left for the holy land, she lived a few blocks away from me. We were practically sisters; I saw her or at least spoke to her practically every day. Her enthusiasm and uplifting words of encouragement when I was working on the manuscript warmed my heart and *neshamah*.

I would like to extend my deep appreciation and *ahavah* to all of my friends at Yeshiva Darchei Torah, Mesivta Chaim Shlomo, and Simcha Day Camp, as well as my friends in the Far Rockaway / Five Towns community. Their interest in the book, as well as their encouragement and support mean a great deal to me.

My wonderful husband and life partner, Paul, stood by me every step of the way, encouraging me to complete this lengthy project, despite the occasional setbacks and delays. His unconditional support injected me with the *koach* to keep moving forward: not to become discouraged when I occasionally had to take a few steps back. His professional advice, brilliant insights and his extensive knowledge and expertise of world history, particularly the events of World War II, contributed tremendously to my work. He also spent many hours proofreading my chapters, offering constructive suggestions and assisting me in making revisions.

My children were also very supportive during the project. They showed a great deal of interest in the subject material, and continually cheered me on. As the years passed, our (then very young) children accompanied us on our visits to the Rubins where they felt very much at home. The Rubins enjoyed our children's company and candidly answered their questions about Chassidic life in prewar Europe and the harrowing war years that followed.

My husband and I were very moved by the *ahavah* Rabbi and

Rebbetzin Rubin displayed toward our daughter, who suffers from autism. Rabbi Rubin would often give her a *berachah*, and the Rebbetzin would shower her with affection. I have no doubt that our daughter, in her own way, remembers and appreciates every moment that she spent with the Rubins.

My children's patience, as well as my husband's, is to be applauded, especially during the crucial years when I was writing the book. Sometimes I would have to shut the door and literally block out everything around me for hours at a time in order to slip into the Rebbetzin's world and write her story as if I had lived it. May Hashem repay their kindness and understanding with much *hatzlachah, simchah* and *berachah* in the years ahead.

Laura Deckelman
Tamuz 5760

Preface

I T IS UNCOMMON FOR A CHASSIDIC REBBETZIN OF A DISTINGUISHED dynasty to write a book, but, because I am an eyewitness survivor of the Holocaust, *rabbanim* and Torah historians have urged me to provide a written testimony of what happened to me, to my family, to my husband's family, and to the European Jewish community during those horrendous years. I, too, feel that it is imperative to relate our experiences. Although a great many Holocaust books have already been written, I hope more accounts are still to follow, because every story is unique and there can never be enough told about the European *Churban* (destruction) of our era, its interpretation, and the great miracle of surviving — the *nes* of *hatzalah*.

I personally testify before the Heavenly Court and before all those who read this book that the information contained herein is true. I was there; I saw it all with my own eyes; my own body suffered. I was one of those captured by the Germans and their Hungarian collaborators in Selish-Sevlüs, Hungary. Along with my fellow Jews, I was cruelly forced into a ghetto, then later marched to a train, pushed into a boxcar, and transported to Auschwitz-Birkenau. From there, I was sent to several other death camps, enduring marches during which thousands of innocent victims died. With the help of the A-mighty I survived, was liberated, and eventually built a new life in America with my husband, Grand Rabbi Menachem Mendel Rubin.

Until recently, reliving and telling my story was painful. Often, my children and grandchildren would ask me about my experiences during the war years: *What was Auschwitz really like? What did Hitler do to you? Why did he and they do it? What happened to your parents?* — and so on. My response was to relate brief, scattered episodes of my personal experience. But what was I really accomplishing by doing that? I was not fulfilling my sacred obligation to provide my family with an unabridged account of what really happened.

Our friend and neighbor, Rabbi Avraham Klein, *z"l*, the Tornalyer Rav, told us that every Pesach, during the *sedarim*, he felt an obligation to recount to his entire family not only the story of *yetzias Mitzrayim*, the Exodus from Egypt, but *yetzias* Auschwitz as well, and urged us to do the same. My husband, however, believes it is preferable not to disrupt the festivity of the *seder* by discussing the tragedy of the *Shoah* (Holocaust). He wrote a *teshuvah* (responsa) in which he advocates designating the twentieth day of the month of Sivan as a day on which all *shuls* and schools should emphasize the *Churban* of European Jewry, as well as the *nes* of the survival of the Jewish people as individuals and as a nation.

I came to the realization that the only way I could tell my whole story was to have a book written on the subject. My husband, the Rebbe — a scion of a distinguished rabbinical family and, like myself, a Holocaust survivor — agreed that we must put our first-person testimonies into the public record, a mission that could be achieved only by producing a written document. I am greatly indebted to him for his advice and supervision of this project.

Indeed, my husband told me that he had already thought of recording his story of survival in the 1980's, when he was scheduled to undergo serious surgery in New York City's Memorial Hospital. As he was about to be anesthetized, a nurse recognized him from two previous visits and exclaimed, "It's you again!" Suddenly my husband was troubled by pangs of conscience demanding why he had not yet told his story.

Although by the grace of the A-mighty my husband survived the operations, it was to be some years before we got down to the serious business of actually recounting our ghetto and concentration-camp experiences. At that time, when we were approached with the idea of producing a book on this subject, one rabbi even quoted the *Rosh Yeshivah*, R' Avraham Pam, who said, "If you want a reliable story, ask the Muzsayer Rebbe and his Rebbetzin."

We decided that the time had finally come to bear witness. I would tell my own story, as well as that of my husband, and along the way also recount the experiences of other family members who were caught up in the European *Churban*. I would tell the stories of those innocent martyrs who, tragically, did not survive, and those other relatives who, thankfully, did.

Once this decision was reached, our friend, Mr. Sender Schwartz, a member of our *shul*, introduced us to the Deckelmans, who were to put in several years of hard work collaborating with us on this project. I dictated my story to Mrs. Laura Deckelman, who wrote the book and, in the process, became my dear friend. She listened to my experiences with sensitivity, insight and understanding, and spent endless hours transcribing, compiling, editing, revising and writing the manuscript before submitting it to Mesorah Publications. I am greatly indebted to Mr. Paul Deckelman as well, for sharing the project with his wife.

The day I commenced the task of retelling my memories for public consumption, I sat down with my husband and began talking into a tape recorder. When the tape was played back, the full impact of what we were doing hit me with a jolt: my words were being recorded for posterity! Both the Rebbe and I felt that we had to document our experiences. The terrible secrets that the German-Austrian Nazis and their apologists and fellow travelers wanted so ardently to cover up, bury, hide and forget had to be revealed to the world by yet another survivor. So the Rebbe told me, "Record your concealed thoughts out loud. There are certain things regarding which *daas Torah* says, 'The more and the louder, the better.' This applies to your story." I decided to have this book written now in English rather than in *lashon hakodesh* (Hebrew) or Yiddish. The primary language for many in our younger generations today is English. Furthermore, English is a universal language, and I want people the world over to be able to read and comprehend what we lived through.

Yet in order to truly convey what happened, new words would have to be added to the dictionary. The barbaric, brutal behavior of the Nazi German government has no precedent in history. On Shavuos, we read the lyric poem called *Akdamus* which says: "If all the seas were ink and all the reeds were quills, it would still not suffice to describe the Torah." By the same token, the *Churban* of European Jewry and the degree of the crimes committed against the Jews are almost beyond description, and the breakdown of democracy and civilization to the subhuman level to which they sank is beyond comprehension.

I hope and pray that what I am doing is correct. I must ask for forgiveness if I have inadvertently omitted mention of anyone whom I should have included in this work. I also wonder if I can do full justice to the story itself. Is there any way I can fully describe the tyranny and criminality of the Nazis, or what we felt, experienced, or saw with our own eyes? Can I adequately put into words the horrible scenes I witnessed: the twisted limbs of those who threw themselves against electrified fences; the tortured bodies dropping one after another into the muddy earth; the filth which surrounded us wherever we went; the flames spewing the ashes of our martyred brethren into an angry sky? How can I fully describe the putrid odors which penetrated our nostrils, the noxious smells emanating from the crematoria and the decomposing flesh of the innumerable martyred innocents? How can I commemorate the lives and deaths of the beautiful children that the subhuman SS burned? How can I describe our broken hearts as we were brutally and mercilessly torn from our loved ones? How is it possible to fully and completely recount the constant psychological and physical torture we were subjected to minute by minute, both in the concentration camps and on the death marches?

It is generally true that when a witness to an event does not tell the whole story, he fails. Yet, regarding the *Churban Beis HaMikdash* (the destruction of the Holy Temple), we find that the degree of the disaster cannot fully be expressed — but we must recount whatever we are capable of. The same should hold true for *Churban* Europe. Therefore, despite the difficulties in trying to convey the sense of the Holocaust to those who did not actually witness it, we must make every effort to do so. When Moshe *Rabbeinu* spoke to the Israelites after the Exodus from Egypt, he said, "… lest you forget the things that your eyes have beheld … and make them known to your children and your children's children" (*Devarim* 4:9). This is exactly what we must do: to tell our children and everybody else exactly what we saw with our own eyes, and how we interpreted it, and the miraculous survival.

I would like to conclude with an incident that I witnessed in *Konzentrationlager* Stutthof. Among us were a mother and her 13-year-old daughter who managed to remain together in the camps. I didn't know their names but I remember that the mother completely devoted her every waking moment to her daughter. Although a walking skeleton herself, the mother always shared her meager ration of food with her child. One day, the daughter was extremely hungry and wanted more than her mother could provide. At that point, perhaps sensing her own impending demise and inability to further care for her daughter, she looked straight into her daughter's eyes and said, "With the A-mighty's help, you will survive, but you will badly need a new mother." The tears of both the mother and her daughter did not dry after that. When, saying *Selichos*, I recite the *pasuk*, "A–mighty, put our tears in Your flask," I remember those tears in Stutthof.

Over 50 years have passed since then. Despair turned to hope as the remnants of the *Churban* continued with their lives and rebuilt a proud Torah generation. Today there are (*kein yirbu*) thousands of Jews living in the United States, Israel, Europe and other places around the world, survivors and rebuilders.

The tears of Stutthof are replaced daily by tears of happiness every time we stand under the *chuppah* (marriage canopy) or attend a *bris, opsherin, bar mitzvah, siyum, vort, sheva berachos* or other memorable *simchah* of our children or grandchildren. We, the survivors of the *Churban,* and all of our future generations, *iy"H,* are living proof that Heaven makes all the final decisions; hence, *The Final Solution Is Life*: *A Chassidic Dynasty's Story of Survival and Rebuilding.*

Rebbetzin Chana Rubin
of Sighet-Ropshitz-Muzsay

CHAPTER 1
Nightmare Before Our Eyes

Selish Ghetto, Hungary: Erev Shabbos,
Friday, June 5, 1944 / Sivan 5704

Farewell to
Selish-Szöllös[1]

"JEWS, OUT!"

I had barely rubbed the sleep from my eyes when the Hungarian gendarmes, supervised by the German SS, ordered us to evacuate our homes and line up outside. Our time had come to be transported out of the Selish ghetto.

With fear in his eyes, my new husband, R' Menachem Mendel Rubin, the Muzsayer Rebbe, placed his two pairs of *tefillin* (phylacteries) back into the *tefillin* bag and packed them inside his rucksack. My mother, the revered Rebbetzin Hesse Teitelbaum-Horowitz, *zk"l*, and I quietly double-checked to make sure that we

---

1 Called "Sevlüs" while under Czechoslovakian rule, the town's name was changed to "Szöllös" [in Yiddish, "Selish"] — its name before World War I — after the Hungarians took it over years later.

had what we needed for Shabbos, while my husband ran downstairs to the basement to dig a hole in which to hide our most valuable possessions. His eyes brimming with tears, my husband gently placed the last unpublished *sefer* (book) of my departed father, *ztk"l*, inside the hole, along with some jewelry — precious family heirlooms — and sealed the opening as well as possible.

We were never to see those priceless items again. After our deportation, our gentile neighbors ransacked the apartment and basement — as they did to the other Jewish homes in the ghetto — and discovered the valuables. We can only surmise that the thieves stole the jewels — the items of lesser value — for their own personal enjoyment, and used my father's precious *sefer* — of infinitely greater value to us — for scrap paper, or even discarded it right away. Years later we were to speculate that had we buried the items in the nearby Jewish cemetery, our treasures might have remained intact. The looters would never have thought to search there for buried valuables.

Other families sharing the house with us in the ghetto were also preparing to leave, as were the hundreds of others confined within the ghetto. The cruel irony of this situation was that I had grown up in this very house. For the other families forced to share our home with us, it was just a stopover until the next transport. For my mother and me, this place had once been our *rebbishe* home, and was now filled with a lifetime of sweet memories.

We bore no resentment toward our fellow Jews who had been forced into our home by the SS and the Hungarians. However, we resented the casual, almost easy way the uniformed gendarmes swaggered through what was truly and legally our house. They ordered people about arrogantly, knowing that no one would dare oppose them or even protest. Yesterday's enforcers of law and order had, seemingly overnight, turned into lackeys of the criminals. People all over the world should take this lesson to heart and remember it well!

Life and conditions in the ghetto were tense, yet somehow we did not truly realize the danger we were facing. One day, the alarming bellows of the town crier informed us that we were to be transported out of the ghetto and "resettled." Soon afterward, we were given our departure date. Just a few days prior to our departure, the gendarmes told us that we would be taken to a labor camp called Könyörmezö, located somewhere in Hungary, where working conditions were not too difficult, and where families would be permitted to remain together. In reality, there was no such place. This fiction was part of the Great Lie invented by Eichmann. (In Hungarian it means "the place of mourning.")

Upon hearing of our destination I felt relieved, believing that I would not be separated from my husband and my esteemed mother. We felt that no matter how difficult the conditions in the labor camp would be, with the help of the A-mighty we would survive.

Now, as we gathered outside, the morning sun blazed into my sleepy eyes and I could already feel the humidity rising on that early spring morning. Nobody thought, however, that this would be the last day we would see the sun rise over the Jewish community of Selish — although the gentile townspeople were well aware of this.

We formed lines and were led by the gendarmes through town. A menacing gauntlet of townspeople lined the sidewalks and streets, many jeering and shouting insults as we walked past. Others, however, expressed sorrow and disbelief.

At first we hesitated, shocked by the hostility of the crowd, but our captors prodded us forward. Trying not to look at our tormenters, willing ourselves not to look back, we marched on.

Soon we found ourselves at the train station. Before us stood a long chain of cattle cars, and before we knew what was happening, the gendarmes started pushing us inside them.

We could not have known that this was just the beginning of our nightmare. I found myself being swept along with the crowd and tried desperately to hang on to my mother. Fragile as she was, I was afraid that she would be trampled by overwhelmed, frightened people, so I grabbed her arm and tried not to let go.

The intoxification of hatred was visible in the eyes of both the SS and the gendarmes as we were manhandled onto the train. Stumbling and nearly tripping on the ramp leading into the cattle car, I gasped for air as I felt myself being hemmed in by the hordes of people behind me. I was later to find out that there were approximately eighty of us in each car. Even when cattle traveled in these cars, they were treated more humanely! Not too long ago, we were true, good, decent citizens of Hungary. All of this had changed overnight, and suddenly we were being herded into cattle cars by human animals.

As more people crowded in, panic overcame me. Wedged tightly among so many others, there was no room for us to stretch out and achieve any measure of comfort. From a distance, I saw others whom I knew from the *kehillah* (community), including my closest friend, Parry, and some of my other girlfriends from home. I wanted to call out to them, but they seemed so far away.

A single young Hungarian soldier, dressed in SS attire, was assigned to our car to maintain order. He was no more than 18 or 19 years old, yet his frozen expression and forbidding demeanor caused my blood to run cold. Carrying a loaded rifle, he took his place on a small wooden platform outside the car.

THE DOORS TO THE BOXCAR WERE SLAMMED SHUT WITH A CHILLING clang. After what seemed an eternity, we felt a sudden jerk and the

The Death Train

train began to move. I grabbed my mother's hand. It was icy cold, even in the stuffy boxcar. I realized that my mother's lips were moving almost imperceptibly; she was saying *Tehillim*. Her inner strength and *bitachon* (trust in the A-mighty) never faltered, even inside this hell on earth. This was the mentality of the "Sigheter House" in which she grew up.

As the train began to rock monotonously, my thoughts temporarily wandered off. It had only been a few weeks since my husband and I had been wed in Nyir-Bator, Hungary. Despite the turmoil of the outside world, even with German troops in full control of Hungary, we had remained sheltered within our

Chassidic lifestyle and circle. However, after a tense Pesach, we were brutally taken away from our homes and locked into a local synagogue. From there, we were dragged off to the Selish ghetto, and now we were being held under gunpoint in a crowded, sordid boxcar. All sense of civilization, humanity and logic had died overnight ... It was impossible to comprehend all that was happening ... except to say that is must be a Heavenly decree.

There was virtually no light in the boxcar. Except for the meager rays that streamed in through a small, barbed-wire-covered opening in the wall, it was dark and gloomy inside. Soon our eyes adjusted to the darkness, and my husband and I devised a way of keeping track of time by monitoring the varying degrees of light and darkness in the freight car.

At one point, the train stopped in Kashau, Hungary, and in the station a bucket of water was passed into our car. Try to imagine sharing one bucket of water among eighty thirsty people, including small, whimpering children! Now try to imagine that this was all the water we were going to get for many hours.

From what I could see through the open doors, the trainmasters seemed to be moving unusually fast in their efforts to rush us out of the station. It became obvious that the train we were on had to make way for the arrival of the following one, whose piercing whistle sounded from afar even as we pulled into the station.

Suddenly we heard soldiers marching quickly toward us. Seconds later, an SS man stormed into our boxcar. Smirking diabolically, he shouted, "*Juden!* From now on, you are under the control of the German Government! You are to take orders only from us!" We had been smuggled over various borders until we were handed over to the Germans!

Deathly silence ensued as the officer continued to glare balefully at us. Suddenly shouting into the silence, he promised to shoot on the spot anyone trying to escape. Then he wheeled on his polished heel and stalked out as abruptly as he had entered. In his wake rose the stunned murmur of the captives inside the cattle car.

Thoroughly shocked, my husband and I gazed numbly at one another. Tears welled in my eyes as I turned to my delicate mother, who also remained silent. What words could come at a time like this?

The doors to the boxcar were slammed shut once again, this time by our new German captors. A piercing whistle split the silence, and our train briskly pulled away. I shuddered with dread. What lay ahead?

ALTHOUGH THE UNBELIEVABLE NEWS THAT WE WERE NOW UNDER direct German rule left us in a state of utter shock, we remembered

Shabbos in the Boxcar

that it was *erev* Shabbos. We would have to usher in the Shabbos as best as we could under the circumstances. Long afternoon shadows had already formed inside the car, and we could tell that the sun had begun to set. It was time to welcome *Shabbos HaMalkah*, the Shabbos Queen.

There were various problems to deal with. The first was the dilemma of how to *daven* (pray) and to recite *Kiddush* in such an unsanitary environment. It is against Jewish law to *daven* in the midst of excrement and filth. My husband decided that we could observe Shabbos in the boxcar because the tiny corner in which we were wedged was relatively clean, although he cautioned us that it would be improper to mention the A-mighty's holy Name in such generally impure surroundings.

In the history of our family this was the first Shabbos when candles were not lit, even though we had brought some with us. My mother and I beckoned in Shabbos, as did many of the other women. Together, my mother and I recited part of the *berachah* (blessing) without mentioning the A-mighty's name. The holy words were mixed with our tears, and soon the car was filled with the sobs of other pained, heartbroken women and children. I located the two loaves of *challah* that my mother and I had baked prior to our journey, and I gently took them out, taking great care not to break the soft braided loaves which were still intact.

A horrible thought came to mind. We were the last transport out of Selish. For the first time in hundreds of years, Selish was void of Jews except for the few remaining in a bunker or two. All of the *shuls* would be empty; the Torah scrolls and prayer books would remain idle.

Throughout the night I dozed fitfully. Towards dawn, I came fully awake and found myself bathed in perspiration. This, combined with the unpleasant damp morning chill inside the boxcar, made me shiver. I worried about my mother becoming ill under these appalling conditions and prayed to Hashem to have pity on her.

The men were *davening Shacharis*. Just as on the previous evening, each man *davened* "alone" in his own cramped "Eastern Wall seat." Afterwards my husband told me how difficult it had been to stand for the *Shemoneh Esrei* in the midst of the wall-to-wall crowd, adding that it helps to keep one's eyes closed in such a situation.

Although by this time we had precious little water left for quenching our constant thirst — let alone for washing — my mother poured a bit of her tiny portion over her fingertips as required prior to reciting her morning prayers.

Sometime during the afternoon, my mother recounted a very special story which filled us with hope. When her father[2] was a small child, one Pesach he accidentally blew out a candle during the *seder*. His mother worried over the incident and said that snuffing out candles in such a fashion was not a good sign. The boy's father, my great-grandfather,[3] turned to his wife and told her not to worry; he promised that their son would someday light "nice candles." And so he did. Years later, my grandfather fathered two special sons, my two uncles: R' Chaim Hersh Teitelbaum, the Sigheter Rebbe, *zt"l*, and R' Yoel Teitelbaum, the Satmar Rebbe, *zt"l*, who were both to become leading lights in their generation.

In the *zemer* for *motza'ei* Shabbos we say, "*B'motza'ei yom menuchah, hamtzei le'amcha revachah* (At the end of the Sabbath,

---

2. My grandfather, the famous *Rav* of Sighet, known by his *sefer* (book), *Kedushas Yom Tov*.
3. Known by the name of his famous *sefer*, *Yetev Lev*.

bring your people relief)." Never before in our lives had this prayer been so important.

Sunday, June 7, 1944

AFTER ANOTHER SEEMINGLY ENDLESS NIGHT OF SEMICONSCIOUS slumber, I peered through the dark at my gruesome surroundings.

The Awful Truth Revealed
Soon I saw the first rays of sunlight poking through the small, barred opening in the wall of our freight car. I heard others moaning in pain or crying in discomfort as they slept. Some who had just risen began to recite the morning prayers.

Overnight, the odor in the boxcar had become even more unbearable and nauseating than before. In later years my husband often said that the Germans had purposely planned to make the journey as miserable as possible in order to ensure that the weak Jewish victims died swiftly in the cattle cars. For those who managed to cling to life, the horrible conditions were so degrading that many of the imprisoned travelers lost their dignity and their will to resist.

My husband stirred and awoke in this sea of human misery. Sickened by the horrible odors in the cattle car, he opted not to put on his *tefillin* because of the filthiness of our surroundings. I remember him telling me that he would not put on the *tefillin* until we got off the train and were in a clean environment again. Little did we know that the Germans would take away his *tefillin* — along with everything else we owned.

Next to me, my mother was also awake. She looked extremely pale and was moaning softly. Tears filled her weary, bloodshot eyes. Although extremely weak and uncomfortable, she did not complain.

My husband managed to remain next to me on the other side, and he leaned back against a corner of the cattle car. His face, usually filled with vigor and energy, looked ashen and sallow. Beads of perspiration formed on his forehead, and I could tell that he, too, felt acutely uncomfortable. As frightened as I was, however, it was still a comfort to know that my husband was by my side. We tried to uphold and strengthen one another's morale and belief, although we felt impending danger ahead.

By this time, the muffled whimpers of babies and children were coming from various sections of the car. Soon the whimpers turned into wails, and the din became nerve-racking. As my husband and I exchanged glances, I saw an expression of sadness and concern in his eyes. Those poor children! How could their parents adequately explain to them what was happening? Many were too young to understand.

One of our fellow travelers on this terrible journey was the *tzaddik*, the *Dayan* of Üjlak. At some point that morning, my husband noticed that the *Dayan's kapote*, or robe, had become tattered and torn to shreds in the crush. I noticed this also and, concerned about the *Dayan's* dignity, reached into our baggage to find another *kapote* for him to wear. By chance, I pulled out my husband's beautiful new Shabbos robe, which was decorated with colored flowers. It had been a wedding present, and was still brand new.

The *Dayan* of Üjlak wore that robe when we arrived in Auschwitz. He was still wearing it when he was led into the gas chamber building to hand over his soul to Heaven.

It is written that the clothing of a Kohen helps to forgive our sins. One can similarly say that the *kapote*, along with countless other *tzitzis* and clothing of other *tzaddikim*, testified in Heaven to the crimes of the Nazis and their collaborators, and to the noble martyrdom of their victims.

At some point that morning, our train stopped at a station where we were able to discern a sign with the words *Nove-Sacz* printed on it. We were in the famous town of Sanz, Poland, where my husband's great-uncle, R' Yitzchak Tovyeh Rubin, *zt"l*, and his famous great-aunt, Rebbetzin Chumele, *z"l*, had lived. If only we could have stood before the tomb of the Sanzer *tzaddik* for a few moments!

Harsh reality hit us as we understood the implications of the words on the sign. My husband turned pale. Why were we in Poland when we had been told that we were going to remain in Hungary? Were our captors perhaps taking us to a work camp in Poland instead of to Könyörmezö?

My husband was peering through a small crack in the wall and talking to someone outside. Moments later, he crumpled down next to me. His face was ashen. My heart began to pound.

Almost choking on his words, my husband said, "I just learned that we are not being taken to a work camp, but to an extermination camp in Poland."

Shock waves shot through me.

"What are you talking about?" I whispered back, not wanting my mother to hear. "Whom did you hear that from?" Wide-eyed with fear, he replied, "I heard this from the teenage Hungarian guard who has been riding with us. He was outside on the platform and saw me looking out through the small opening. Our eyes met, and he approached me. He spoke to me in Hungarian through the little crack."

Haltingly, my husband disclosed what had been revealed during this conversation. The sneering guard told him that all of us had been fooled. The reality was that in a few hours, our train would pull into the extermination center known as Birkenau (which, we would later learn, was a subcamp of Auschwitz). All of us would be reduced to ashes by nightfall.

"What are you talking about?" I protested. "You don't believe him, do you?"

"Yes, I do," he replied. "I have every reason to believe him."

"Why?" I asked in astonishment.

"It was the expression in his eyes," answered my husband. "The intense hatred he feels for me, for you, for all the *Yidden* (Jews) on this train is very obvious; the way he smiled when he said we would all be reduced to ashes before nightfall."

"This is too incredible, too bizarre to believe!" I argued. "Why would they tell us that we were being sent to a work camp and then send us somewhere else?"

"They lied to us and we all fell for it, perhaps because we wanted to believe we were not in such imminent danger," my husband explained.

I wondered whether we were the only Jews on the train who

possessed this horrifying information. I felt the blood draining out of my face.

Tears were streaming down my husband's cheeks. He turned to me and said, "We must say some final words to one another now because I don't know if we will ever see each other again once we leave this train."

I could barely speak after hearing that. My entire body was shaking, and I found myself sweating and in tears.

We opted not to tell my mother, although we suspected that she might have instinctively known of our impending danger because of the intense way she was saying *Tehillim*.

Many piercing questions plagued my mind. How could this have happened? How could I, a young Chassidic *kallah* (bride) from a *rebbishe* background wind up in a filthy cattle car bound for a death camp?

I vowed that no matter what lay ahead for me or my family, I would never forget my *yichus* (lineage) and Chassidic upbringing. The words and lessons taught me by my esteemed and holy parents would remain with me and I would come to rely on my memories to get me through whatever lay ahead. Above all, I would remember that Heaven rules over all of us, even in the cattle car, in that place called Birkenau, and anywhere else the SS might take us.

My husband nodded and began to quote from *Tachanun*."*Habeit miShamayim u're'ei, ki hayinu la'ag vakeles bagoyim* ... (Hashem, look down from Heaven and see: although we are degraded, debased and insulted, taken like sheep to the slaughter ... we don't forget Your holy Name, Hashem!)"

CHAPTER 2
My Early Years

I WAS BORN IN THE TOWN OF SIGHET, ROMANIA IN THE EARLY 1920'S, but was raised in the town of Selish, Czechoslovakia. My parents named me Chana after my grandmother, the wife of the

A Special Gift From Heaven

Sigheter Rebbe known by his Chassidic work, *Kedushas Yom Tov.* At the time of my birth, the very religious couples in Europe were married with *chuppah* and *kiddushin,* by a rabbi. In these circles, the Jewish marriage ceremony was all that mattered; it was even considered preferable not to obtain a civil marriage license. Consequently, the offspring of Chassidic couples carried the last names of both mother and father, rather than the one conventional "legal" last name — that of the father — which is mandated by civil marriage. Therefore, my full maiden name was Chana Teitelbaum-Horowitz. My mother carried the Teitelbaum name from the Teitelbaum dynasty, and her name was followed by my father's name, Horowitz.

*The Rebbetzin's grandfather's Ohel, with
the Rebbetzin speaking to Polish caretakers*

הקמת מצבה
באהל דזיקוב

גילה ורעדה. זיינען מיר מודיע
ז אי״ה אָנפאָנג אלול הבע״ל
וועט פאָרקומען אַ הקמת לוחות
מצבה אין אהל פון די דזיקוב׳ער
צדיקים זי״ע ועכי״א.

אליעזר ומינא פרעסער
(212) 435-3048

אדות פרטים בבקשה לפנות
לאדמו״ר גאב״ד מונשאי שליט״א
● (212) 375-9292 ●

*A tombstone and memorial plaques in the ohel in Dzikov,
as well as the announcement of the unveiling of the plaques*

A city shul in Selish, now a pharmacy

My father, originally from Galicia, Poland, was R' Chaim Meir Yechiel Horowitz, *zt"l*. He was the *Av Beis Din* (Head of the Rabbinical Court) of Ranziv, Galicia, and was known as the Ranziver Rebbe. The Horowitz name originates with the Melitzer-Dzikover Rebbe of the great Ropshitzer dynasty (the Polish name for Dzikov is Tarnobdze).

My mother, Rebbetzin Hesse Teitelbaum, *zk"l*, was born in Sighet, a town in Marmarosh, Romania. She was the sister of the renowned Sigheter Rebbe, R' Chaim Hersh Teitelbaum, *zt"l*, and of the famous Satmar Rebbe, R' Yoel Teitelbaum, *zt"l*.

The Teitelbaum dynasty was — and is — one of the most famous in the Chassidic world, tracing its roots back to its founder, R' Moshe Teitelbaum, of Üjhel, Hungary. Born in 1759 in Galicia, R' Moshe ultimately settled in Hungary and became a founder of Hungarian *Chassidus*, one who was greatly respected by many European *gedolim* of the time. The first R' Teitelbaum was considered a giant in Torah learning and authored various Chassidic and

My father, R' Horowitz ztk"l, myself (as a child) and one of our Chassidim, Mr. Kestenbaum a"h. The photo was taken in Kneutiz (country place)

halachic volumes using the name *Yismach Moshe*, the title of one of his works. His descendants continued to live up to the standards of piety and scholarship their ancestor had established.

After their *chasunah* and *sheva berachos*, my parents settled in the Galician town of Ranziv, but were forced to move during World War I along with other famous Galician *rebbe'im*. They established their new residence in the town of Selish, Czechoslovakia.

The years passed, but much to their sorrow, my parents were unable to bear children. Although worried about their situation, they strongly believed that if the A-mighty willed it, they would be presented with a child and would see fruit on their tree. Besides *tefillos* (prayers), my father and mother undertook various folk remedies, and to everyone's astonishment, a miracle finally occurred. Much to her surprise and delight, my mother discovered that she was expecting a baby after 22 years of marriage.

My mother'sadvanced age caused both my parents a great deal of anxiety at first. But as the months passed uneventfully, their fears

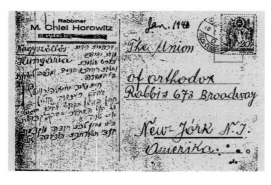

were gradually alleviated. However, my mother still insisted on delivering in Sighet, Romania, her birthplace as well as the town in which her father was buried, just in case of complications. My mother stipulated that were she to die during or following childbirth, Heaven forbid, she would want to be buried near her father.

On a steamy, scorching summer day the midwife was summoned to my mother's bedside, and several hours later she helped deliver my mother of a beautiful baby girl. The birth went smoothly, and my arrival was celebrated by Chassidic families throughout the country. When my esteemed parents proudly returned to Selish with their famous new daughter, people greeted them with extraordinary *simchah*.

Written by my venerable father, ztk"l,
to the Agudas Rabbanim in N.Y.C., in 1940

As well as bringing joy to my venerable father and ecstatic (but tired) mother — both past 40 — the birth of this long-awaited child was especially welcomed by our family's distinguished Chassidic dynasties; rumors even circulated that each group took credit for enabling this miracle to occur.

In the Chassidic book, *Kadosh Yisrael*, the writers claimed that my birth was the *mofes* of my great-uncle, the Vizhnitzer Rebbe, R' Yisrael Hager, *ztk"l*.[1] My father once recounted a story at a Friday night *tish* in Mihaly-Falva, Romania,[2] about himself and my mother and the Vizhnitzer Rebbe, R' Yisroel Hager.

One Shabbos, when my father's uncle, the Vizhnitzer Rebbe, R' Yisroel Hager, was in Selish, my parents invited him for Shabbos morning *Kiddush*. During a *l'chaim*, my father asked the Vizhnitzer Rebbe to give him and my mother a *berachah* for a son. R' Hager looked at my father and replied, "Wouldn't you be satisfied with a daughter?" At that moment my mother entered the room, and my father excitedly told her, "I think my uncle just promised that the A-mighty would send us a son." The Vizhnitzer Rebbe corrected my father with a smile, saying, "I am a man of my word!" A short time later, my mother learned that she was expecting.

Mr. Lipa Lefkowitz from Oradea learned in my uncle's yeshivah in Sighet. He said he witnessed his Rebbe, R' Chaim Hersh Teitelbaum, the Sigheter Rebbe (also known as the *Atzei Chaim*), promise my mother (his sister) that she would be blessed by Heaven with a child.

Early Childhood Memories

AS AN ONLY CHILD BORN UNDER THE CIRCUMSTANCES DESCRIBED above, my parents focused all their loving attention on me, and the three of us formed a special bond. However, since I was an only child and a daughter, my father and I had a special closeness all our own. He enjoyed taking me for walks, telling me stories, and singing to me in his own special way. Also because I was an only child, there were a few instances when my father treated me as if I were his son. When I was around 3 or 4 years old, he and I would

---

1. The husband of my grandmother's sister, who was one of the Dzikover Rebbe's daughters.
2. The residence of my husband's elder brother, the renowned R' Yosef Mayer Rubin, *ztk"l*.

walk hand in hand to *shul* on Shabbos morning. Once inside, my father would steer me to his regular seat at the Eastern Wall in the men's section and allow me to remain by his side as he prayed.

I felt special standing by his side in *shul*. I watched him *daven* with Chassidic fervor, sometimes with tears in his eyes as he gazed Heavenward. It was a special treat to be with my father in *shul*, although we occasionally received quizzical looks from others. When people asked my father why I remained with him in *shul* instead of going with my mother, he would smile and answer, "To me, Chana is like a son."

I was also treated "as a son" on Pesach nights. During our two *sedarim*, my father would call upon me to ask the Four *Kashes*. Since it is customary at a Chassidic *seder* for a boy, not a girl, to ask the Four Questions, I felt somewhat awkward with the honor. Every year I would assume my special place at the table and proceed. From the other end of the table, I would see my father nodding in approval, his brown eyes twinkling as I continued. When I finally concluded, he would graciously express his appreciation before he answered the questions.

My father spent his days learning Torah, telling Chassidic stories, writing *sefarim*, and advising and blessing people. He would often pore over his books or write until the early hours of the morning, saying that Torah learning took priority over sleep. A descendant of the Dzikover dynasty, its members famous for their strong voices, my father was a powerful singer and made use of his melodious voice for *tefillah*. He was also famous for his Chassidic stories, and often after *Shacharis* he would relate various anecdotes to his fellow congregants about past *tzaddikim*. These fascinating narratives were passed down to him from his forefathers. To this day, a number of survivors from Selish still remember many of my father's stories and the deep impressions they left.

Among Galicians it was customary to sip steaming hot tea from a glass through a sugar cube held in place between the teeth. Night and day my mother would keep a samovar simmering over the flame on the portable gas stove so that we always had hot water available for tea, especially because my father found it relaxing to drink tea while learning. Often after meals, my father would retire to his study, and it became part of my routine to bring him his tea without his actually asking me for it. My father would always smile warmly to show his appreciation.

I have fond memories of my father tucking me into bed at night. He would ask me to recite the *Shema* and, upon my doing so, would smile at me with a sparkle in his tired eyes. After quietly leaving my side, my father would extinguish the light and walk out of my room, leaving the door slightly ajar so that I would not have to sleep in the dark, since light chases away evil. The dim light from the hallway would filter into my room along with the gentle creaking sounds of the floorboards as my mother and father softly walked about the house. I enjoyed the silence and stillness of our house at night and the warm feeling of security, tucked under my covers, knowing that my parents were nearby.

I did not know my grandparents from either my mother's or my father's side. They had all passed away before I was born. Every year, my mother took me to visit their tombs, where a large crowd gathered from all over. *Zechusam yagen aleinu* — may their merit guard over us.

ALTHOUGH MY FATHER HAILED FROM POLAND AND REMAINED A Polish citizen while living in Czechoslovakia, he chose not to take us back to

Vacations   his homeland. Many Chassidic newcomers from Poland felt that Hungary was a safer place in which to raise daughters. The Polish Chassidic women were changing faster with the times and becoming more modern. My father did not want that kind of environment for me.[3] My father did not completely break his ties to Poland, however; he maintained his *rabbanus* and returned

---

3. That was the reason my father-in-law settled in Szaszregen, Romania, and my great-uncle, the Vizhnitzer Rebbe, settled in Oradea, also in Romania.

every summer to be with the congregation of Ranziv in Galicia.

My mother and I did not accompany my father to Poland during the summer; rather, we traveled to a town with mineral springs such as Bardiav, Czechoslovakia. Our small cabin was surrounded by tall trees, and every morning I would wake up to the pleasant sound of birds chirping. The view from our cabin was breathtaking, and after a leisurely, light breakfast, my mother and I would take a brief walk through the countryside. In the morning my mother usually took mineral baths, which were considered to be beneficial to health, while I played with Chassidic girls from neighboring cabins whose families were vacationing there. On hot days we would draw ice-cold water from the local spring and share a pitcher of the refreshing liquid under the shady trees. On *erev* Shabbos, my mother and I would extend invitations to other families to join us for the Shabbos *seudos* (meals).

My mother and I always returned to Selish at the end of the summer feeling rejuvenated and ready for the upcoming *yamim tovim* (holidays). My father usually returned to Selish after we were already home. We would anxiously await the telegram advising us of his arrival. Then, together with his followers, I would meet him at the train station where, looking healthy and invigorated, he always greeted me with the affection of a father who has only one daughter.

Shabbos in Our Home

R' YITZCHAK LURIA, THE GREAT 16TH-CENTURY TEACHER OF Kabbalistic mysticism, taught and wrote about the great and mysterious power attached to eating, and about how in each food there exist sparks of holiness, inserted by G-d at the time He created the trees

---

My uncle, the Satmar Rebbe, married the daughter of R' Horowitz, the famous Plancher Rav, when he was 17. At that time his father, the Sigheter Rav, was already gravely ill. Nevertheless, he still had it in mind to tell his young son, who was marrying into a Galician *rebbishe* family, not to move to Poland.

and the paradise in the Garden of Eden. According to the writings of Kabbalah, from which many of the Baal Shem Tov's teachings later evolved, a pure, holy leader knows how to select the holier remnants of the food that have lain dormant from the time the Creator created them — and his followers deem it an honor and a *zechus* to eat at the same table and thus to consume some of that same holy food.

Based on this teaching, the Chassidic rebbe presides over his table, or *"tish,"* at which he eats together with, or in front of, his *Chassidim*. Besides eating, a physical act which becomes sublimated by thinking spiritual thoughts, singing *zemiros* (hymns) in praise of the A-mighty constitutes another part of the *avodah* of a *tish*.

Every Friday night, my father hosted his *tish* in our dining room and led the men in singing the *zemiros* for which Dzikov was famous. His beautiful voice served as an inspiration to all at the table, and everyone followed his lead with heartfelt enthusiasm. The effect of *nigunim* (melodies) and *zemiros* is well known; *Chassidim* know how to make use of melody and song to inspire the *neshamah* (soul) towards *emunah* (faith). The happiness barely contained within the walls of that room was contagious, and everyone was swept up by the feeling.

Meanwhile, my mother and I quietly ate our *seudah* (meal) in another room after seeing that the men in the dining room had settled in with their meal. On Shabbos afternoon after lunch, the women joined my mother and me for tea and cake.

During the week, my mother wore a *tichel* (head kerchief) and ordinary clothing, but on Shabbos she shone in her special white *shirtzel* (apron) and exquisite *stern-tichel* — a pearl crown worn on the forehead by European rebbetzins on Shabbos. Her holy face was radiant with an inner glow that I did not see during the week. As she lit the Shabbos candles every Friday night, the bright lights illuminated her lovely face, and the *kedushah* (holiness) of Shabbos permeated our home.

The girls school in Selish, in 1940. I am sitting in the bottom row, first on the left.

When I was of grade-school age, my parents chose not to send me to the local Bais Yaakov school. Their decision was influenced by the Sigheter and Satmar Rebbes' opinion that the Bais Yaakov schools of Czechoslovakia and Hungary were too modern, and thus inappropriate for Chassidic girls; that the influence of such schools would diminish the girls' sense of modesty and *yiras Shamayim* (fear of Heaven). Our local Bais Yaakov schools were also part-time; many religious girls in our area attended regular public school during the day, then went to Bais Yaakov in the late afternoon for *limudei kodesh* (religious studies). (By way of contrast, the same *rabbanim* who opposed the Bais Yaakov system of Hungary and Czechoslovakia viewed the Polish Bais Yaakov system, consisting of a full, all-day program, as a savior of *Yiddishkeit* [religious Judaism] among the young generation.)

The result of this opposition was that I remained at home and studied with private tutors, while many of my girlfriends, daughters of fine, religious families, attended public school during the day and Bais Yaakov later in the afternoon. It was a somewhat lonesome experience for me, staying home all day while my girlfriends attended school. The only time I was able to see them was on Shabbos and Yom Tov.

One year, after I had become a *bas mitzvah* at the age of 12, another Bais Yaakov school opened near our home. Many of my girlfriends were attending, and I asked my parents if I could go. Although my parents had some reservations, they agreed to let me go, not as a regular student, but to attend one or two *shiurim* (lessons) each week. The teachers were truly inspiring, and I came home excited about what I had learned.

I especially looked forward to *Shabbos Mevarchim* because that was when the Bais Yaakov school hosted its *Oneg Shabbos* (festive gathering on Shabbos). Every month, on the Shabbos preceding *Rosh Chodesh* (the first day of the new month on the Jewish calendar), a different girl was asked to deliver a thought on the *parashas hashavua* (Torah portion of the week). My topic was Pesach. I remembered feeling somewhat nervous making the presentation. However, my teacher and the girls later praised me for an enlightening speech. I returned home for the *shalosh seudos* (Shabbos evening) meal, excited to tell my mother and father about my successful presentation.

Dress Up Chasunos

MY FRIENDS AND I DREAMED ABOUT THE DAY WHEN WE WOULD BE escorted to the *chuppah* (marriage canopy). Even though most of us did not attend many *chasunos* (weddings) while we were growing up, our mothers and grandmothers told us about their weddings, and we marveled at every story.

We would hear about how the *shadchan* (matchmaker) arranged the *shidduch* (match) and about the preparations that went into making a beautiful *chasunah*. Our mothers and grandmothers would reminisce about their *tenayim* when, in front of family, friends and the community, the engagement would be made official by contract. They told us about the *chasunah* itself: about the *mesader kiddushin* (officiating rabbi) and the *kesubah* (marriage contract); about the people who recited the *sheva berachos* (seven blessings) under the *chuppah*; about the music and the elegant *seudah*. Then we would hear about the elaborate *sheva berachos* banquets, hosted by family or friends, that followed over the next seven days.

Was it any wonder that at age 14 or 15, when my friends and I got together on Shabbos afternoon, we spent many hours talking, giggling and daydreaming about the day when our turn to stand under the *chuppah* would come? We wondered who our *bashert* (intended) would ultimately be and where we would live. Would we remain near our parents or *mechutanim* (in-laws)? Or would we reside in a town which was distant from all family? We talked and dreamed a great deal because books and games appropriate for Shabbos, which are readily available today, were a rarity in Europe.

One particular rainy Shabbos afternoon, my friends and I decided to have a "pretend *chasunah*" in the house. As my mother was not entertaining company at the moment, she happily partook in our "*simchah*" (joyous celebration) and helped us dress up. We enjoyed planning our *chasunos* so much that this game became a regular Shabbos afternoon event. My friends and I took turns playing the parts of the *chassan, kallah,* (bridegroom, bride) and different family members. Four of the girls would act as bearers of the *chuppah*.

When it was my turn to be the *kallah*, I found the makings of the perfect wedding gown right in our linen closet. I wrapped snowy white sheets around the clothing I was already wearing and then reached further into the closet for a white cloth which I would use as my "*stern-tichel*." I then found a lace runner to use as a veil. My mother's drawers were filled with ribbons of different colors and styles, and she allowed me to select whichever ones I wanted to accentuate my "lavish" gown and crown. When my real wedding day came years later, I looked back on those wonderful Shabbos afternoons and felt well rehearsed for the main performance.

ONE SUNNY SPRING MORNING, WHEN I WAS 15 YEARS OLD, my parents received a letter from the Teitelbaums, inviting me to

A Special Visit to Satmar their house in Satu Mare, Romanian Transylvania, for a few days. This was the first time that I was invited without my parents. Evidently, my uncle and aunt felt that I was mature enough to travel alone.

Although I was excited about receiving a personal invitation, I had mixed feelings about traveling alone, something that girls in those days rarely did. Although this would be a great new adventure for me, I was also apprehensive. My mother sensed my apprehension and assured me that I would have a traveling companion to accompany me to Satu Mare and back.

On the day of my departure I met the woman my father had designated as my traveling companion. My mother accompanied me onto the train where, trembling slightly, I found my assigned seat. As my traveling companion sat down next to me, I looked out the huge window next to my seat and saw my mother waving to me from the platform one more time, then turning to walk away. The train whistle blew — what an exciting, happy sound it was to me! — and the engine began to generate huge amounts of steam. The jolt of the train's unlocking brakes made me jump, and before long, the train began moving. We were on our way. The trainmaster came around to check the passengers' tickets, and I felt my hand shake as I presented mine to him. After a while I settled down and soon, lulled by the rhythmic movements of the train, I dozed off.

Finally, we arrived at Satu Mare and the Teitelbaums' home. Rebbetzin Feige, the Satmar Rebbetzin, looked as majestic as ever and greeted me with her usual warm smile. Eagerly she inquired about the trip, my parents, and whether I was hungry or tired from the journey. We placed a call to my parents from a neighbor's house because even the Teitelbaums did not have their own telephone, a common situation in prewar Europe.

I unpacked quickly before joining my honored aunt in the dining room for tea and cookies. As I settled in, memories of previous visits bubbled up. In my mind the Teitelbaums' spacious apartment seemed larger than life, and I always enjoyed exploring the majestic rooms, one leading into the other. Some of their furniture pieces were huge and impressive — the plush sofa in the parlor, for example, and the polished oak dining-room table, chairs and china closet. I was also awed by the high ceilings of the house, the ornate chandeliers and the elegant drapes over huge windows.

I remembered how, when I was younger, I would watch the many *Chassidim* and other people coming to my uncle's house day after day, wondering who they all were. As I grew up, however, I learned that my uncle, the Satmar Rebbe, was quite an important man in the country and in the Chassidic world, and a leader of the United Orthodox Rabbinate. His fame as a Torah scholar and a holy man was by no means limited to Chassidic circles alone; there were non-Chassidic Jews as well who sought his advice or his blessing. On some occasions, even non-Jews, such as village officials or functionaries of the government from Bucharest, came to consult with him.

Rebbetzin Feige was (and still is) a fabulous cook and baker. Everyone from miles around looked forward to attending my uncle's Shabbos *tish*, which was accepted as a "*tish*" of holiness, not only to hear him say his *chidushei Torah* (original Torah thoughts), to share a *l'chaim* and to sing *zemiros* with him — but also to savor Rebbetzin Feige's *seudos* — from her golden, tender loaves of challah to the hearty plates of *cholent*, chicken, and noodle *kugels*, and the scrumptious, sweet fruitcakes and chocolate babkas served for dessert.

Rebbetzin Feige informed me that she had made arrangements for a Chassidic girl in the *kehillah* (community), one approximately my age, to visit me and to accompany me on walks around the neighborhood. Rebbetzin Feige was very health-conscious, and she saw to it that I enjoyed the benefits of fresh air and sunshine every day.

Sometime during the mid-morning hours my friend would walk over. After lunch, later in the afternoon, we would go outside into the courtyard or walk through the town, where we would see many of my uncle's *Chassidim* walking about in their *kaftans,* and women pushing baby carriages. Various stores, including a fruit market, a tailor shop and a bakery, lined the paved blocks. A few merchants milled about, trying to sell their products. Sometimes my companion would take me on a quick tour of the outskirts of the town. We talked about our families and our dreams for the future. We enjoyed each other's company and kept in touch, even after I returned home.

One evening I started to feel incredibly dizzy and nauseated. My body seemed to ache everywhere, causing me to moan in pain. My aunt checked my temperature, then rushed out of the room. Moments later she returned, explaining that she and my uncle had reason to believe that someone, possibly an elderly, childless woman, had placed an *ayin hara* (evil eye) on me!

The effects of the *ayin hara* were making me sick. My aunt told me that my uncle had prepared a remedy to wipe away the spell. I was to count backwards while my aunt dipped remnants of bread into water. Before long the remedy worked, and I began to feel better. I was able to sit up in bed, and soon felt my appetite returning.

How can one explain this phenomenon? Nowadays, when a child feels ill, his parents rush him to the doctor. In Europe, however, it was common to consider certain sicknesses the result of an *ayin hara,* which is mentioned even in the Talmud. When European-born people of my generation compare stories of their childhood, many discuss illnesses that were caused by the *ayin hara.* My husband, who was brought up in Szaszregen, told me that he remembered members of his family and others in the *kehillah* being treated with folk remedies. Every *kehillah* had people who specialized in mixing various herbs and other substances to create a potent remedy to treat the patient suffering from the *ayin hara.*

After that one awful night, I did not get sick again during my visit, and the rest of my stay with the Teitelbaums was very pleasant. All too soon it was time to return home. My aunt prepared a nutritious lunch for me to take on the train. Once again, I was provided with a companion for the journey.

My mother was waiting for me at the Selish train station when I arrived. Supper at our house lasted several hours as we caught up on each other's news of the last ten days. Later that evening I wrote a thank-you letter to the Teitelbaums. Finally I went up to my room, delighted to be sleeping in my own bed again.

No matter how good it is to be away, there is no place like home.

DURING THE 1930'S, A DARK CLOUD BEGAN TO LOOM OVER THE JEWS OF Eastern Europe, unlike any other in our history.

Days of Darkness Arrive
It was with both horrified fascination and a strange sense of detachment that European Jewry observed the events leading to the rise of the wild dictator Adolf Hitler. I was not even 9 years old when he grabbed power in early 1933. Truth be told, Germany seemed very far away, and I did not at the time give much thought to what was happening there.

Of far greater concern to people in our part of Czechoslovakia in those years were neighboring Hungary's demands for the return of Czech territory that Hungary claimed as its own. By March of 1939, Hungary and Germany together had virtually dismembered and swallowed up little Czechoslovakia. Hungarian troops occupied our Selish district and we became subject to their laws and authority.

We did not welcome this change. Almost alone in Europe, the Czech Republic had functioned as a democracy while it existed, and Jews enjoyed full civil and religious rights there. While we experienced some anti-Semitism from the non-Jewish population, it was not encouraged by the government. In contrast, official anti-Semitism had been worsening in Hungary for some years, with several political parties openly modeling themselves after the Nazis and demanding ever tougher anti-Jewish measures. New laws subjected Jews to employment quotas, property seizures and other forms of harassment.

Now we Czech Jews would suffer under those same unjust laws.

AS A POLISH CITIZEN, MY FATHER HAD A VISA WHICH ENTITLED HIM to live in Czechoslovakia. As long as the status quo held, and

Hard Times Ahead Selish remained part of Czechoslovakia, his visa was automatically renewed every two years. The situation changed, however, when the Hungarians took over our area of Czechoslovakia in 1938. Following the infamous 1938 Munich agreement, which stripped Czechoslovakia of the Sudetenland, Hungary silently dealt with Berlin to reclaim its "lost" territories and began strongly pressing its claim to those areas. Hungary and the Czechs held talks in Vienna at which Hitler's Minister, Joachim von Ribbentrop, and Italy's Minister, Count Ciano (Mussolini's son-in-law), acting as supposedly impartial arbitrators, awarded those territories to Hungary on November 2, 1938. Later, Hungary took over much of Transylvania (including Szaszregen) from Romania, helped by Germany's pressure on the Bucharest government. In return for this support of its claims, Budapest was later obligated to hand over thousands of Jews to the Nazis.

The impact of these political and diplomatic maneuvers hit us personally soon after the Vienna conference, when the Hungarian officials who assumed control over affairs in Selish refused to renew my father's Polish visa. Without an authorized visa, on alien soil, my father now faced imminent deportation to Poland.

Although life at home continued as usual, we now lived in fear and uncertainty over the future. Rumors circulated throughout various Jewish townships to the effect that Hungarian gendarmes would soon be arriving to deport Polish citizens, but nobody knew when this would happen, which town the gendarmes would strike next — or whether they would strike at all. My mother and I worried constantly about my father and his possible deportation. The Jewish authorities in Budapest and other cities did not involve themselves with this problem; it was a problem of the "Polish" Jews.

The dreaded moment came on Shabbos *Rosh Chodesh*, 30 Tammuz 5701 / August 23, 1941. On that day Hungarian gendarmes, armed with high-powered machine-guns, burst into town to round up the Polish Jews whose names appeared on their list of non-citizens. The Hungarian government had made a deal with the Germans to transfer 20,000 non-citizens to Poland.

My father and I were just getting ready to leave for *shul*; my mother had already gone on ahead. Suddenly we heard an unusually loud knock on the door. Our hearts stopped.

My father slowly opened the door and peered outside. Two big, burly Hungarian guards pushed him back inside and forced their way into our home. Looking directly at my stunned, fragile father, one of the guards shouted, "Pack a small suitcase and come with us to the train station! You are being deported today!"

The cruel significance of these words was lost on my father, who spoke only Yiddish, but he sensed the urgency of the situation. Since I spoke some Hungarian, I translated the gendarme's words to my father.

"Please, can't I have a little more time … an extension on my visa?" pleaded my father, innocently thinking in terms of the law and order which had prevailed in Hungary for the last thousand years.

"You must pack a bag and come with us now! Hurry!" repeated the gendarme harshly, proof positive that lawlessness now reigned.

They did not give my father time to think, time to contact my mother, his wife, who had already left for *shul*, time to say farewell to his loyal followers, time to do anything but go! My hands were trembling as I helped my father put a few things together. I packed some of his clothing and ran into the kitchen to get some food for his journey. Since it was Shabbos, I wrapped two *challahs* in a towel and included some other food items.

My father suffered from a chronic stomach condition, so I wanted to make sure he did not leave without his medication. Usually I knew where to locate the bottle, but now, in my panic, I could not remember where it was. I frantically searched the house. Without medicine to provide relief for his weakened stomach, I knew that my father could become quite ill, especially under severely stressful conditions such as those which now confronted him. I tried to calm down and remember where I had last seen his medication.

"Let's go!" shouted the impatient gendarme. Just then I located the medicine and stuffed the bottle into my father's valise. "Should I pack your *tefillin*?" I asked my father. "Yes," he responded. He would take his *tefillin* along. Although a Jew is not supposed to touch *tefillin* on Shabbos, my father had no choice in this particular situation. He was being forced to travel against his will, and when going on a long journey, a Jew must take his *tefillin*. I quickly added his *tallis* (prayer shawl) as well, along with several *sefarim*.

"Where are you taking me?" queried my father, turning to the gendarme, his voice quivering. I continued to translate.

"You're being deported to Poland!" the policeman shot back.

"Where in Poland?" asked my father.

"No more questions! Just finish packing and let's move out! You have a train to catch!" Fury and hatred blazed in the man's eyes.

The other gendarme, who had been standing by the door, now took out his watch and checked the time. Scowling menacingly, he began to pace back and forth, his body language reinforcing his partner's impatient orders.

Although only in his early 60's, my father appeared extremely weak and vulnerable at that moment. I wanted to somehow protect him. He had always sheltered me as a child, and now I wanted to help him. But how? Was there any way I could talk the policemen out of taking him away? Short of that, would they allow my mother and me to go with him so he would not have to face an uncertain future alone? I knew that I would have to act quickly, because at that moment, time was our biggest enemy.

"Why are you taking him?" I demanded, ignoring the possible danger to myself in challenging these two thugs.

"We have our orders!" snapped the gendarme.

"Can my mother and I go with my father to Poland?" I pleaded.

"No, absolutely not! Our orders are for your father only!"

Stunned silence reigned in the room for what seemed an eternity.

"Can I ... can I at least go with him to the train station?" I begged, choking on my words and fighting back the tears. "Very well," answered the policeman, relenting a tiny bit. "But we must depart now!"

I wanted to run to *shul* to inform my mother of what was happening, but the officer would not allow it. Vigorously he shook his head in a negative response to this final entreaty, and I felt myself go pale.

Tears filled my father's eyes. I am sure that at that moment he wondered whether he would ever see my mother or me again. What would become of my dear mother, the gentle *tzadekes* (righteous woman)? The poor woman was at that moment *davening* in *shul*, totally unaware that her life and her family were being destroyed.

The gendarme opened the door and, brandishing his rifle, motioned to us to step out. My father took one last look at his beloved home, so filled with happy memories of his cherished family and *kehillah*.

Whose pain was deeper — my father's or mine? Who could measure? Slowly, my father picked up his valise, turned toward the door and walked out, his hand gently brushing the *mezuzah* as he whispered a prayer. I followed him, accompanied by the two gendarmes. The door was slammed shut behind us, and we stepped out into the street.

Word had gotten out that the policemen had come for my father, and crowds of neighbors were standing outside or staring out their windows, pulling back the curtains to see what was going on. The only person allowed to say farewell to my father was the venerable Selisher *Av Beis Din*, R' Shlomo Yisrael Klein, H"yd (may the A-mighty avenge his soul!), an outstanding *baal middos* who was also our close friend. Aware of the danger my father was facing, he hugged him and gave him a blessing. (His only surviving son, R' Oyzer, today lives in Boro Park and we maintain a close friendship.)

The policemen pushed the spectators away and dragged my father to the train station. For a saintly person such as my father, the thought of being forced to travel by train on Shabbos was more agonizing than physical torture.

Remaining by my father's side during the long walk to the train station, I did what I could to comfort him, but what mere words could reassure a person at such a time?

Soon I began to find it difficult to keep up the pace forced on us by the gendarmes. I was young; how much harder it was for my fragile father to maintain the brisk pace all the way to the train station! His face turned a ghastly shade of gray-white, drops of perspiration formed on his forehead, and his breathing became labored. I feared that he might collapse in the street.

Finally we arrived at the train station. It is a great irony that prior to the Holocaust, train stations were generally places of happy anticipation. The arrival of a train signified the coming of a beloved relative, an important visitor, a great rabbi or, for a merchant, some long-awaited merchandise. But during the Holocaust, train stations became places from where Jews were deported, and the arrival of a train meant the beginning of a journey which usually ended in a place such as Auschwitz. That Shabbos it was past imagining that such a pretty place, with its neat benches surrounded by colorful flowers, would come to symbolize the introduction of so much unhappiness into our lives. It was from this station that my father would be kidnaped by international murderers acting under a make-believe form of "law."

The gendarmes finally allowed my weary father to rest. Pointing to a nearby bench, they ordered him to sit and wait until the designated train arrived. I rushed to his side and, under the watchful eyes of the gendarmes, sat down next to him.

Glancing around, I noticed some nicely dressed non- Jewish passengers standing or sitting on the same platform, waiting for the same train. Unaware of what was happening to my father, to our world, they looked happy and carefree as they chatted with their relatives or acquaintances on the platform. My world, however, seemed to be coming to an end.

No longer able to keep up a strong front for him, I sobbed

uncontrollably on my father's shoulder.

"Sh-h-h-h, my Chanale, don't cry, please don't cry," said my father gently. He sighed quietly. "We are believers in *hashgachah pratis* (Divine Providence). If this is Hashem's will, let's hope for the best."

I continued to cry on his shoulder.

"Chanale," he insisted, "instead of shedding tears for me, my darling daughter, I would like you to do something special."

"What is that, *Tatti*?"

"Please don't ever lose your belief in the A-mighty, even though I am being taken away, and remember to take care of your mother and yourself ... and pray for all of *Klal Yisrael* during this turbulent, uncertain period. It can only help, and your *neshamah* (soul) will feel uplifted. Will you do that for me after I leave, my Chanale?"

I noticed a slight glimmer of hope in his tired eyes as he smiled gently at me, almost as if his happiness depended upon my reply.

"Yes, *Tatti*," I answered, wiping away the tears.

"You will explain to Mama what happened and you will be a pillar of strength for her; she is a delicate lady," he continued. "You and Mama will need to take care of each other while I am gone. The *kehillah* will look after you both, and your uncle, the Satmar Rebbe, will temporarily take my place as your father until I return. Above all, I want you never to forget that the A-mighty is watching over us all the time, and that our destinies, come what may, lie in His hands. Don't ever doubt His intentions, no matter how much pain and suffering you may feel. Remain steadfast to your faith, my precious child."

"Yes, *Tatti*, I shall."

We sat quietly for a couple of moments.

"You'll contact us when you arrive at your destination, won't you, *Tatti*? Perhaps when we know where you are, we can join you." This was more in the form of a question than a positive statement — I was hoping against hope that I would somehow, somewhere, see my beloved father again.

"I don't know if that will ever happen, Chanale," said my father. "When I get to wherever it is that they are taking me, I will try to get in touch with you to let you know that I am safe. But it is all up to Hashem. Always remember what I am telling you now, Chanale, just … just in case …"

"I've always dreamed of you dancing at my *chasunah* …" I sobbed, tears streaming down my face.

My dear father had just started to say something when the piercing sound of a whistle in the distance interrupted our conversation. His tense body jerked, and we turned our heads to watch the dreaded train come down the tracks. Slowly, ever so slowly, the train moved in our direction, and I prayed that it would not come to a stop, for once it did, my father would be taken away — probably forever. But the train did eventually halt, and I felt my heart stop as the gendarmes came to forcibly escort my fragile father onto it.

I stood by my father's side for one last precious moment. Just before he was shoved onto the train by the Hungarian gendarmes, my father put his hand on my head and blessed me with the ancient words: *"Yevarechecha Hashem veyishmerecha* … (May Hashem bless you and watch over you …)."

"Bleib gesunt, stay well, my darling daughter," he said, tears rolling from his loving eyes. "Remember what I told you, and always carry those words in your heart — and in your soul."

Standing inside the train with the hateful, armed gendarmes on either side of him, my father appeared pathetically alone. Generally it was the Nazi system to take the rabbis first, and that is probably the reason that the other non-Hungarian Jewish civilians — the other victims of this first round of betrayal by the Hungarian government of its inhabitants — were not delivered into the crushing hands of the Germans at the same time as my father. Their turn, alas, would not be long in coming.

A few minutes later, the trainmaster blew the whistle and the train slowly started to pull out of the station, taking my beloved father away — far, far away — ultimately all the way to *Gan Eden*.

Smiling weakly, he waved good-bye to me from inside the train. My final memory of him consists of his sorrowful expression and that helpless wave.

Frightening thoughts filled my head as I stood on the train platform until the train was out of sight. I silently prayed that Hashem should help me find the strength and courage to face my frail mother. Slowly I walked back home, weeping silently.

Lost in thought and deeply in shock, I did not realize that I was finally approaching my parents' house, and would have to find a way to tell my mother the tragic news. Looking up suddenly, through my tears, I saw the blurry image of my sweet mother standing in front of the house, waiting for me.

She already knew. She had been told by the crowds of people who had seen my father taken away. Since then she had been suffering a double agony, fearing that the Hungarian gendarmes might have impulsively shoved me onto the train along with my father. We looked at one another for a moment, then clung to each other tightly and cried piteously in each other's arms, feeling the gravity of the situation, but not really aware of its true, final impact. I could feel my mother's tiny, fragile body trembling in my arms, and I tried to soothe her. We finally walked back into our house, looking at each other but saying nothing.

Through my hot tears, I saw many of my father's friends and other families in the *kehillah* waiting for me. They surrounded us and attempted to offer *chizuk* (encouragement). My mother had set *Tatti's* place at the Shabbos table before she left for *shul* that morning. We ate dispiritedly and *bentched* (recited the Grace After Meals), then my mother politely told our guests that we wanted to lie down.

Once we were alone, the house was incredibly silent. The sunlight streaming in through the front windows was suddenly too bright, and I drew the drapes. My mother wearily dragged herself to the couch. I quietly followed her, sat down next to her and held her hand. The two of us stared into nothingness; in our minds we could almost hear the precious moments ticking away and see the distance widen between us and *Tatti*, knowing that as each moment passed, he was being pulled farther away from us. It chilled me to the bone to think of *Tatti* being forced to travel on Shabbos, wondering what he could be feeling — or thinking — at that moment?

The rooms around me were empty, yet I felt my father's presence everywhere. Many loving memories of him at different stages of my life filled my throbbing head. Wasn't it just yesterday that I sat in his lap on that chair in the corner while he rocked me gently, singing Chassidic melodies? Wasn't it just last week that my father and I were seated at the dining-room table, talking about life? He had sighed and noted that I was growing up so fast — soon he and my mother would have to arrange a *shidduch* for me … There had been a twinkle in his eye as he said that.

Now I gazed at my mother, worried about her. She sat silently; she did not utter a word for the longest time. What was going through her mind? What could I say to try to ease her suffering somewhat, while dealing with my own pain at the same time?

The bottomless void that we felt in our house and our hearts that afternoon cannot be described adequately in words. Never in my wildest imagination did I envision what the house would be like without my father's glowing presence there — particularly on Shabbos. He lit up our home when he entertained guests at his Shabbos table, especially when he hummed his favorite Chassidic *nigunim* in his haunting, melodious voice or led his guests in singing *zemiros* on Friday night. My mother and I would be in the next room, listening to him. Tears of happiness often shone in my mother's eyes as she proudly listened to her husband.

After her long silence, my mother finally turned to me. Whispering through her tears, she asked me to tell her everything that had happened, from the time the gendarmes burst into our home until the time my father's train pulled away. I painfully described the scenes. "What were his last words?" she asked. I gently told her what he had said.

As soon as we found the strength, we began to say *Tehillim*, beseeching the A-mighty to keep my father safe from harm, and to bring him safely back home to us.

AFTER THE INITIAL SHOCK OF MY FATHER'S DEPORTATION HAD DULLED slightly, my mother and I still firmly believed that he would

My Rescue Journey to the Polish Border

return to us.

Days passed, but we did not hear from him. We also did not receive any news about him.[4] Perhaps it was more difficult than we had ever imagined for him to get in touch with us, or maybe he was in some kind of trouble.

Through the grapevine, we learned that there were non-Jewish men who could be hired to cross the border into Poland, look for exiled relatives, and smuggle them back to their families in Hungary. They usually worked under cover of darkness to minimize the chance of being caught. Had these paid rescuers been discovered in the act of returning exiled Jews, either by the guards on the Hungarian side of the border or by the German soldiers on the Polish side, they would have been summarily shot. But despite the danger, there was no dearth of gentile men willing to make extra money this way, even at the risk of their lives, and there was certainly no shortage of Jews willing to pay sizable sums to get back a loved one.

My mother and I were hopeful that we would be able to hire someone to bring my father back safely to our side of the border. We had already heard rumors that once Jews were taken to the other side of the Polish border, they were in danger. We feared for my father's safety.

While we were awaiting word of my father's whereabouts, word reached us that the Munkacher Rebbe, *HaRav* Baruch Rabinowitz, *shlita*, and his son — both of whom were Polish citizens — had also been deported to Poland. We learned that

---

4. At the same time, however, we did hear that our next-door neighbor, the venerable Belzer *Chassid*, R' Pesachye Klein, also a Polish citizen, had similarly been taken away.

R' Rabinowitz's mother-in-law, the Munkacher Rebbetzin, Rebbetzin R.P. Shapira, *H"yd,*(the widow of R' Chaim Elazar Shapira) had hired someone to find R' Rabinowitz and his son and smuggle them back over the border. Since my mother was elderly and unable to travel, it was decided that I alone would accompany Rebbetzin Shapira to the Hungarian-Polish border. I took along money and a basket of food prepared by my mother.

After traveling a few hours by car, we arrived at the border town of Yassin. We asked members of the *kehillah* for directions to the

The Rebbetzin of the Minchas Elazar of Munkach

border. At the border, I could see Polish territory off in the distance. A wire fence marked the frontier between Poland and Hungary, and here and there I could see guards on either side of the fence. A young man approached us and asked what we were looking for.

The earlier Munkacher rebbe, zt"l, R' Chaim Elazar Shapira, author of Minchas Elazar

The Munkacher Rebbe's son-in-law, HaRav Baruch Rabinowitz, zt"l

He startled me at first. What if he were one of the border guards, out to arrest anyone found sneaking around near the crossing? Much to our relief, however, he was not a soldier or a police officer, but a young, robust man, dressed in rugged clothing and boots. He explained that he was a Slovakian peasant, skilled in the ways of the outdoors and very familiar with the local geography, including, importantly, the various points at which the border could be crossed without attracting the attention of the border guards on either side.

"Is there someone you're trying to find on the other side of the border?" he inquired.

"Yes," I said breathlessly, "that's it exactly. There are several people we must find."

"Whom are you looking for?"

We told him, and it turned out that he was waiting for Rebbetzin Shapira.

"I have brought people over the border and have never been caught," he said confidently.

I asked him for more information about how he would cross the border, find my father, the Munkacher Rebbe, and his son, and bring all three safely over. He said that it would be tricky, but that it could be done.

"What is your final decision?" he asked tensely. "Time is short."

Rebbetzin Shapira and I left him for a few moments to speak privately. Could we trust him? Would he keep his word and bring back our family members? We decided that we really had no other option and hired him. Handing him a roll of money, we promised to pay him an additional fee once he brought the three men back, safe and sound.

The young man requested a description of the three men. I reached into my bag and handed him the most recent photo I had of my father.

The young man looked at my father's picture intently, closing his eyes once or twice as if to memorize the details and contours of my father's face. "He is a very distinguished looking man," he said.

Rebbetzin Shapira took out a picture of her son-in-law and grandson, which were also studied intently by the young man.

We sat in silence for a moment. The humid summer evening air was thick and hazy. The buzzing of insects in the surrounding thickets intensified the tension of the moment.

"How quickly might you find them?" I asked.

"I can't say," he replied. "Each situation is different. I can be on the Polish side of the border in a matter of hours. As quickly as I find them, I will bring them back to you. You must remain in town for a few days and wait right here, but only after nightfall."

"We'll wait for you here after nightfall, starting tomorrow night," we answered.

"Very well. Now we must end our meeting because we don't know who is within earshot. Turn away and walk in the other direction," he insisted.

I took one last look at him before leaving. "Please find them," I pleaded.

"Don't worry," he replied confidently. Those were his last words.

I was filled with high hopes, but was so nervous that I could hardly eat or sleep. Would the young man find my father? Could my brittle father keep up with the young peasant in the thickets? Suppose my father injured himself along the way by falling or stumbling over a hidden branch, or suppose the young man succeeded in finding them, only for all of them to be caught sneaking back over the border?

I shuddered over those horrifying thoughts, but remembered my father's reassuring words at the train station. The Munkacher Rebbetzin, Rebbetzin Shapira, and I both *davened* intently for the young man's success in his mission.

After sundown the following day, Rebbetzin Shapira and I returned to the same spot where we had stood with the young man we had hired. I strained my eyes to look past the border, hoping to see several male figures approaching the border site. My heart pounded every time I heard a noise in the brush. We sat on a tree stump and waited for hours. Much to our disappointment, the skies started getting brighter and the young man had not returned with our loved ones. With a heavy heart, I followed Rebbetzin Shapira back to the house where we were staying.

Another day passed, then another. Much to our sorrow, the young man failed to return. Discouraged and disillusioned, we finally left Yassin and returned to Selish alone and empty-handed. How could I tell my mother that our rescue attempt had apparently failed? It would break her heart.

One part of my mind clung to the slender possibility that perhaps the young man might still find him, and that my father would contact us. Much to my disappointment, no further attempts were made by anybody else to find him, a fact that remains troubling to this day.

Our friend Mr. Mann, *a"h* (*alav hashalom*, may he rest in peace), later told my husband that he had found a Hungarian officer who, for money, drove the Munkacher Rebbe and his son safely back over the border in his car. After his return, the Munkacher Rebbe spoke publicly about the mass murdering on the other side of the border, but only a few people believed his story.

JUST A FEW WEEKS AFTER MY FATHER WAS TAKEN AWAY, MY MOTHER and I left Selish to spend the fall *yamim tovim* with the Teitelbaums.

Glimmers of Hope Slowly Fade Friends and neighbors from the *kehillah*, who had been somewhat hopeful initially, remained silent now.

That Rosh Hashanah, as we spent many hours *davening* in *shul,* we had a special *tefillah*: to inscribe my father into the *Book of Life* along with the other deported victims. My mother prayed fervently at my side, her weary eyes filled with tears. Although the Satmar Rebbe's *tefillah* was extremely inspiring, our hearts broke when my uncle's great, holy voice rang through the *shul.* We were used to hearing my father's beautiful voice praying out loud, as he normally filled the dual roles of rabbi and *baal tefillah* (leader of the prayer services) in his *shul.*

Yom Kippur came. My heart pounded as the sun set; would this be the day of my father's return? *Kol Nidrei* was especially painful without my father's blessings; in years past, his haunting melodies used to soar out of the *shul* toward the Heavens. The following day I cried in *shul,* arguing, as it were, with Heaven, to seal my father in the *Book of Life* and bring him back to us.

The last service of Yom Kippur is known as *Ne'ilah* — Hebrew for "locking" — a metaphorical reference to the gates of Heaven slowly swinging shut as the sun goes down and the worshipers fervently address their final prayers of the Day of Atonement to the A-mighty. Humbled and exhausted after a full day of intense, soulful prayer and weakened from an entire day of fasting, we make one last supreme effort to pour out our hearts and utterly throw ourselves upon Hashem's great mercy. That year, as my great uncle cried out, *"Vechasmeinu besefer hachaim!* (Seal us in the *Book of Life!),"* I wept and prayed as never before, hoping to avert an evil decree from falling on my beloved father, relying especially on the great *zechus* of my uncle's *tefillos.*

With the arrival of Succos (the Feast of Tabernacles) and Simchas Torah (the Feast of Rejoicing with the Torah), there was still no word regarding my father's whereabouts. My uncle's *succah* (tabernacle) was spacious and majestic, and normally I would have enjoyed decorating it with needlepoint works, fruits, figs and pictures. Usually I found the Yom Tov of Succos invigorating. I loved being out-of-doors in the cool, fresh air and simply sitting inside my uncle's beautiful *succah.* I usually enjoyed greeting and talking to guests who stopped by, and my aunt's savory dishes were always the delight of the *kehillah.* But that year my mother and I could not really enjoy Succos — without my father we felt like a body without a head. The stress was taking a toll on her. New lines were etched on her forehead, and she was beginning to look wan and thin.

With a sinking heart, I came to the realization that my father might never be found. At the conclusion of the *yamim tovim,* my mother and I returned to our empty home in Selish.

Life went on, somehow. Days and months passed, still without any word from my father. There were days when my heart ached so much that I did not want to get out of bed. My father even appeared in my dreams at night. In many of them, he and my mother would be walking me to the *chuppah;* then he would be dancing the *mitzvah tantz* after the *seudah.* Sometimes I would wake up smiling or laughing, but then reality coldly set in, and I would quickly remember that my father was not there.

For the next two years, we still clung to the distant hope that maybe, just maybe, my father would still come back to us.

CHAPTER 3

Engagement During Perilous Times

AS TIMES HAVE CHANGED, SO, IN GENERAL, HAVE ENGAGEMENT rituals, with men and women selecting their mates themselves instead of having their parents arrange their marriage. However, based on today's statistics of divorce and separation, one may wonder whether it might not be better for matrimonial arrangements to be made again today as they were when I was a girl.

Coming of Age

In previous years, many members of my family became engaged when they were as young as 5 years of age! Some people think this practice goes back to Czarist Russia when soldiers grabbed young, unmarried boys in the street to serve in the army. The only way a boy could be saved from the draft was by getting married at a young age.

A story is told of a Russian soldier seizing a 10-year-old Jewish boy who wasn't wearing long trousers.

"You can't take me, I'm married!" cried the boy.

"Why aren't you wearing pants?" snapped the soldier.

"I had to give them to my younger brother for his wedding!" the boy answered back.

Thus, in Russia, it became commonplace to arrange early engagements so that young Jewish boys could avoid being drafted. But my husband believes that our Chassidic ancestors were married at a young age for other reasons. His grandfathers, for instance, lived in the Austro-Hungarian empire under the rule of Franz Joseph, where such cruelties did not exist. Even so, they too became engaged and married very early in life. My husband's grandfather, the Rebbe, R' Baruch Rubin, *zt"l*, for example, was actually engaged when he was but a child of 5 years and his prospective *kallah*, the daughter of the Zidichoiver Rebbe, was all of 6. They were, of course, married some years later, but the engagement was formalized when they were small. The same held true for my uncle, the Satmar Rebbe, *zt"l*, who became a *chassan* way before he became a *bar mitzvah*. (The Satmar Rebbe, *zt"l*, told us that once his father came home from Galicia and told him, "Yoilish, you became a *chassan*.")

These early engagements were hardly atypical. There was a tendency among *Chassidim* to have parents or close relatives arrange early engagements for the younger generation, for Torah-based reasons. Just as the Patriarch Avraham sent Eliezer as his emissary to find a mate for his son, Yitzchak, so too did our devoted parents of later generations take special care in arranging *shidduchim* for their children. It was generally understood that parents, with their broader life experience, knew better what was good for their sons and daughters, who, no matter how intelligent, were still young, callow and inexperienced in the ways of the world and human relationships. In today's world, we see young people making unbelievable, illogical choices based on flimsy whims, transient infatuations and inaccurate portrayals of human relationships by the mass media.

In the past, purity of family life also included the teaching of "purity of mind." Therefore, the *chassan* did not meet his *kallah* until after the *chuppah*. Before the Second World War, this practice started to change. In fact, I met my *bashert* (intended) on the day of the *tenayim*, the formal engagement, although my *bashert's* elder brothers had adhered to the custom of not seeing their *kallahs* before the *chuppah*.

All the details leading up to our engagement and marriage are still vivid in my mind's eye.

In the early spring of 1943, while my mother and I were staying with the Teitelbaums, my uncle told me that it was time for me to get married. He would start interviewing prospective *chassanim*, he said, and I trusted that he would be very careful in selecting the best *shidduch* for me. My uncle explained that it was customary for the prospective *chassan* to be tested on his knowledge of Torah, and assured me that the overall appearance and temperament of any young man under consideration would be examined thoroughly as well.

My uncle made it clear that he would not rest until he found someone of whom he knew my father would approve. Moreover, since it was my uncle, not my father, who would be selecting my future mate, I would be allowed to meet the prospective *chassan* before the *tenayim*. If for some reason I did not feel comfortable with the young man, the *shidduch* would not take place.

As a child, I had looked forward to the day I would stand under the *chuppah*. Now that the time was approaching, I felt overwhelmed by the prospect. Circumstances had drastically changed my life, and at that time, I did not feel ready to get married. My delicate mother still needed me by her side, and I continued to cling to the hope that my father would return in time to help arrange my *shidduch*.

I was also hesitant because we were in the midst of war, and young Jewish men were being dragged away from their families to become part of labor brigades. Many did not return alive. I feared that my new husband would be taken away from me soon after we were married, and I could not bear the ache of yet another loss in my life. I expressed these feelings to my uncle, but he felt differently. His *bitachon* was so intense that he strongly believed my *chasunah* should take place, even in the middle of such adverse conditions. Reminding me that I was 19 years old already, he insisted on starting the interviews. My mother and my aunt, Rebbetzin Feige, agreed. Even as the storm clouds of war gathered over Germany and Poland, in Hungary we assumed that life would go on.

In the weeks and months that followed, my uncle began to find out about prospective *chassanim*. Whenever he announced that he had scheduled an interview with a young man, my heart would jump into my mouth. I realized that if my uncle approved of the young man, I could be a *kallah* that very same day. On the designated time of the meeting, my mother, my aunt and I would wait in another part of the Teitelbaum home, not knowing what was being said behind closed doors. As promised, my uncle was very discriminating when it came to finding the most suitable *chassan* for me, and I realized that it might take some time before he found the right man. At times I was somewhat relieved, because I still hoped beyond hope that my father would make his much-awaited appearance at the front door. The pain of imagining a *chasunah* without my father present gnawed at me day and night.

The Shidduch

ON A JUNE MORNING IN 1943, MY AUNT CAME TO ME AND SAID, "Tomorrow morning, a *bachur* (young man), the son of the Rabbi of Szaszregen, Hungary, is coming to see the Rebbe." With a twinkle in her eyes, she continued, "He is the son of a distant relative of mine, the Rebbe, R' Yaakov Yisrael V'Yeshurin Rubin (Eichenstein), *ztk"l*, whom I hold in great esteem. The young man's name is R' Menachem Mendel Rubin, and he is a descendant of a long chain of Chassidic dynasties. From what I am told, at 21 years of age, young R' Rubin is quite a *talmid chacham* (Torah scholar), handsome and very personable."

A strange feeling engulfed me. I had never seen my aunt so

enthusiastic over a *bachur*. Could this young man be the one?

As scheduled, R' Menachem Mendel Rubin arrived at my uncle's apartment early the following morning. I remained elsewhere in the Teitelbaum home while the interview between my uncle and R' Rubin took place in my uncle's library.

By lunchtime my uncle happily announced that he was highly impressed with young R' Rubin, and was more than satisfied that he would be a most suitable husband for me. As promised, I would be introduced to my *chassan* later that afternoon at a small family gathering.

I felt myself blush as my mother took my hand and we smiled at one another. Rebbetzin Feige embraced me and also wished me only the best. I was happy that my uncle had found my *bashert*, and I could tell by the glow in his eyes and by his reassuring smile that he was pleased with his decision. I still had many questions to ask him, however. Somewhat flustered, I did not know where to begin. Everyone smiled affectionately at my excitement. Imagine! That morning, I was a single girl; that evening, I would become a *kallah*! But there was so much to be done first.

My aunt immediately began making preparations for the gathering that afternoon which would take place in the Teitelbaum home, and for the *tenayim* which would follow later that evening. Soon other women came to help my aunt prepare for our company, while my mother and I took off to the guest room to get ready.

My mother and aunt had an engagement dress custom-made for me when my uncle began interviewing *bachurim*, so that I would have something beautiful and appropriate to wear when the time came. When I was dressed, my mother combed my hair and tied it back with soft, silk ribbons. I stood in front of the full-length mirror and saw not a little girl, but a young *kallah*.

My mother told me to sit in the guest room and wait to be called. My aunt knocked on the door to announce that my distinguished *chassan* was on his way, and marveled at how beautiful I looked. I learned that R' Rubin would not be accompanied by his father since by that time it was dangerous for Jews, especially older ones, to travel by train, for there they could be subject to official scrutiny and harassment. Instead, his older brother, R' Yosef Mayer Rubin, *ztk"l*, who lived nearby in the town of Mihaly-Falva, had come to Satu Mare as their father's representative. One of their father's devoted *Chassidim*, Mr. Tuvia Blei, would also be attending.

The two women left the room. I sat alone, lost in thought. While my uncle's enthusiasm was contagious, I was quite nervous and anxious about meeting my new *chassan*, the man with whom I would spend the rest of my life. Would I like him? Would I feel comfortable around him? How would he feel about me? Evidently, my uncle seemed to think we would be very happy together. Then a wave of sadness washed over me as I remembered that my father would not be with me to share in my *simchah*. I began to weep. My father's absence left an empty feeling in the pit of my stomach, and no matter how I tried, I could not feel completely happy about my impending marriage — not without my father's presence.

I walked to the window and looked out. The sun was shining and the flowers were blooming in Rebbetzin Feige's small garden near the wall of the building. I held my hands out in front of me and turned them slowly, letting the sun's rays warm my icy-cold fingers. When I sat down again, I heard someone knocking at the front door. Since a long hallway separated the parlor from the room in which I sat, I could only hear muffled voices. My *chassan* had just arrived!

Some time passed, and soon my mother returned and asked me to step out. Even though my knees felt shaky, I managed to follow my mother to the parlor where she steered me to the sofa and motioned me to sit down. I heard voices coming from the front hallway; my cousin, Rebbetzin Roisele, *z"l* (the daughter of the Satmar Rebbe from a previous marriage and the wife of the Rebbe, R' Lipa, *zt"l*, the head of the *Beis Din* in Satu Mare) was addressing my *chassan*, and then I heard his voice for the first time. I strained to hear their conversation; they seemed to be talking about R' Rubin's trip to Satu Mare. Immediately I noticed that he had a soft, gentle voice.

As I waited for them to enter the parlor, I looked around and was very impressed with the beautiful way Rebbetzin Feige and my cousin, Rebbetzin Roisele, had prepared for this gathering. My aunt's best china, silverware, glassware, teacups and embroidered linen napkins were laid out buffet-style on the tables, which were elegantly covered with white lace tablecloths. Assorted cakes and cookies were arranged on glass serving dishes. Silver teapots were placed at both ends of the table, and wine, schnapps and shot glasses were lined up for the *l'chaim*. Rebbetzin Feige had also adorned the tables with lavish vases of fresh violets and lilies from her garden. The flowers gave off a sweet scent, filling the room with their pleasing aroma.

After what seemed an eternity — actually, only a few moments — my future husband entered the room. My mother nodded at him politely, her kind smile a bit cautious, then stood up and formally introduced herself. My heart was pounding as I watched the two begin their conversation. He had dark-brown hair and eyes, was thin and attractive, and stood straight and tall in his neatly pressed Chassidic garb. I did notice that he was somewhat pale, and realized that he was probably just as nervous as I.

As a way of breaking the ice with her future son-in-law, my mother explained how our family and his were related through the Ropshitzer and Kozshnitzer Chassidic dynasties. They spent a few moments discussing our *yichus*. In the meantime, a crystal bowl filled with fruit, including grapes and oranges, was brought out and placed on the table. My mother politely asked, "Would you like an orange?"

I still remember his response.

He said that while he looked forward to eating the orange, a rarity in Hungary, he could not eat it — or any other fruit — before having grapes first. "According to *halachah* (religious law)," he explained, "one has to make a *berachah* (blessing) on grapes before eating any other fruit because *Eretz Yisrael* was praised for its grapes."

I could tell by my mother's smile that she was favorably impressed with his explanation — and with this young *bachur* himself.

After a few moments, he and I were introduced. Nervously I stood up and finally faced my prospective husband-to-be. He nodded cordially, and I smiled shyly. At first, I didn't quite know what to say. My first words to him were to inquire about his trip. He answered that it had been uneventful, which, for a Jew traveling on a train through Hungary in 1943, was a very good trip indeed. He led the rest of the conversation, and we chatted for a few moments. Then my family and I were introduced to his brother, R' Yosef Mayer Rubin, and to his older sister, Rebbetzin Leah, the wife of R' Zalmen Leib Gross, the Rav of Sugatag (a town near Sighet). She had traveled to Satu Mare to meet my family and me, and to attend the *tenayim*. I was disappointed at not meeting my new parents-in-law, but I understood why they could not attend.

My uncle led the men with a *l'chaim*, and after the toast everyone enjoyed my aunt's refreshments — especially the plump, juicy oranges. All told, it was a pleasant and successful meeting, and I was happy to have had the opportunity to meet my *chassan*.

Before long, it was time for my *chassan* and his family to leave. They went to the apartment of the Rebbe's son-in-law and daughter Roisele to await the *tenayim* that would take place in a few short hours, that very evening.

Once back in the privacy of the guest room, my mother, my aunt and I happily discussed our first impressions of R' Rubin. They agreed with my uncle's assessment that he was a perfect match for me. In the short time that I had seen him and spoken with him, I found him to be intelligent, sensitive and kind. I asked my mother and my aunt to convey my impressions to my uncle, and, remembering my uncle's offer to cancel the *tenayim* should I not be happy with the *bachur*, I agreed that the *tenayim* should go on as scheduled. But happy though I was at becoming engaged, my feelings were bittersweet; my heart ached for my father to share my *simchah*.

Much later, my husband recounted the events which led up to his interview with my uncle, the Satmar Rebbe.

R' Menachem Mendel's father, the Rebbe R' Yaakov Yisrael V'Yeshurin Rubin (Eichenstein), *ztk"l*, received a letter from the Satmar Rebbe, suggesting a *shidduch* between R' Menachem Mendel and me, his niece. The Satmar Rebbe sent along my photo, but for reasons of *tzenius* (modesty), Rabbi and Rebbetzin Rubin did not allow their son to see it.

The Satmar Rebbe invited R' Menachem Mendel to Satu Mare for an interview. This was not the norm in European Chassidic circles; usually the girl's father or guardian would visit the prospective *chassan's* home and interview him there. However, since it was too dangerous for the Satmar Rebbe to travel to Szaszregen, the prospective *chassan* would have to go to the Rebbe.

Since it was also too dangerous for R' Menachem Mendel's father to accompany his son to Satu Mare, Mr. Blei would go as his representative. Arrangements were made for R' Menachem Mendel and Mr. Blei to stay with R' Menachem Mendel's uncle, R' Chaim Halberstam, *zt"l*, (the son of the Rebbe, R' Shulem Eliezer, *H"yd*, and the husband of his father's sister Chava) during their stay in Satu Mare.

Although R' Menachem Mendel was looking forward to the meeting with the Satmar Rebbe, he was apprehensive about traveling. There was always the possibility that he or his companion would be detained by the Hungarian police and dragged off to a labor camp. He worried about his family, who would be frantic with worry were he to disappear.

Despite these misgivings, the travelers arrived safely and proceeded to R' Chayemel's home as planned. Later that evening, R' Menachem Mendel went to his room to prepare for the meeting with my uncle, the Satmar Rebbe, the following morning. Eager to impress the Rebbe, R' Menachem Mendel stayed up all night, preparing a *dvar Torah* from *Maseches* (Tractate) *Nedarim* (Vows).

R' Menachem Mendel's appointment with the Rebbe was scheduled for a quarter to 8 in the morning. Mr. Blei accompanied R' Menachem Mendel to the Rebbe's home. When they arrived, they were first greeted by a confidant of the house, R' Yaakov Hirsh

Tarner Szojchet. He and R' Menachem Mendel engaged in a brief discussion about Torah and *Chassidus*. R' Yaakov even used a few worldly terms that R' Menachem Mendel was acquainted with (except for one, "physiognomy").

A few moments later, R' Menachem Mendel was ushered into the Rebbe's library. Mr. Blei remained outside so that the Rebbe and R' Menachem Mendel could meet privately.

The Rebbe greeted his young visitor warmly and motioned to a comfortable chair facing his huge *sefarim* table. The large and majestic room was filled with many holy books of Torah and *Chassidus*.

"What are you learning now?" the Rebbe asked R' Menachem Mendel.

R' Menachem Mendel took a few moments to answer. Then the Rebbe spoke to him at length about the *maseches* that R' Menachem Mendel had started to discuss. R' Menachem Mendel had another few moments to respond, and then the Rebbe spoke again for a considerable length of time. R' Menachem Mendel was immediately impressed by the Rebbe's warmth and kindness, and felt comfortable in his presence.

After some time had passed, the Rebbe looked at the clock on his desk and noted that it was already a quarter to 10. Looking directly at R' Menachem Mendel, the Rebbe said, "Our meeting is over. I must *daven* now."

"The meeting is over?" repeated R' Menachem Mendel, somewhat disappointed. "But … I didn't have a chance yet to tell you the *dvar Torah* I prepared …"

The Rebbe smile reassuringly and said, "I can tell much about a person by how he listens to a *dvar Torah*. As I spoke to you, I was testing you — not so much on what you said, but on how you understood."

Having said that, he wished his guest a good day. R' Menachem Mendel left, not knowing what kind of impression he had made on the Rebbe.

Mr. Blei was then called into the Rebbe's study. He returned a few moments later, and informed R' Menachem Mendel that the Satmar Rebbe was impressed with him and wanted the family, including his niece, to meet him that very afternoon.

WORD ABOUT THE SHIDDUCH AGREEMENT AND IMPENDING TENAYIM was sent to my future parents-in-law's home in Szaszregen via **Our Unusual Tenayim** telegram. I could only imagine their excitement and happiness upon learning the wonderful news; if only they could have been with us to share in this joyous occasion! Word also spread to various cities about the wonderful *shidduch* between the two Chassidic dynasties.

Much needed to be done to prepare for the *tenayim*, just hours away. Rebbetzin Feige and other women in the community gathered in her kitchen to help prepare the *seudah* and to set the table. The tables in my aunt's lavish dining room were once again covered with elegant tablecloths and set with her finest china. Just as was done at the small gathering earlier that afternoon, bottles of beer, wine and schnapps were placed at the head of the table for the *l'chaim*.

Although the Teitelbaum home was full of activity and excitement that afternoon, and much still needed to be done, I was told to rest until it was time to get dressed for the *tenayim*. At the designated hour, my mother came in and helped me get ready.

In the meantime, my future *chassan* stayed at Rebbetzin Roisele's house for the remainder of the afternoon. Rebbetzin Roisele, the perfect hostess, told him that she had had a decisive say in the *shidduch* arrangements, for which my future husband thanked her politely. R' Yosef Mayer stopped by with a fresh white shirt and pressed *kaftan* for my soon-to-be *chassan* to wear that evening.

At the designated hour Mr. Blei escorted my *chassan* to the Teitelbaums' home. By the time they arrived, I was already seated with my mother and the other women. The well-lit room was somewhat warm as a result of all the baking and cooking, and my aunt opened the windows. Soon guests began to show up, and the sounds of cordial greetings in the front hallway could faintly be heard from where I waited. After the Satmar Rebbe arrived from his *beis midrash*, the *tenayim* ceremony began.

My *chassan* was seated at the head of the table with the Satmar Rebbe, R' Teitelbaum, and his brother, R' Yosef Mayer Rubin, surrounded by other distinguished relatives, friends of my uncle, and Mr. Blei. Unfortunately, my *chassan's* uncle, the Rebbe, R' Chaim Halberstam, *H"yd*, and his aunt, Rebbetzin Chava, *H"yd*, were not able to attend the *tenayim*.

Even though this was supposed to be a happy event, it turned out to be, at best, a bittersweet gathering because of the constant danger looming over our heads. At every moment we were aware that any one of us could be taken away by the Berlin-dominated Hungarian authorities for no other reason than that we were Jewish. Even the sounds of footsteps outside the window made our hearts pound, causing tension to mar the atmosphere of this joyous evening.

About halfway through the *tenayim*, a beer bottle on the men's table spontaneously exploded. It had undoubtedly blown up because its contents were under extreme pressure, but at the time, the explosion sounded like a gunshot. I was later told that my uncle turned ashen for a few moments, but quickly regained his composure upon realizing that it had been an accident and no one had been injured.

We resumed the proceedings, although the abrupt interruption had shaken me profoundly, serving as a harsh reminder of this terrible war which caused us to jump at every unexpected sound. This train of thought led to thinking about my father, who was not with us, and I began to weep silently at the table.

Soon the *tenayim* celebration ended, another *simchah* darkened by feelings of fear and loss brought on by the anti-Semites of the European world.

DAYS AFTER THE TENAYIM, THE SATMAR REBBETZIN, IN THE PRESENCE of my revered mother, gently broke to me the news that I had **Bitter News** hoped never to hear: my father was no longer alive. Taking my hand, my aunt tried to comfort me by saying that my father had been a wonderful and holy man, who both lived and died with *mesiras nefesh* (whole-hearted dedication) to the A-mighty.

I could not speak for quite a while. Even though deep in my heart I probably knew that my father had in all likelihood passed away by then, I still clung to the hope that maybe — just maybe — he was alive somewhere. As long as I had not received definite word of my father's death, there was always that small ray of hope …

The finality of the news shattered me: I would never again see my father in this world. He would not stand under the *chuppah* with me, nor would he share in the *nachas* of his grandchildren someday. There were so many things I had wanted to talk to him about; so much I had wanted to say to him — but now it was too late. My heart broke into a thousand pieces. Numb with shock and grief, I gazed into my mother's tear-filled eyes — and abruptly chastised myself for thinking only of my own pain. Imagine what my mother must be going through!

It was then that my aunt explained that she and my mother had found out about my father's death several weeks before my engagement, when a young Jewish Hungarian army laborer was finally able to reach my mother in Selish, and tell her the tragic news. Prior to that time, he had not been able to break away from his labor brigade to travel to Selish. He attempted to comfort my mother by telling her how brave my father had been before he was shot. The young laborer, who was part of a forced labor detail, had halted next to my father and managed to speak a few words to him. My father apologetically stopped him, saying, "I am preparing myself to die as a Jew *al kiddush Hashem* (to sanctify the name of the A-mighty). I do not want to be disturbed." [1]

Upon receiving confirmation of her worst fears, my mother did not know whether to immediately tell me about my father's death

---

1. This story is mentioned in the book of the Kiviashder Rav, R' Shapiro, *z"tl*, in the Chanukah portion.

or to wait. She sought the advice of various family members including the Teitelbaums, and it was decided that I not be told until after I became engaged. At the time, interviews for my *shidduch* had begun, and they feared that the news might upset me to the point that I would be unable to proceed emotionally with preparations to get married.

Was their decision to temporarily withhold the information of what had happened to my father a true act of *chesed* and mercy? To this day, although I am fully aware that my mother, uncle, aunt, and other relatives had felt that they were acting in my best interests, I am still not sure whether I would have preferred to be told the full truth as soon as it was known, rather than being allowed to cling to false hopes for several more weeks.

I spent the next few days weeping bitter tears. How could the subhuman German SS soldiers, aided, as we were to learn, by the ignorant, drunken Ukrainian peasant rabble, kill such a pious, gentle, soft-spoken man as my father? How could they kill thousands of other innocent Jewish victims, including infants?

It was not until some years later that I learned exactly what had happened to my father.

A young Jew from Selish, Mr. Yisrael Green (now living in Toronto, Canada), had been conscripted into a *munka tabor*, one of the forced hard-labor brigades organized by the Hungarian Army, and happened to encounter my father twice. The first time he saw my father was in the town of Horodenka, located in the German-occupied Polish-Galician side of the border; the second time was on the way to Kamenetz-Podolsk, a town in the German-occupied Ukraine, right before my father was murdered in a mass grave.

From the station at Horodenka, the SS marched my father and the others from his transport to stables and warehouses, located some distance away. The SS informed them that they would stay there temporarily, and then they would be taken to an undisclosed location. The SS left the stables and warehouses unsupervised, and in the absence of the guards, many of the detainees left the buildings and wandered off into the street.

Mr. Green was driving by in an army truck and passed the stables in which the Jews were housed. He spotted my father outside, on the road, sitting on a suitcase, and waved to get his attention. My father, pale and weary, looked up at Mr. Green and acknowledged his presence. Without saying a word, Mr. Green quickly tossed bread and cans of kosher sardines in my father's direction. My father thanked Mr. Green with a nod.

Over the years, people have asked me why my father did not escape when he had the opportunity to do so. Of course, I have no answers, but I would like to suggest a few possibilities. Physically, my father was drained, and the simple act of walking away from the warehouse might have been too difficult for him. And even if he could have walked away, what then? As a frail, obviously Chassidic man, he would have been an easy target for the hostile Poles living in the surrounding town, who, without a doubt, would have either murdered him in cold blood or seized him bodily and handed him over to the SS.

After a brief absence the SS returned. They rounded up the Jews and ordered them onto the trucks which were waiting to take them on what was to be the final journey of their lives. The trucks came to a halt at Kamenetz-Podolsk. The date was Monday, August 25, 1941 / 4 Elul 5701.

I could only imagine how my dear father was roughly dragged off the truck along with the other Jewish passengers; how he was led to a wooded area where, to his shocked surprise, he found himself among thousands of other frightened, bewildered Jews who had been brought there from Hungary, Russia, Poland, and Czernowitz, a town in the Ukraine. Wearing his *tallis*, my father, along with thousands of other Jews, was forced to run into a clearing in the woods.

"Stop here!" barked the German-Nazi SS soldiers. Thousands of innocent victims — men, women and children — halted in front of a large clearing. They were handed shovels and ordered to dig.

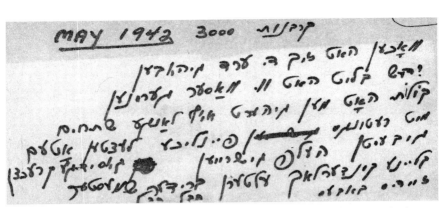

Handwritten statement by an eyewitness regarding the massacres at Kamenetz-Podolsk,
"For weeks the Earth rose. Jewish blood ran like water…"

When the order was given to the adults to dig quickly, they knew they were about to dig their own graves. It was then and there that the encounter occurred between my father and the young Jewish laborer who brought us the news of my father's death.

Moments later, the sounds of weeping and *davening* were drowned by the sounds of reverberating gunshots. A chilling haze from the massive rounds of submachine-gun fire hovered over the mass pits. Thousands of innocent, G-d - fearing *neshamos* separated from their bodies and began their ascent to Heaven. These innocent souls were victimized there in a historically unprecedented manner.

The mass killings at Kamenetz-Podolsk took place over a number of days in late August of 1941 (5701). The *yahrtzeits* of approximately 40,000 victims are marked on 4 Elul and 5 Elul.

In 1987 my husband and I visited the mass grave in Kamenetz-Podolsk to erect a plaque with my esteemed father's name on it. While there, we were told by some elderly inhabitants who managed to live through this *Aktion*, the truly gruesome story of what had actually happened, including the involvement of local Ukrainians in the killings.

At my venerable father's grave in Kamenetz-Podolsk;
I made a tomb in Vienna and established the monument there.

On one of the days of the mass murder, the sadistic SS German *Einsatzkommandos* (shooting squads) gathered together a group of Ukrainian peasants. The SS told the Ukrainians to liquidate the thousands of Jews at the grave site, offering them food and vodka as a reward. "Kill them however you can," directed the cold-blooded Nazis. "We are giving you, collectively as a group, one hundred bullets. For every bullet you bring back, you will get a bottle of vodka."

The Ukrainian peasants did not need to be asked twice. The Germans had found the perfect collaborators to brutally carry out their orders. Eager to "earn" their vodka, the greedy Ukrainians, supervised by the SS, used every possible instrument — including bayonets and large knives, even shovels — to murder the innocent Jewish martyrs and save the bullets as well. We are told the peasants "earned" fifty bottles of vodka for their efforts.

On all the other days of the mass killings, the *Einsatzkommandos* slaughtered the Jews with machine guns. However, the Nazi murderers did not wish to waste bullets on infants and small children, so they ordered the Ukrainians to brutally snatch the squirming, crying tots out of their parents' protective arms, toss them alive into another pit, and cover them with a thin layer of dirt.

Transporting several religious Russian boys to a summer camp in Budapest during visit to Kamenetz-Podolsk

The tomb explains in Hebrew what transpired there and mentions my father in particular

Some former members of the Hungarian labor brigade told us that as they went past the mass grave two days after the *Aktion* they saw movement under the thin layer of earth covering the bodies of the *kedoshim*. The earth was rising as those still half alive tried to inch their way out from beneath the huge mass of corpses. From what we were told, the earth rose in this fashion in many other places as well.

CHAPTER 4
My Husband's Early Years

MY HUSBAND, R' MENACHEM MENDEL RUBIN, WAS BORN ON June 22, 1922, in the town of Szaszregen in the section of Romania known as Transylvania. At the time of his birth,

Zachor — Remember!

the town was known as Reghin and was a part of Romania. Its name was changed to Szaszregen following the transfer of this area to Hungary in August, 1940. My father-in-law was the distinguished and prominent Chassidic Rebbe, the *Admor* R' Yaakov Yisrael V'Yeshurin Rubin-Eichenstein, *ztk"l*. The Rubin name comes from his father's paternal side, which traces its ancestry to the noted Ropshitz Chassidic dynasty through his great-grandfather, R' Usher of Ropshitz, *zt"l*, the son-in-law of R' Naftali Tzvi Horowitz who was the son of R' Mendel Rubin of Liska, *zt"l* (the founder of the dynasty, whose name my husband bears). The Eichenstein name comes from his father's maternal side. His grandmother was the

Our first project in Ropshitz was to protect the cemetery by surrounding it with a gate

My dear son, Admor M'Ropshitz R' Chaim Rubin, was influential in building a new gate at the cemetery and a new Ohel on the Ropshitzer R'Usher Yeshayah's grave, pictured here

Rabbi Rubin's efforts to save the cemetery in Ropshitz from destruction

Workmen beginning to dig the foundation for the new fence around R' Usher Yeshayah's grave

The temporary fence installed around the Ropshitzer's grave

When I came to the Ropshitzer's grave site (center) some time after the new fence had been installed, imagine my shock upon discovering that the fence was gone! It had probably been stolen by the locals for use as firewood. To my husband's right is the Dejer Rebbe shlita, from Boro Park.

R' Rubin's father and mother. My venerable father-in-law was recognized as a great scholar in Torah and halachah. He was highly respected by leading rabbis and Chassidic leaders – and was also well-regarded even by many non-Jews.

daughter of the Zidichoiver Rebbe, R' Mendele Eichenstein, *zt"l*, the son of R' Yitzchak Eizik Eichenstein, *zt"l*.

My venerable mother-in-law, of blessed memory, Alta Nechama Malka, from the Koritzer-Kosover family, was a famous *tzadekes* of exceptional *yichus*. Her father was the Sereder Rebbe, *Admor* R' Chaim Dachner, *zt"l*, a descendant of R' Yisrael ben Eliezer, *zt"l* — better known to the world as the Baal Shem Tov. Thus, my husband can trace his *yichus*, or line of descent, back to the very founder of the entire Chassidic movement, with Chassidic courts in every generation of his family from the inception of *Chassidus* until the present. In fact, his family is among those whose *yichus* can actually be traced back some 3,000 years in a golden chain from King David down through tens of generations of scholars and rabbis, including Rashi, the great medieval Torah commentator.

My husband's father, R' Yaakov Yisrael V'Yeshurin Rubin, was born in Zidichoiv, Poland (his mother's home) in 1885/5645, the firstborn son of his family. My husband tells an interesting story about how his father was named.

Generally, children in Chassidic circles are named after illustrious deceased relatives. However, shortly before my husband's grandmother, Sara Shlomtza, gave birth to my father-in-law, her father, R' Mendele, the Zidichoiver Rebbe, dreamt that his new grandchild would be a boy and that the infant should be named Yaakov, after the third of the great Biblical patriarchs. R' Mendele, who lived some distance from his daughter, sent her a letter in which he wrote her about his dream.

Soon afterward Sara gave birth to a son, just as her father had foretold. Word of the baby's arrival reached R' Mendele. The *bris* (circumcision) was to be held on the seventh day of Teves, 5645, in the town of Brizdovidz, Poland. Concerned that his daughter might not have received his letter regarding the naming of the infant, R' Mendele overcame the difficulties posed by traveling and attended the *bris*. When the time came to name the baby, he called out all three names of the Biblical Yaakov: *Yaakov Yisrael V'Yeshurin*. It is interesting to note that the Zidichoiver Rebbe selected the name Yeshurin even though it is common only among Sephardic Jews.

In the East Galician Chassidic circles in which my father-in-law was raised, he was considered an *ilui*, a child prodigy. My husband was told that by the age of 10 or 11, his father had already learned much of *Yoreh Deah*, the first part of the *Shulchan Aruch*, by heart. Famous *rabbanim* who traveled from different townships heard this young child expound on what he learned and were highly impressed. His family had no trouble making a *shidduch* for him when was just 11 years old, and he married into the family of the Shotzer-Zlotchover-Premishlaner Chassidic dynasties of Sulitza, Romania. As was customary in Chassidic circles, the young couple moved into the bride's house after the wedding and the *chassan* continued learning Torah and *Chassidus*.

A short time later, the Rabbi of Sulitza, R' Babad, *zt"l*, passed away, and the *kehillah* of Sulitza unanimously elected my father-in-law to be the *Rav* of the township. His wife learned that she was expecting their first child, and their future looked rosy. Soon their child, a daughter, was born, and they named her Chana.

Tragedy struck when the young Rebbetzin became ill and passed away shortly after her daughter's birth. Her untimely death filled everyone's heart with grief. It was especially painful for the young *Rav*, knowing that his little daughter would have to be brought up by her grandparents. (The child later became the wife of the famous Spinker Rebbe, *zt"l*, of Bnei Brak, Israel.)

Some time later, a *shidduch* was arranged between R' Rubin and my mother-in-law, a lovely, pious young woman named Alta Nechama Malka. She was the daughter of R' Chaim Dachner, *zt"l*, the Rebbe in Seret, Bukovina, whose distinguished family was descended from the Baal Shem Tov and his famous disciples.

In 1916, my in-laws got caught up in World War I, which saw most of Eastern Europe become a battleground for the contending armies of Austria-Hungary, Germany and Imperial Russia. Together with many other Jewish and non-Jewish citizens of Austria and Poland, they were at one point detained in an internee camp in Romania. Torah-observant Jews living in the camp turned to R' Rubin for decisions on unusual *she'eilos* (questions of religious law) that arose under these difficult circumstances. My esteemed father-in-law had no *sefarim* (books) to consult because he had been forbidden to take them with him after his arrest. Instead, he depended on his vast knowledge of *halachah* (religious law), and managed to answer the complicated *she'eilos* entirely from memory.

After the war, my in-laws, along with other Chassidic leaders and their families, resettled in Transylvania, which was then part of Romania. R' Rubin held court in the town of Regen, which over the years became famous for its Torah and its *chesed*. In his house, my father-in-law taught his followers: "Love your neighbor as yourself."

The 1920's were years of turbulence for European Jews, many of whom had been uprooted during World War I. Besides the vast political changes the war had wrought, changes in technology, ideas and customs challenged the old ways on many fronts. My in-laws were a bastion of conservatism and tradition in their efforts to keep their followers from falling under the influences of the modern world.

People who knew my parents-in-law during those years in Szaszregen say they remember them for their Chassidic sensitivity and particularity and for their strict adherence to long-established *minhagim*, the traditional ways of life. Even wearing buttoned shirts was, at the time, considered a modern innovation in Chassidic circles. In my father-in-law's house, no shirt had buttons; shirts were fastened with string ties (a tradition which would not be broken, ironically enough, until it was time for our own wedding some 20 years later). In fact, my venerable brother-in-law, the Sulitzer Rebbe in Far Rockaway, still adheres to this custom. The matter of shirt buttons may appear trivial, but I cite it as an example of R' Rubin (Eichenstein)'s devotion to even the smallest details of the traditional Chassidic ways — the kind of devotion which had helped to protect the *neshamos* (souls) of many generations of Jews from the encroaching influences of the secular world.

It was into this very pious, tradition-minded environment that my husband, R' Menachem Mendel Rubin, was born. He was the fourth of nine children born to R' Rubin and his second Rebbetzin, Alta Nechama Malka. The names of the children, from oldest to youngest, were: Leah, *zk"l*, Yosef Mayer, *ztk"l*, Usher Yeshayah, *ztk"l*, Menachem Mendel (the Muzsayer Rebbe), Shmuel Shmelka (the Sulitzer Rebbe, now residing in Far Rockaway, New York), Mordechai David (the Szaszregen Rebbe, now living in Flatbush, New York), b. 1927; Yocheved, *zk"l*, Mirel (Rebbetzin Meisels, the Sarvasher Rebbetzin), now residing in Boro Park, New York), and Shprintza, *zk"l*.

Menachem Mendel's *bris* was held in his father's *beis midrash*. The entire *kehillah* attended, and his pious father himself circumcised him in accordance with strict Chassidic tradition. The infant was named after his great-grandfathers, R' Menachem Mendel of Zidichoiv and R' Menachem Mendel of Glogov, both of whom were affectionately known to their followers as Reb Mendele. The *sandek* (person who holds the infant during the *bris*, considered a great honor) was the Vizhnitzer-Borsher Rebbe, and the name was given by the Keresterer Rebbe, a brother of my father-in-law.

My husband's childhood years were filled with happiness, *chesed*, and order, permeated by the warm, loving security of close ties to family and *kehillah*.

His formal education began around the time of his *upsherin*, as is customary in Chassidic houses. There was great rejoicing in the Rubin household as 3-year-old Mendel got his first haircut. His *peyos* (sidelocks) were left long in the Chassidic fashion, and only then did he receive his first pair of *tzitzis* to wear.

R' Rubin-Eichenstein did not wish to send his sons to the town *cheder*, so he hired private, full-time tutors to instruct them at home, despite the considerable expense involved. Their typical school day lasted from before sunrise until well past sundown, sometimes as long as 14 hours a day. Learning was interrupted by time for *davening*, meals and recess. The learning week began on Sunday morning and ended at noon on Friday. The entire process was closely supervised by the boys' father and, as is customary in Chassidic families, by the older brothers.

When the Rubin home turned into the boys' *cheder*, R' Rubin's role changed from that of kind, forgiving father to strict teacher/supervisor. A spiritual wall of discipline and respect was always present between R' Rubin and his sons. The boys had to work hard, be on their best behavior and pay attention at all times, just as in any other *cheder*. At the end of the school day, R' Rubin reverted to his role of father once again.

It never occurred to young Mendel or his brothers that they were working too hard; they never felt drained or exhausted. In fact, as my husband looks back on those years, he remembers the joy and satisfaction he felt when his father *farhered* (tested) him and his brothers on what they had learned, and praised their knowledge.

Rebbetzin Rubin also played an important role in their learning process. As a result of her efforts, her husband and sons were able to spend as much time learning as they did.

In those days, the houses in town didn't have steam heat or running water. Water was pumped from a well, and rooms were heated by built-in ovens or wood-burning iron stoves. In order to heat such a stove, thin slivers of tinderwood had to be prepared and lit to start a fire. Then pieces of wood were added to the fire, which warmed the stove, which, in turn, heated the rooms.

During the week, Rebbetzin Rubin rose earlier than the rest of her family to prepare the fire in the oven. By the time everyone else awoke, the rooms in the apartment were heated. When the boys' school day began at 5:30 in the morning, they had their mother to thank for providing them with a warm "classroom." Even though the Rubins did not have modern heating, they did have electricity, so before daybreak and late into the evening the boys studied by the light of electric lamps. More important than their physical comfort, however, were the Torah values that the Rebbetzin instilled in the children, in particular the desire and knowledge necessary to properly perform the *mitzvah* of *hachnasas orchim* (welcoming and helping needy guests), and making the next person's needs as important as — or more important than — their own.

The stress placed on this *middah* (character trait) made their home very unique and special. My in-laws taught the children *ahavas Hashem* (love and devotion to G-d), *ahavas Yisrael* (love of one Jew for another), *ahavas Torah* (love of Torah), and the various aspects of *gemilus chasadim* (acts of kindness), at an early age. They worked hard to instill the proper *middos* (character traits) in each member of the family, and to raise them in an environment which was true to the basic tenets of *Chassidus*.

Many times Mendel and his siblings were asked to give up their bedding for overnight guests. The boys would then sleep on the floor with blankets, and the girls would either share one bed, or sleep in the women's section of the *shul*. Giving over one's bed to a stranger was considered fundamental to the *mitzvah* of *hachnasas orchim*.

The Rubins' home included both the *beis midrash* and the family's living quarters. The *beis midrash* was on the first floor, and the family lived on the second floor. The women's balcony, overlooking the *beis midrash*, was also located on the second floor. Members of the *kehillah* met my father-in-law in his library to learn, or to ask him *she'eilos*.

The impressive study contained one shelf after another of *sefarim*: huge folio volumes of Talmud and Responsa, commentaries and the works of sages. My husband recalls that when he was a small child, his father's *sefarim* seemed to reach way up, far beyond the confines of the ceiling. Right before Pesach young Mendel, his brothers, and the *gabbai* of the *shul* would remove all the *sefarim* from the shelves and take them to air out in the open. They would lay the *sefarim* out in the yard, and the wind would blow away any *chametz* that might have been trapped between the pages. It is written that the Gaon of Vilna, R' Eliyahu, *zt"l*, personally searched his books the night before Pesach, as he searched his rooms, but in my husband's home, as in other *rebbishe* homes, they cleared the *sefarim* of *chametz* by placing them outside on a windy day.

The Rebbetzin and her daughters worked from dawn until dusk, baking, cooking, serving, and counseling the visitors who came day and night. Often the Rebbetzin would offer *chizuk* to guests who were overwhelmed by problems of poverty, ill-health and lack of family harmony. Sometimes my father-in-law would come to the Rebbetzin to seek her advice and counsel. Rebbetzin Mirel says that her father would stand by the door of the kitchen and speak to the Rebbetzin from there. The Rebbetzin would listen closely to her husband while tending to her work in the kitchen, and would offer him helpful opinions.

Three of my five sisters-in-law: from left, Yocheved zk"l, who died in Bergen Belsen; Shprintza zk"l, killed in the gas chamber at Birkenau along with my mother-in-law; and Mirel, who survived the war and is presently the Sarvasher Rebbetzin of Boro Park, Brooklyn.

The Rebbetzin did not serve any food that was store bought or ready made. She and her daughters made everything by hand from raw ingredients. Even the butter spread on the slices of freshly baked bread was hand churned. My mother-in-law also supervised the milking of the cow to make sure that the milk was, indeed, that of a cow, and not that of a non-kosher animal. (This is the same principle behind today's *chalav Yisrael* milk supervision.)

Since home refrigerators were virtually non-existent at the time, the Rebbetzin stored the perishables and large quantities of cooked food in ice buckets in the family's lower cellar — a cold, clammy, windowless room enclosed by thick and heavy walls. My husband tells me that it was cool there in the summer and freezing in the wintertime.

THE REBBETZIN KEPT AN ORDERLY SCHEDULE, BUT THE CENTRAL focus of the latter part of the week was preparing for Shabbos.

Shabbos Kodesh

Preparations began as early as Wednesday, when my sisters-in-law accompanied their mother to the *shochet* (ritual slaughterer) at the *shecht shtebel* (slaughterhouse). The girls would help their mother select the most robust chickens to be slaughtered. The chickens were taken home for *kashering* and cooking.

There was always more fuss and activity than usual on Thursdays. Every Thursday night my sisters-in-law Mirel and Yocheved prepared the *challah* dough. On Friday morning the girls assisted the Rebbetzin in rolling out the dough and braiding the *challahs*. Then they would cut off a piece of dough, recite the appropriate *berachah* over it, and place it into the oven to burn. Following that, they would bake the rest of the *challahs*. The delectable aroma of the *challahs* baking filled the entire house.

Then the Rebbetzin and the girls prepared the potato and *lukshen kugels*, fish, chicken and chicken soup with large cooked beans according to the Chassidic custom. They cooked carrots and *farfel* (toasted barley) — a legacy from the Baal Shem Tov who, it is told, said to eat *farfel* Friday night — and fruit compote for dessert. The *cholent* and *kugels* were left to simmer overnight.

Both *erev* Shabbos and Shabbos were engulfed in *minhagim* (traditions). Every Friday morning, breakfast consisted of *roselle*, made from chicken legs, and freshly baked *challah*. On Friday evening before *shul*, the men enjoyed the custom of *ta'ameihu*, and happily tasted the fish and *farfel*. There was a Friday night *peiros* (fruit) *tish*, with a special meaning.

My sister-in-law Rebbetzin Mirel Meisels, the Sarvasher Rebbetzin, recalls a time in the early 1940's when approximately one hundred young observant boys, forced into slave labor by the Hungarian gendarmerie, would come to her parents' home for the Shabbos evening meal. One particular Friday night, after the boys finished their meal, my father-in-law asked them, *"Ihr megt bentchen?* (Are you allowed to *bentch*?)"* Young Mirel ran into the kitchen and asked her mother why her father was asking the young men whether they were allowed to *bentch* after completing a full meal. Wasn't it obvious that they were obliged to recite the *Bircas HaMazon* after eating bread and consuming a meal? My mother-in-law explained that if one goes away from a meal hungry, one is not allowed to *bentch*. My father-in-law simply wanted to make sure that his guests had had enough to eat.

The Kapote and Rebbishe Clothing

IT GOES WITHOUT SAYING THAT MY HUSBAND ALWAYS ADMIRED his noble father — a pious, kind and brilliant *tzaddik*. Standing approximately six feet tall, R' Rubin (Eichenstein) was a handsome man who always dressed in traditional Galician (Polish) Chassidic clothing: an old-fashioned white shirt without buttons, a large woolen *tallis katan* over the shirt, and a black or colored *kapote* (robe). On Shabbos and Yom Tov, my father-in-law wore a white vest over the *tallis katan*, a silk *kapote*, white knickers, long socks, and comfortable slipper-shoes specially made by the shoemaker in the traditional style. He covered his head with both a *yarmulke* and a velvet, Galician-style hat at all times — even in the privacy of his home. When he met with his *Chassidim* or led the *davening* in the *beis midrash*, he wore a special *kaftan*. On Shabbos, he wore a Galician-style *shtreimel* (fur hat).

My father-in-law was admired and highly respected in the community. His many Chassidic followers who learned with him or sought his help — either in issues of *halachah* or with personal problems — appreciated the fact that they were dealing with a special and uncommon personality. Many people in the United States, Israel and Europe still speak of the uniqueness of the Sulitzer-Szaszregener Rebbe.

During the *yamim tovim*, especially during the period from Rosh Hashanah through Yom Kippur, many men would come from other towns to attend my father-in-law's *tefillah* (prayer services) and *rebbishe tish*. Among those were Rav Elyeh Weiss, *H"yd*, from Vasarhely, a well-known *Chassid* and *talmid chacham*, and R' Yehoshua Kain from Tekendorf, the *baal Shacharis* on the High Holy Days. The venerable Mr. Yechiel Liberman, *H"yd*, was among the regular congregants on Hoshana Rabbah. (His son Eliezer now lives in Boro Park, Brooklyn.)

R' YOSEF MAYER, MY HUSBAND'S ELDEST BROTHER, WAS THE FIRST among the boy siblings to get married. His *kallah*, Rebbetzin

First Separations Esther, was the daughter of R' Chaim Gliner, who was the son of the well-known Rebbetzin Gitshe, the daughter of the famous Sanzer Rebbe. After Esther's father passed away, her mother married the famous Kosoner Rebbe, R' Yisrael Rotenberg, *H"yd* who became Esther's stepfather. R' Yosef Mayer was highly respected by all who knew him.

R' Usher Yeshayah married Perye, the daughter of my husband's uncle, my father-in-law's younger brother, R' Mayer Yosef, the famous Keresterer Rebbe. R' Usher Yeshayah, too, was an authentic product of the Szaszregener house. In 1943, R' Usher Yeshayah was a guest in Budapest at the home of the Shalgo family. This family was prominent in the Orthodox community; they were devoted *Chassidim* of the Belzer Rebbe in Poland and the Kereterer Rebbe of Hungary. While at the Shalgo family's home, R' Usher Yeshayah was invited to deliver a *derashah*, and his *charifus* (sharpness of mind) and *bekius* (breadth of knowledge) were the talk of the town.

My brother-in-law, R' Yosef Mayer Rubin (top left) standing next to his stepfather-in-law, the Kosoner Rebbe, R' Yisrael Rotenberg. The man at bottom right is unidentified.

After R' Yosef Mayer and R' Usher Yeshayah married, the rest of the family rarely saw them. The situation was different for their oldest daughter, Leah. After her marriage to R' Zalmen Leib Gross, the son of the *Rav* of Berbesti-Kruli, R' Shmuel Gross, *zt"l*, the couple stayed with the family for a few years. My husband recalls learning *Yoreh Deah* with R' Gross during that time.

A few years later, R' Gross became the *Rav* of Sugatag, a town near Sighet. Sugatag was best known for its healthful mineral baths. From Sugatag, the family was interned in

R' Schulem Eliezer Halberstam of Sanz, the grandfather of R' Yosef Mayer Rubin's wife Esther

the nearby ghetto of Berbesti, from where they were transported to Auschwitz. Tragically, R' Zalmen Leib, Leah, and their eight sweet children perished in the gas chambers.

R' Ben-Zion Mendelowitz of Bnei Brak, Israel, was one of the last people to see my revered brother-in-law alive. Mr. Mendelowitz and his father, Shlomo Mendelowitz, *zk"l*, stood behind R' Gross on the line of men waiting to be "looked over" by Mengele. Mengele asked R' Gross, "What is your profession?" R' Gross truthfully replied, "Rabbi." Mengele sent him to the left, even though he was physically fit to work.

The fond memories my husband has of his parents and of his childhood remain embedded in his heart and soul. The values, traditions and customs that he and his siblings learned in their parents' *rebbishe* house have been passed down to our beloved children and grandchildren.

These high values are rare in today's egocentric society. The *Midrash* tells us that the characteristics of Torah Jewry can be compared to those of a fox. By nature, a fox runs forward, but looks backward. Torah-true Jews must think along the same terms: to progress with the technological advance of mankind, to understand humanity and be patriotic and loyal citizens, but to look back and refer to Torah-true values and behavior.

CHAPTER 5

My Husband's Memories and Impressions of the Early War Years

MY HUSBAND WAS 17 YEARS OLD AND VISITING BUDAPEST with his father on September 1, 1939, when Germany invaded Poland. The alarming news blared from the radio and spread via word of mouth. Young Mendel asked his father about the significance of this latest development, and R' Rubin responded to his son's questions without a trace of fear or concern. Mendel noticed that the Jews did not seem much disturbed by the news, going briskly about their daily business as if nothing had happened. It was obvious that for the Jews of Budapest, the invasion of Poland seemed far away; they felt the war would not reach them. This delusion remained constant, accompanying them even into the ghetto.

They could not have been more mistaken.

Although anti-Semitism was rife in Romania before World War II, the Jews were, on the whole, not treated too harshly by the government. A fairly good relationship continued between King Carol II and the Jewish community. However, Jews had to constantly be on their guard in public, always watching for malicious gentiles who would yank their beards and side curls, or even beat them — especially on the trains. With aid from Berlin, the more organized Romanian anti-Semites had formed such fascist organizations as the Iron Guard movement, which openly imitated the Nazis and called for suppression of the Jews.

Romania was officially neutral at the beginning of the war, but Hitler used lies and threats to pressure King Carol into ultimately severing his ties with the Allied nations and proclaiming his country a "neutral ally" of Germany in mid-1940. Later that year, Germany forced Romania to cede Transylvania, my husband's native region which included 150,000 Jews, to Hungary. My husband remembers that when the Hungarian army marched into Szaszregen, people were not sure what to think: Was this development good or bad for the Jews?

The local Jews feared this change, and with good reason. Hungary appeared to be a close ally of Hitler, with powerful fascist groups such as the Arrow Cross making life difficult for the Jews there. At the urging of the anti-Semites, the Hungarians had enacted anti-Jewish employment quotas and property confiscation laws. Just as it did when taking over our Selish district in Czechoslovakia the previous year, Budapest quickly imposed these laws in formerly Romanian Transylvania.

The Hungarians also issued a new decree, ordering every boy 11 or older to participate in public-service work on Wednesday afternoons. For the first time in their lives, Mendel and his brothers would be working alongside non-Jewish boys, doing hard physical labor. The Jewish boys, conspicuous with their *peyos* and Chassidic garb, were often abused by their gentile work partners. The local police, appointed to supervise the boys' work, did not intervene.

The close of the workday brought relief to Mendel and his brothers in the knowledge that they would not have to confront their tormentors for another week. The boys often returned home limping slowly and painfully. After a hot meal, they would head straight for the security of the *beis midrash*, joining the people already there to learn and to *daven Maariv*. The soulful, intense *davening* at their father's side diminished the aches and pains caused by the hard work and beatings, replacing the anguish with tears of thankfulness that they were once again home, away from those who would hurt them. But as the following Wednesday approached, feelings of anxiety once again gripped the boys, and their parents' faces settled into the now-familiar expressions of worry.

Overnight Anti-Semitism

SZASZREGEN, MY HUSBAND'S HOMETOWN, GOT ITS NAME BECAUSE a large percentage of the population was composed of Saxons who had originally emigrated from Germany. *"Sas"* stood for Saxons in Hungarian, and the word *"regen"* meant reign or kingdom. Thus *Szaszregen*, loosely translated, meant "Saxon Region."

Practically overnight, the Rubin family and their Jewish neighbors were startled to discover that they were detested by their German neighbors. For many years the Rubins had lived directly across the street from the Greifs, a German family. The Griefs appeared to be fine, friendly people, and they and the Rubins shared a mutual respect. All of that changed as soon as the poisonous winds from Berlin blew in.

By 1939 the Greifs, along with everyone else in the community, had become corrupted by the vicious propaganda and lies Hitler was spreading via his radio broadcasts and other propaganda activities. My husband shudders at the memory of hearing Hitler's voice trumpeting from across the street, blaring out of the Greifs' radio, hysterically vowing to wipe every Jew off the face of the earth. Sometimes the Rubins would catch the Greifs staring directly at them through the open windows with expressions of hatred while their radio, turned up to full volume, continued to spew venom.

The Schillers were other longtime neighbors of the Rubins. It was later discovered that Schiller had been a secret underground Nazi prior to about 1939, after which his beliefs were out in the open. What caused Schiller to finally reveal his anti-Semitic feelings? My husband believes Hitlerism conquered the hearts of so many Germans because of the hope and promise of *"Deutschland uber Alles* (Germany Above All)*,"* the belief that the German *"ubermenschen"* (supermen) would rule over the *"untermenschen"* (inferiors). This was the basic principle of German Nazism, and it was this ultimate goal that captured the German heart in Austria, in the German Rhineland (taken from Germany by France in 1918), in the Sudetenland — and in Szaszregen.

Haven for Refugees

AS UNCOMFORTABLE AS CONDITIONS WERE BECOMING FOR THE Hungarian Jews, it was nothing compared to the plight of Polish Jewry, where there was not even a charade of humanity or mercy to shield them from the merciless Third Reich murderers. Some Polish Jews attempted to escape, with a portion of them successfully reaching Hungary. Once in Hungary, they learned through the grapevine that they could seek refuge with the Rubins anytime, day or night.

As youngsters, Mendel and his siblings often awoke in the middle of the night to the sound of their father, the Rebbe, rushing downstairs. The next morning, the Rubin children would learn that there were new runaways in the house. For everyone's protection, R' Rubin opted to hide the fleeing Polish Jews in the basement instead of in the main part of his home. This way, in the event of a raid by the Hungarian police, the refugees would have a better chance of escaping. If the refugees had to flee in a hurry, they could climb through a hidden opening carved into the gate behind the Rubins' home. The Polish Jewish refugees stayed with the Rubins until safe escape plans were devised for them by R' Rubin and other members of the *kehillah*.

Staying in the basement for any length of time was not at all pleasant, but when the refugees considered the alternative, they were relieved just to be alive. The Rubins tried to make them feel as comfortable and secure as possible under the circumstances.

Although food and money were not plentiful during those years, the Jewish community, especially the followers of the esteemed Rebbe, went out of their way to provide food for the Rubins to give to the hungry people hiding in their basement. The Rebbetzin was then able to prepare steaming hot meals for the refugees to warm their shivering bodies.

The entire Rubin family became involved in helping those hiding below. The Rebbe and Rebbetzin, as well as their children, spent time with the frightened Jews, offering them words of encouragement. The refugees tearfully told the Rebbe horror stories about how they were forced to live in ghettos, starving and subjected to insufferable conditions. Men and teenage boys lived in fear of being rounded up and taken away to work in forced-labor brigades. It was a nightmare as well for the mothers, wives and children who remained behind, not knowing if the men would return.

My sister-in-law, then a young girl, recalled that some of the refugees arrived with their children. The Rubins were aware that the simple sound of a baby crying could betray the presence of the entire group to nosy neighbors, who would report them to the police and get all of them — refugees and hosts alike — imprisoned. However, all of the children — many of whom had been forced to grow up at a tender age — remained silent and cooperative. As if by instinct, they remained huddled closely in the arms of their siblings and parents as they awaited yet another move.

It was extremely courageous of my father-in-law to harbor these refugees. Had he been caught performing this act of *chesed*, he would have been subjected to limitless punishments by the Hungarian gendarmes or by their German masters. Inevitably, though, despite all the efforts of the Rubin family to be as secretive as possible, word somehow leaked out to the police that they were hiding runaway Jews. Was the informant Schiller? Somebody else?

Without warning, the authorities began to stage a series of raids at the Rubins' home. The raids took place at unexpected times; violent pounding on the front door rudely interrupted many a family meal. One of the daughters would answer the door and calmly greet the authorities, her cool demeanor lending an air of normalcy to the gathering within the house. Yet as prepared as the Rubins were, the frenzied banging always created a feeling of panic.

Almost upon arrival, the people hidden in the basement were taught how to escape during a raid. The sound of pounding from above was a signal to them to run for their lives. Without a moment to waste, they fled from the basement and crawled out through the secret opening in the gate. It was a dangerous maneuver for many of these people, weak and emaciated as they were from constant flight. Those who were unable to crawl through the gate and run away remained huddled in the courtyard. Miracle of miracles, the police did not think to look for them there. Hashem caused the Rubins' careful planning and strategy to keep them all from being caught.

BY MARCH OF 1942, THE WEDNESDAY AFTERNOON COMPULSORY WORK brigades had evolved into a full-blown, forced-labor conscription

Tragic Shabbos for Imprisoned Bachurim

system for young Jewish men and teenage boys. They were carted off to labor camps to do backbreaking work from sunup to sundown. Many of the boys, accustomed to studying in yeshivah all day, were neither physically nor emotionally up to the work. Parents and wives were afraid to let their sons and husbands out the door; they never knew from day to day whether they would return.

My esteemed brother-in-law, the Sulitzer Rebbe, *shlita*, recounted to me a heartbreaking incident that involved the Rubin family coming to the aid of some of the Jewish *bachurim* forced into hard labor.

One Shabbos morning in 1944, his father, R' Rubin, received a message from the local stationmaster explaining that there was a large number of Jewish boys and young men locked in a cattle car at the train station. For some reason, the train was detained at the station over Shabbos, and the workers would not be moving on to their next assignment until the following day. The employees at the station house were forbidden to feed them, nor were they allowed to open the doors of the car so that the boys could step out for a little fresh air.

The pathetic cries of pain and hunger emanating from the cattle car touched the stationmaster, who felt compelled to help the confined boys. In his note to R' Rubin, he suggested that the rabbi make arrangements to send over large quantities of kosher food so that the boys could eat a proper Shabbos meal.

Later, the Rubin family was to find out that these Jewish youths were very weak from starvation, torture and work injuries. Shivering in their sweat-soaked clothing, they were exhausted to the point of collapse. Not surprisingly, some were sick with high fever and infections. Although the boxcar in which they were locked was chilly and damp, the boys felt suffocated within the cramped confines of the train. And with only one waste bucket among them, the odors inside the boxcar were overpowering.

After reading the stationmaster's message, R' Rubin convened an emergency family meeting and explained the grim situation to his Rebbetzin and children. Then he sent the children around the neighborhood to request contributions of food for the confined boys. The neighbors supplied generous portions of *cholent* and *kugel*, along with loaves of *challah* and wine for *Kiddush*. In the meantime, R' Rubin arranged to have some non-Jewish neighbors help the younger children carry food and other necessities to the train station. Since there was no Shabbos *eruv* in Szaszregen, the only ones permitted to carry anything were gentiles or minors (in a case of *piku'ach nefesh*, however, even adult Jews are allowed to carry on Shabbos).

As soon as they were ready, R' Rubin wished his children and all the others accompanying them a speedy completion of their mission of mercy. Eagerly, the long line of people embarked on this wonderful act of *chesed*. My husband recalls how he and his siblings swelled with pride, knowing that they were performing this very special *mitzvah* on Shabbos. They were eager to meet the boys inside the cattle car, but when they arrived, the gendarmes guarding the train would not allow the boys out.

The attitude of the gendarmes discouraged argument, and the group had no choice but to heed instructions and leave everything on the train platform, hoping the police would distribute the food among the captives as promised. Reluctantly turning their backs on the sounds of muffled groans and sobs coming from inside the cattle cars, the children returned home and resumed Shabbos with their parents.

After *Havdalah*, R' Rubin personally called on the stationmaster and asked him to release the boys for the night, promising to assume full responsibility for them and to have them all back at the station the following morning. The stationmaster reluctantly agreed to release the boys into R' Rubin's custody, but with a warning that if any of the boys would be missing the following morning, the Rebbe would be held responsible — and the consequences would be severe.

The revered R' Rubin took a huge risk because he did not know the boys personally. Would any of them try to run away? Nobody had any way of knowing. It was simply a matter of trust.

Word quickly got back to the *kehillah* that approximately two hundred and fifty boys and young men from the transport would soon be arriving with the Rebbe and would require overnight accommodations. One of the neighbors, who owned a huge barn, contributed piles of straw for the boys to sleep on, and a concerted effort was made to spread it throughout both the men's and women's sections of R' Rubin's *shul*. In the meantime, Rebbetzin Rubin and her daughters, along with other women from the neighborhood, prepared many huge pots of hearty, nourishing potato soup.

The boys were not released from the station house until 1 o'clock in the morning. R' Rubin and other men from the *kehillah* were horrified to see how filthy and emaciated the boys were. Their worn, thin clothes had been reduced to rags. Some of the captives had their feet bound in strips of cloth; others had on dirty shoes peppered with holes and slits.

R' Rubin and the other men slowly accompanied the youths back to town. Many limped; unable to walk on their own, they leaned against their companions. One of the youngsters had lost a foot, and others were suffering from frostbite.

By the time the youths arrived at the Rubins' home, the women and girls were ready to serve the steaming soup. Since there was such a large group, the boys were asked to form a line to receive a piece of *challah* and a bowl of soup. Some quickly gulped the soup down and bashfully asked for more. Others ate slowly, savoring it, dipping the *challah* in the bowl to get every last drop. The soup warmed their chilled, emaciated bodies and put a smile on their cracked, parched lips. After the meal, the boys settled down in the soft straw, temporarily safe in the comfort and serenity of the *shul*, and drifted off for a few short hours of peaceful slumber.

At the appointed time just after dawn, R' Rubin walked the boys back to the train station. It broke his heart to send these poor, wretched boys back to the labor camps, but he had given his word of honor to the authorities. To go back on his promise now would be a great *chillul Hashem* (desecration of the A-mighty's name), proof to the gentile officials that the word of a rabbi was not be trusted. Besides, it would leave not only himself, but also the rest of the family — and, indeed, the entire *kehillah* — open to severe repercussions from the vengeful authorities, and the Rebbe had no desire to see others put in danger because of his actions.

YOCHEVED AND MIREL, MY HUSBAND'S YOUNGER SISTERS, OFTEN displayed tremendous courage and *mesiras nefesh* (self sacrifice)

The Gendarme or the Wolf? during those uncertain years. Once, on Tishah B'Av, the Rubins heard about a group of Hungarian Jewish men stationed in a work camp about four or five kilometers from their house. Many of these young men continued to observe the laws of *kashrus* in the camp, even though it was almost impossible to do so.

Rabbi and Rebbetzin Rubin learned that the young men would be fasting on Tishah B'Av, even though they had to work. Rebbetzin Rubin prepared a meal for the young men over which to break their fast and asked Yocheved, then 14, and Mirel, approximately 2 years younger, to bring baskets of food to the labor camp.

Even though it would be a long walk in the hot summer sun and they were, of course, fasting themselves, the girls obliged without hesitation. They also knew that if they were caught by the gendarmes, they would be punished.

A short time after setting out, the girls spotted a soldier walking toward them from a distance. Yocheved grabbed Mirel's hand and pulled her into a nearby wooded area. Shielded from sight by the trees, they decided to remain hidden for a few moments in order to give the gendarme ample time to walk away.

Suddenly they heard a sound coming from some shrubs. They turned and saw a pair of eyes staring at them from inside the bushes. It was a wolf! Hearts pounding with fright, they quietly walked away, putting as much distance as possible between themselves and the woods.

Safe for the moment, the two young girls now had to decide whether to return to the woods or to stay on the main road. They knew that either decision could be life-threatening. If they remained in the woods, they faced potential attack by the wolf, but if they traveled on the open road, they risked encountering another gendarme and being taken away for interrogation, or even being carted off to jail. Finally they decided to chance walking the rest of the way to the labor camp on the main road.

When they finally arrived at the Hungarian military labor camp, they saw that the slave laborers had not yet returned from work. All the girls could do was remain absolutely still in their hiding place and wait.

Some time after sunset, Yocheved and Mirel heard the sound of marching feet. Their hearts skipped a beat as the girls ran over to the barbed wire fence which separated them from the slave laborers. Motioning to a group of men, Yocheved and Mirel told them they had brought food on which to break the fast. Mirel flung the loaded basket over the barbed wire fence. Tears filled the eyes of the young men as they thanked the girls profusely for the meal.

Once satisfied that the men had eaten enough, the girls began their long walk home. It was late when they arrived, and they were cold, hungry, and weak. Rebbetzin Rubin, who had been waiting up for them, greeted them at the doorway and served them a hot meal. She lauded her tired daughters for their bravery and *mesiras nefesh*.

More Acts of Chesed

DURING THOSE YEARS, YOCHEVED AND MIREL PERFORMED THE SAME *mitzvah* on *erev* Yom Kippur. Rebbetzin Rubin prepared a hearty *seudah*, placed it in a basket, and sent the girls with the basket off to a labor camp in search of religious slave laborers who needed to observe the *mitzvah* of eating a *seudah* before the fast. Again the girls had to walk many miles, and once at the labor camp, they had to wait until late afternoon for the young men to return from work before giving them the basket. Yocheved and Mirel remained in the camp until the men had completed their meal — and only then did they return home.

One particular *erev* Yom Kippur, the girls were late in coming home. It was already sundown and they feared that they would not arrive home in time to eat the *seudah*. R' Rubin was waiting for them outside, holding a *netilas yadayim* (hand-washing) cup in his hand. He handed them each a piece of *challah* after they had washed their hands, and instructed them to hurry inside to eat the *seudah*. The girls ate quickly and rushed to *Kol Nidrei* services. Exhausted as they were that evening, their father's expression of pride and approval gave them renewed strength to face the fast day.

Yocheved and Mirel were to continue their brave acts of *chesed* before other *yamim tovim*, including Pesach, when they brought matzah to the observant laborers. What a tragic irony it was that Yocheved was to pass away on *erev* Pesach! May her holy *neshamah* be remembered.

As previously mentioned, Rebbetzin Mirel survived the war. She is now the Sarvasher Rebbetzin in Boro Park, Brooklyn. Over the years, she and her husband, R' Shabsi Meisels, *zt"l*, carried on the beautiful Chassidic way of life they had lived at home, and together they raised a Torah-true generation — of which my in-laws, *H"yd*, would have been proud.

CHAPTER 6
Storm Clouds on the Horizon

AFTER THE *TENAYIM* IN SATU MARE, MY *CHASSAN* RETURNED to his parents' home in Szaszregen for the nine months of our engagement.

Since it was wartime, I was reluctant to get married right away. I was worried that my *chassan* might be carted off to a labor brigade soon after our wedding. If that were to happen, would I ever see him again? Or would he become a war statistic? The thought of another forced separation — and the possibility of being emotionally wounded again so soon after learning of my father's death — was overwhelming. Every day saw large numbers of young men being dragged away from their homes, and many young brides were ultimately turned into young widows. I tried to convey my fears to my family, but they had their minds set on the wedding taking place as soon as possible. My *chassan's* family agreed.

By early 1944, my uncle decided against waiting any longer and, despite my reservations, set a date for the *chasunah*: Tuesday, March 15, 1944 / 19 Adar, 5704. (Coincidentally, our youngest child, Malka, was born to us years later on this same date.)

Even though Selish was my hometown, it was decided that the *chasunah* would be held in Nyir-Bator, Hungary. The Satmar *Chassidim* had discovered that the gendarmes there would not arrest a large gathering of Jews if they were bribed with a considerable sum of money. My family also found out that in Nyir-Bator it would be easier to obtain the great quantities of food needed for the *seudah*. The town's community leader, R' Avraham Lefkowitz, *a"h*, a devoted Satmar *Chassid*, saw to it that everything went according to plan. R' Moshe Dresdner, *a"h*, who doubled as the town's *shochet* (ritual slaughterer) and *sofer* (scribe), was appointed to write our *kesubah* (marriage contract). (R' Dresdner survived the war; he immigrated to the United States and resided in Boro Park. His son, R' Yaakov, heads a well-known Chassidic house in Williamsburg, Brooklyn.)

A distant cousin was kind enough to make all the wedding arrangements. Even under the best of circumstances, planning a *chasunah* for hundreds of guests is a monumental undertaking. Doing so in spite of all the wartime obstacles in our path was nothing short of a miracle.

Although traveling conditions were dangerous and potentially life-threatening for Jews, my in-laws, accompanied by their younger children, arrived safely in Nyir-Bator for the *chasunah*. Upon meeting them, I was immediately impressed by the venerable R' Rubin and his *aishes chayil* (wife; literally, "woman of valor"), Rebbetzin Alta Nechama Malka Rubin, and felt honored that they would be my parents-in-law. The younger Rubin children — my *chassan's* brothers Shmuel Shmelka and Mordechai David, and his sisters Yocheved, Mirel, and Shprintza — were all there, and they made me feel completely at ease. Seven-year-old Shprintza was especially delightful and adorable — not to mention precocious. Only her smile outshone her soft, blond, curly hair.

We had no way of foretelling the tragic future at the time, of course, but cheerful little Shprintza was to be victimized along with my revered and holy mother-in-law inside the Birkenau gas chambers just a few short months after that meeting. Sweet, quiet Yocheved, who smiled graciously and appeared quite the elegant young lady with so much to look forward to, was to perish in Bergen-Belsen, in the loving arms of her sister Mirel (the only one of my sisters-in-law to survive the war), shriveled from starvation and illness, just days before liberation. Within a short time as well, my oldest sister-in-law, Leah, and her innocent, endearing children, were also sacrificed in Birkenau, as was her husband. I was also to lose two of my new brothers-in-law, my husband's older brothers Usher Yeshayah and Yosef Mayer, the latter of whom had stood in for his father at our *tenayim*.

Despite my initial fears about getting married during the war, when I saw the happy, hopeful expressions in the eyes of my future in-laws, my trepidation seemed to fade away. Temporarily blocking out thoughts about the morose situation surrounding us all, I eagerly anticipated our future together. As I became better acquainted with my new family, I dreamed of the future when the A–mighty would grant children to my husband and me, and how, in a safer time, we would travel together to Szaszregen to visit his parents, the grandparents of our children. What pride we would all feel to be links in the dynastic chain of this illustrious Chassidic family!

Yet in the midst of all of this happiness a deep grief lurked — the knowledge that my beloved late father would not be there to know his grandchildren.

My dear, revered in-laws were never to see us again after the *sheva berachos*. However, in the few short moments that I spent with them the evening before my *chasunah*, all seemed well in our little corner of the world.

Later that evening a large *seudah* was prepared in my cousin's *shul*, but I did not attend. Many of our wedding guests were there, among them *Chassidim* from my *chassan's kehillah*, including long-time followers of my father-in-law. Besides our family, friends and acquaintances, poor people in the community were all invited and welcomed, as was the custom.

The *chasunah* took place in the late afternoon on the spacious grounds of the *beis midrash*, surrounded by still-bare trees, under clear blue skies with silky white, puffy clouds.

Traditionally parents escort their children to the *chuppah*, but in Galician *rebbishe* circles, such is the custom only for the oldest child. Thereafter, an older married brother escorts his sibling to the *chuppah*. In my case, however, as I had neither my father nor an older brother to take me to the *chuppah*, a cousin was assigned. My cousin, R' Lipa Teitelbaum and my brother-in-law, R' Yosef Mayer, escorted my *chassan* to the *chuppah*, and their wives, Rebbetzin Roisele and Rebbetzin Esther, escorted me. My revered mother and about-to-be mother-in-law walked near us.

I felt radiant and somewhat nervous in my delicate, custom-made, off-white silk gown. (I wore an off-white gown instead of a white one because Chassidic women, in an attempt to not imitate non-Jewish traditions, do not traditionally marry all in white.)

Under the *chuppah*, Rebbetzins Roisele and Esther led me around the *chassan* seven times. There are many schools of thought regarding why this is done: According to Kabbalah, the *kallah* circles the *chassan* seven times because the phrase "And when a man takes a wife" is written seven times in *Tanach*. It is also written in *Sefer Yirmiyahu* that "a woman shall go around a man." My husband once wrote a *teshuvah* (responsa) citing a number of sources in Kabbalah and mystic teachings as to why this is done.

Customarily the local rabbi performed the *Kiddushin* (wedding ceremony), but because our families were so renowned, the Rav of Nyir-Bator bestowed the honor of being *Mesader Kiddushin* upon my revered uncle, the Satmar Rebbe. In turn, my uncle passed the honor to my pious father-in-law, R' Yaakov Yisrael V'Yeshurin Rubin (Eichenstein), the Grand Rabbi of Ropshitz-Sulitz-Szaszregen, as a token of his deep admiration for him. Initially R' Rubin was reluctant to accept, but the Satmar Rebbe told him that since he was the father of the *chassan*, it was fitting that he should perform the *Kiddushin*.

Tears welled in my *chassan's* eyes as he watched his holy and esteemed father take his place in front of us and begin the proceedings. My *chassan* said the *"Harei At"* without being prompted, loudly and effectively — as one who knew what it was all about. I later learned that this is not common among Chassidic *chassanim*; most repeat the words after the *Mesader Kiddushin*. The *kesubah* was read aloud by the venerable Rav of Bator, R' Naftali Teitelbaum, *zt"l*, who then handed it to a designated representative instead of to me, following the accepted custom. We drank the wine from silver cups; then the seven blessings of the *Kiddushin* were recited by the Satmar Rebbe in such an arousing, thunderous voice that I still hear it today; it moved every soul present.

Finally it was time for my *chassan* to break the glass, a ritual which serves as the traditional end of the wedding ceremony. The glass is broken to commemorate the destruction of both the First and Second Temples, and to remind us Jews that even during times of private joy, we bemoan our lost holy glories.

The *gabbai* placed the glass on the ground before my *chassan*, and the silence was shattered by the sound of breaking glass. Our parents and guests shouted *"Mazel Tov"* in unison. In the eyes of the A–mighty, according to *halachah*, and in front of our family, friends and followers, R' Menachem Mendel Rubin and I were now married. Following the *chuppah*, we moved indoors where we proceeded to enjoy a lavish multi-course feast. It was nothing short of a miracle that such a bountiful amount of food was obtained for our wedding. My esteemed aunt, the Satmar Rebbetzin, was credited with this achievement by everyone who attended.

In step with the lively music of the band, nearly one thousand Chassidic men danced to their hearts' content. The pace and fervor of the dancing intensified as the evening wore on. The men danced around my uncle, my father-in-law, my *chassan*, and all close relatives and friends. The women and I joyfully danced on the other side of the *mechitzah* (room divider). My sister-in-law, Rebbetzin Mirel Meisels, remembers our *chasunah* as an exceptionally emotional and uplifting *simchah*.

Since we were in the midst of dangerous and uncertain times, Mirel and the other young children in my *chassan's* family were sent back to Szaszregen immediately after the *chasunah*. Much to their disappointment (and ours), they had to miss the week of *sheva berachos*.

MY ESTEEMED AUNT, REBBETZIN FEIGE TEITELBAUM, ARRANGED our first two *sheva berachos* meals in Nyir-Bator, after which our

Our Sheva Berachos and the Presentation of the Last Konsus in the History of Hungary

family and guests prepared to return to Selish with my mother, who had generously offered to host the remaining *sheva berachos seudos* in her Selish home. Fearfully, we boarded a train and arrived safely in Selish on *erev* Shabbos.

The *sheva berachos* were celebrated in a true *leibedik* manner with guests and elegant *seudos* (meals). On Friday (Shabbos) night, besides the *rebbishe "tish,"* my uncle, *zt"l*, and father-in-law, *zt"l*, danced, and the *ruach* of the *simchah* elevated everyone to such great heights that the crowd sang and danced with intense vigor and enthusiasm. That particular *sheva berachos* lasted until 3 a.m.! It would have been a *simchah* to remember for a lifetime, except that while it took place, our European brethren were being tortured and sacrificed at the hands of the Nazis and their collaborators.

The *sheva berachos* scheduled for Sunday, March 19, 1944, was to have special significance and import: this was the evening that my husband was to be officially presented with the Rabbinical contract, known as the *Konsus Rabbanus,* of the congregation of Muzsay, near Beregszaz. The *seudah* and *sheva berachos* was attended by a number of *rabbanim* from various townships and by a large crowd, among them my late cousins, R' Yoel Teitelbaum, the Kiralyhazer Rav, *zt"l*, and the late Bator Rav, *zt"l*. Some close relatives of my husband's who attended are still alive, including the Zidichoiver Rebbe in Queens, R' Isaac Eichenstein, *shlita*.

From the ladies' side of the room, I could just about see what was going on by peering through the cracks in the *mechitzah*, and I strained to hear the entertainment and the speeches which began after the elaborate *seudah*. A *badchan* (official jester at weddings) by the name of Elimelech Kish began the evening with some witty, Chassidic anecdotes. It was also his job to keep the proceedings moving along, and he called upon my *chassan* to deliver a *pilpul* — a lengthy lecture dissecting a particular statement in the Talmud. My new husband chose to discuss a higher level of Talmud called "Ho'il," meaning if it is in one's hands to do something, it might be already considered done. How ironic this is in retrospect. It was in our hands to hide, but it was not done. R' Lipa Friedman, a leading personality and a noted *talmid chacham* of the Selish community, who acted on behalf of the Ranziver House, and who later became a leader in the establishment and building of the Satmar movement in the United States, interrupted my *chassan's derashah* (lecture). He asked a question on the Talmudical question regarding this concept of *Ho'il*. In Yiddish, my *chassan* answered R' Friedman, "*Reb Lipa fregt zehr git* — Reb Lipa is asking a good question."

After my husband completed his *derashah*, the *badchan* returned and lauded the *chassan* for impressing the *mechutanim* (people related by marriage; in-laws) and the public with such a proper answer. As a result, the *badchan* ended each of his paragraphs with the words, "*Reb Lipa fregt zehr git.*" The *badchan* also "reprimanded" R' Friedman and "fined" him one thousand pengos for the charities of Selish and Muzsay because of his "interference with the *chassan's derashah.*" He said that the letters which make up the name "Lipa" are (in reverse order) the initials of the words, "*Elef pengo yiten Lipa,*" which in Hebrew means, "Lipa will give a thousand pengos."

At some point during the *seudah*, the committee from the Jewish *kehillah* in Muzsay, headed by R' Hersh Rubin, a brother-in-law of the late Shoproner Rav, and Mr. Yonah Steinberger entered the hall. In front of the entire crowd they presented my *chassan* with a letter of acceptance, called a *Konsus Rabbanus*. In European Orthodox circles, it was customary for a *kehillah* to present their newly-accepted rabbi with the *Konsus Rabbanus*, written and signed by its members. In my husband's case, the Satmar Rebbe was the first *Rav* in that vicinity — in a township called Orshava — and Muzsay accepted his authority. He then turned over this rabbinate to his sister's new son-in-law, my *chassan*. The *Konsus Rabbanus* contained eighty-two signatures. My *chassan* later told me that my uncle affectionately put his hand on his shoulder and whispered with a smile, "It's a small congregation, but I myself also didn't start out in Satmar [a large congregation]."

The delegates of Muzsay announced that the following day my uncle, father-in-law, and a number of other people would accompany my *chassan* to the township of Muzsay. There, my *chassan* would formally accept his new position and would deliver an acceptance speech at the local *shul*.

The mood in the room as these plans were announced was ecstatic; we were oblivious to what was festering outside our comfortable and orderly world.

A Phone Call to the Estreichers Changes Everything

WHILE OUR *SHEVA BERACHOS* WAS UNDER WAY, THE TELEPHONE RANG in the home of Mr. Moshe Binyamin Estreicher, a Selish resident. Mr. Shimon Namety from the Central Orthodox Office in Budapest was on the line. The Central Orthodox Office was an organization governed by a rabbinical and a lay committee, acting as an overall liaison organization for the Orthodox community's dealings with the Hungarian government. Mr. Namety urged Mr. Estreicher to find the Satmar Rebbe immediately and warn him that he must be on the next train home. Adolf Eichmann with his SS regiment had stormed into Budapest, and Hungary was under German control! All Hungarian Jews were now in grave danger, and starting the following day, Hungarian Jews would be forbidden to travel on trains. If caught, a Jew would be arrested by the German police and taken away.

THE JEWISH OBSERVER

The Satmar Rav זכר צדיק לברכה

As we go to press, we take note of the irreplaceable loss suffered by *Klal Yisroel* with the passing of the late Satmar Rav, Rabbi Yoel Teitelbaum זכר צדיק לברכה on 26 Menachem Av/August 19, at the age of 92.

The Satmar Rav, a direct descendant of both the famed "Yismach Moshe" and the "Chavas Daas" was recognized as a young man for his unusual *lomdus, hasmada* and *tzidkus*—Torah scholarship, diligence and piety, assuming his first rabbinical position as *rav* of Muzheyer at the age of seventeen. During the forty years following his Bar Mitzva, he never slept on a bed, except on *Shabbosos*, so involved was he in Torah study. By the outbreak of World War II, he was *rav* of the thriving community of Satmar and had emerged as one of the leading figures in Hungarian Jewry. (Rabbi Reuvain Grozovsky זצ"ל quoted his father-in-law, Rabbi Boruch Ber Lebowitz זצ"ל: "The Satmar Rav was *the* person to contact whenever the Polish and Lithuanian leadership had need to communicate with Hungarian Jewry.")

A biographical appreciation of the Satmar Rav (from The Jewish Observer) makes note of his serving as the Rav of Muzsay

Before a stunned Mr. Estreicher could ask any more questions, his caller hung up. Mr. Estreicher gathered some of his family who hurried alongside him to the *shul* where our *sheva berachos* was under way.

As soon as the Estreichers arrived, they sought out the Satmar Rebbe's *gabbai*, R' Yosef Askinazy (who now heads a *beis midrash* in Monroe, N.Y.). Since I was on the women's side of the room, I could not actually see what was going on, although I could hear what was happening. My *chassan* later told me that after the panic-stricken Mr. Estreicher relayed his message, R' Askinazy turned pale. Trembling, he returned to my *chassan's* table, and without making eye contact with anyone else, he walked directly toward the Satmar Rebbe, who looked up quizzically. R' Askinazy asked the others, including my *chassan*, to step away for a moment, and whispered into my uncle's ear. My uncle appeared to be distressed by the news.

By then the musicians had stopped playing, and the babble of voices from the celebrants died down as, one by one, people realized that something was seriously amiss. Those standing close to my uncle saw his face turn ashen, and the mood in the room, which had been festive just moments earlier, changed very quickly to one of tension and anxiety. A quiet murmur rippled through the room as our frightened guests turned to one another, asking what was going on. Many turned toward my uncle, seeking an answer. Trying to appear as calm as possible, my uncle said, "We will now *bentch* (say the blessing after a meal). Immediately afterward, everyone must go home. Our trip to Muzsay and the ceremony marking the acceptance of R' Rubin's rabbinate have been postponed."

Everyone was stunned by this unusual turn of events, but not really surprised. Even though the Satmar Rebbe did not offer any explanation at that time, word got out that starting the following day, Jews would no longer be able to travel. Our cousin, the Zidichoiver Rebbe, R' Isaac Eichenstein, *shlita*, later told us that on his way to the *sheva berachos* he heard rumors that the SS had occupied Budapest, and he had anticipated the strong possibility of such a decree. After *bentching*, all of the guests, including the Satmar Rebbe, my father-in-law, and all of our relatives, bid us a hasty farewell and hurried to the train station. This memorable *sheva berachos* had come to an abrupt end, and all of our plans were put on hold. My *chassan*, my mother and I would have to remain behind at my mother's house in Selish for the time being.

Not only were we disappointed over our guests' sudden departure, we also worried about them traveling home under such dangerous conditions. There had been rumors for days that something terrible was about to happen, and now the news that we were dreading to hear had become reality.

In Tractate *Gitin* we learn that while the *Beis HaMikdash* was burning down, unusual events were taking place in the town of Betar. At one end of the town people were rejoicing and dancing in the streets, while in another section of the town, others were murdered.

Our experience can be compared to this tractate. At the very same time that our elaborate *sheva berachos seudos* were being prepared — and while our last one was taking place — the Germans were making murderous preparations of their own, which would ultimately result in the capture of three-quarters of

Hungary's 650,000 Jews[1] — this, despite the fact that the Germans had already been defeated on the Russian front, and they saw that defeat would be inevitable in Western Europe at the hands of the Americans and the British as well. Seizing Hungary would not be strategically advantageous to the Nazis, but it would enable them to gain control over the Jews there — the last sizable Jewish community on the European continent that was still intact. No logical mind could explain the motive of such a demented undertaking. Greed might have been one possible motivation, as huge amounts of gold and jewelry were stolen from the Jewish victims, and the existence of a large pool of potential forced laborers might have been another.

Historically, our *rebbishe chasunah* was the last one to take place in Hungary. Our *Konsus Rabbanus* was also the last to occur among Hungarian Orthodox Jewry. It was also the last time my husband and I were to see many members of our respective families.

As we spent our final moments with my in-laws, my *chassan* and I held on to the hope that we would see them again soon, but deep in my heart I felt a tinge of sorrow as we said our farewells. I remember hearing my mother-in-law asking my *chassan* when she would see him again. Through his tears, he did not know what to say. Little did we know at the time that the answer was "Never."

Several times before their departure, my in-laws expressed deep concern for the fate of *Klal Yisrael* (the greater Jewish community), and although they did not say it in so many words, they were apprehensive about their own impending journey to Szaszregen. They silently worried about their children. Were they safe? Would they still be at home, waiting at the door with smiles and warm

---

1. According to most authoritative estimates, including those quoted by Holocaust historian Lucy S. Dawidowicz in *The War Against the Jews 1933 - 1945*, Hungary proper had a pre-war Jewish population of about 400,000, and then acquired another 250,000 Jews when it took over territories from Czechoslovakia, including my hometown of Selish; from Romania, including my husband's native Transylvania; and from Yugoslavia.

greetings? The terrible truth of what the future held had still not entered the realm of the believable.

The younger Rubin children were at home when they heard the distressing news. Fearfully they awaited the return of their parents, and sighed with relief when my in-laws reached their house. Immediately the children peppered them with questions. The deathly pallor of their parents' faces told the story; the children knew that the situation was critical. Together they prepared for what lay ahead.

EVEN THOUGH OUR FAMILIES HAD DEPARTED FROM SELISH ON Sunday evening, it seemed as though an eternity passed before the

Two Strangers as a Married Couple
sun rose above the horizon on Monday morning. For the time being, my immediate family was reduced to three: my mother — the elderly, widowed, aristocratic *tzadekes*; my new husband — a non-political and non-news-minded Chassidic young man, and I — a young, innocent, 19-year-old *kallah*. My mother had inherited an expensive diamond brooch which she sold before my wedding to purchase a small tenement house for us in Selish. Since it was customary for the *kallah* to provide *parnassah* (financial sustenance) for the first years of marriage, this tenement was to serve that purpose.

Even though raging black storm clouds were gathering over our heads, we attempted to continue with our everyday lives and routines. This was a special transitional time for us; even though we were now married, my husband and I barely knew one another, and we needed the first few days to become better acquainted. In addition, we each had our own obligations and duties to perform, he in the *beis midrash*, and I, setting up our household. As a young, nervous *kallah* I had so many questions, and my venerable mother was always there to supply the answers. She helped me put away our new dishes, and worked with me to prepare my first few meals.

My husband's routine included learning with his *chavrusos* (study partners) and putting together a group for *shiurim* (lessons). After the first *dvar Torah* my husband gave at *shalosh seudos*, R' Avraham Friedman, *o"h*, took him aside and offered him advice on preparing future *shiurim*. R' Shlomo Yisrael Klein, *zt"l*, the venerable *rav* of Selish, was kind and helpful to my husband. Among other things, he showed my husband the local *mikveh* (ritual bath), explaining in detail how it was built and operated according to *halachah*. Later, when my husband was to build a *mikveh* in the D.P. Camp Leipheim, these explanations would come in very handy.

As those precious early days of our newly married life passed, my husband, mother and I were too preoccupied with our new adjustments to fully comprehend the perilous situation that we were in. Who would have thought that in a matter of weeks, the three of us would be packed in boxcars with thousands of other innocent, unknowing Jews, headed for the ghastly, "ultra-scientific," bestial extermination factory of Auschwitz?

WE TRIED TO BOLSTER ONE ANOTHER'S MORALE. YET IN LIGHT OF what was happening around us, that was nearly impossible.

Our Days Are Numbered
Following Eichmann's occupation of Hungary on March 19th, a *Judenrat* (Jewish council which would govern the Jewish community) was formed to carry out German orders. The Selish *Judenrat* was a very honorable one.

On March 29th, anti-Jewish legislation began. Jews were forced out of the professions and ordered to sew the yellow Star of David on all their outer clothing. I still remember sitting next to my mother in my apartment as we sewed the Star of David on our coats.

Jewish property was confiscated, and Jews were isolated from their non-Jewish neighbors and banned to the ghettos. The ultimate plan for the Jewish citizenry was deportation and liquidation.

In order to carry out their plans swiftly and efficiently, the Germans divided Hungary into six zones (Zone I: the Carpathians; Zone II: Transylvania; Zone III: Northern Hungary; Zone IV: Southern Hungary east of the Danube; Zone V: Transdanubia including the Budapest suburbs; and Zone VI: Budapest), and with the help of the Hungarian police and the *Sondereinsatzkommando* (special-duty commando), the Germans began their task of rounding up the Jews, placing them in ghettos within their designated zones, then shipping them off to concentration camps.

In the meantime, Pesach was upon us. This was to be my husband's first Pesach away from his esteemed father's *seder* in Szaszregen, and his first one as a rabbi.

Preparations for the holy Passover went on as usual. My husband and members of the congregation baked matzos. I cleaned and thoroughly scrubbed our new apartment from top to bottom to rid our home of *chametz*. My mother and I, as well as all the other ladies in the *kehillah*, took out the Pesach dishes, polished the silver, and cooked for the *sedarim*.

The night before Pesach, using a wax candle and a feather, we searched our homes for *chametz,* and the following morning we burned all remaining *chametz.* Although the excitement of Pesach was in the air, the same air was polluted with danger as the tension around us intensified.

We heard that Jews were being taken away daily. How ironic: There we were, preparing for Pesach, the holiday which commemorates the Exodus of the Jews from Egypt, the holiday during which we say, "*Hashata avdei* —This year we are slaves." We did not grasp the real meaning of those words, we who were about to be taken into bondage by the Hungarian gendarmes working under orders from Berlin.

In the midst of our Pesach preparations I decided to hide my jewelry. By then we knew we were in imminent danger of being seized and evacuated from our home — but we didn't know when this would occur. I put some of my smallest but most precious pieces of jewelry into the large buttons of my jacket. There were five buttons on the jacket; I removed them and carefully sewed some diamond earrings and a diamond ring into the back part of the buttons, sealed them and sewed the buttons back on the jacket. If we were taken away, I would wear that jacket in the hope that I would be able to hold on to it until the end of the war.

Pesach 1944 finally arrived. Soon after my mother and I lit the Yom Tov candles, my husband returned from *shul* and we began our *seder*. Although he conducted the *seder* eloquently and the food was appetizing, none of us felt much like eating. On the first night the SS knocked on the door, wanting to place an officer with us, but our apartment was not suitable.

During one of the *sedarim* we heard a commotion outside our window. With trembling hands, my mother and I pushed aside the curtain to see what was happening in the street. Fearing the worst, I raced into the bedroom to put on the jacket containing the jewels. I returned to the window and looked outside. As it turned out, the commotion was simply a shouting match between two groups of Hungarian soldiers. Our hearts and temples still pounding, we returned to the table and shakily resumed the *seder*.

Sleep came with great difficulty that night. By that time we were all sleeping fitfully, not knowing what the next moment would bring. We remained tense throughout *Chol HaMoed* (the Intermediate Days of Passover) and the final two days of Pesach, yet were relieved to still be home, unharmed. That relief, however, was to be short-lived.

Seized by Levente (Hungarian Military) Youths

EARLY THE FOLLOWING MORNING MY HUSBAND LEFT OUR APARTMENT to go to *shul*. He was grabbed by two muscular *Levente* youths in the street. Hearing the commotion, I rushed to the window and watched helplessly as my husband was dragged down the street, around the corner and out of sight. A rush of panic overcame me. Would I ever see him alive again? Would they come for my mother and me, too? Where would we be taken? I ran to inform my mother of the latest alarming development.

My husband was taken to the city's main Orthodox *shul*. The *Leventes* shoved him upstairs into the women's section of the *shul*, where he found other rabbis and community leaders already there. We later learned that the German tactic was to first seize the *rabbanim*, the *shul* president, and other prominent leaders of the Jewish community. By taking them away first, the Germans and their Hungarian collaborators hoped to meet less resistance from the remaining masses of people. Once all of the leaders had been locked away, the other men were sought and taken to the *shul*. Even the old Grand Rabbi Yaakov Yitzchak Weisz, the Spinker Rebbe, *zt"l*, who was sick and bedridden, had been taken there — in his bed! This is the way the authorities worked; nobody was spared.

All of the seized men tried to remain calm and assess the situation. In the meantime, the rest of the Jewish community — men, women and children — were ordered to pack whatever they could carry for their move to the ghetto. As already mentioned, our house was within the ghetto's perimeters, so we would be permitted to remain where we were. All we could do was wait and hope that my husband would join us there soon.

My husband and the other prominent men remained locked in the *shul* until evening. The situation grew more tense as each agonizing hour passed. At one point, my husband was standing near a window and he caught sight of a lone German soldier outside, holding a machine-gun in his hand. For a few tense seconds, his eyes and the soldier's met through the window. My husband later told me that he would never forget the chill that seeped through his heart as he gazed into the murderous eyes of the SS soldier.

Sometime that evening the doors to the *shul* were suddenly flung open. Ruthless Hungarian soldiers slammed the butts of their weapons into the men and chased them out of the *shul*. As my husband and the others bolted out the door and into the cold night air, they found themselves surrounded by hordes of angry soldiers. My husband wondered if the soldiers would march them to a wall to be shot, or push them in the direction of the newly established ghetto.

A few tense moments later, the soldiers ordered the men to form a line. Once the soldiers finished a head count, they ordered the men to march. Nobody dared try to run away, lest they be pumped with bullets in the back by the hostile guards. A short time later, the men reached the walled-in ghetto.

Confined to the Ghetto

THE REST OF THE JEWISH COMMUNITY WAS ALREADY IN THE GHETTO by the time the soldiers shoved the men past the iron gates separating the Jews from the rest of the world. Cries and sobs of relief were heard everywhere. We were relieved to see the men returned to us, alive and well.

Despite our attempts to make the best of a desperate situation, we panicked because we did not know where our next meal would come from — or if we would even have another meal.

A *Judenrat* was ordered and its members rationed the prepared kosher food that was sent in by the Hungarian soldiers. Unfortunately, there wasn't enough food to feed the many innocent, imprisoned victims and the *Judenrat* had to carefully and equitably distribute what little food there was among us all.

Even though we were practically starving, conditions could have been much worse. Families were still intact and we continued to hold on to some of our possessions and jewels. The homes we stayed in were still immaculate and we were able to wash our clothing and remain clean. The one advantage of the ghetto was that the Jews had autonomous rule within the confines of its walls.

The Germans, as usual, fed us and everyone else not with food, but with lies. Every day brought another new lie. We were told that Jews who were injured while fighting in the Hungarian army were not forced into the ghetto; neither were Jews of mixed marriages or those with one non-Jewish parent. As earlier mentioned, we were told that we would ultimately be resettled in another Hungarian town, where we would remain with our families.

The late R' Moshe Weiss, *a"h*, (whose son is the son- in-law of the Klausenberger Rebbe, *zt"l*) was in the ghetto with us. One day he approached some community leaders, including my husband, and told them that when it was time for us to be deported, we should protest by refusing to march to the train. He also insisted that we build bunkers so that we should have a place to hide in the event of a raid. My husband later told us that nobody paid much attention to R' Weiss' suggestions. At the meeting, my husband proposed that before considering any drastic actions, we should await word from Jewish contacts in Budapest. As the days dragged on, however, no word came — not even a warning that something horrible was going on.

Finally, news did penetrate the ghetto walls. Our transport, the third, was going to be taken out of the ghetto a few days after Shavuos, and we were indeed going to a Hungarian work camp. The camp's name was Könyörmezö. As we were soon to discover, however, the existence of Könyörmezö was actually a lie they were feeding us.

Days later, on a warm and bright Shavuos afternoon, my husband was leading a *tish* in the courtyard in front of the house. About eighty Jewish men were there, singing traditional *zemiros*. *"U'va'u chulam bivris yachad, naaseh v'nishma amru k'echad* (Then they all joined together in a covenant — 'We will do and we will hear,' they said as one)." As their voices rose in inspirational song, my husband later told me, the group clapped and appeared festive —

not like people who were probably going to be shot a few days later.

In the meantime, one small group headed by Mr. Tullie Rosenberg (who survived the war, now lives in Los Angeles and is a philanthropist) built a bunker. My husband and I were invited to join the group, and returned home to quickly gather our jewelry and necessary belongings. We returned to the site of the bunker with my mother. When Mr. Rosenberg caught sight of my aged mother, his face fell. He took us aside, obviously uncomfortable, and bluntly told us that his group could not allow my mother in, because an elderly person could cause problems and hinder the others in an emergency.

My husband and I looked at one another in despair, and asked Mr. Rosenberg to excuse us for a few moments. We were not shocked by Mr. Rosenberg's request — it was his duty to protect the people in his small group. However, he was asking us to leave my delicate mother behind while the rest of us would remain in the bunker and have a greater chance of survival.

I was in an awful predicament. My husband and I had a chance for life, but how could I abandon my mother? I began to weep. Apologizing to my husband, I wanted to say that I could not allow myself to join Mr. Rosenberg's bunker, not if we had to leave my mother behind. Before I said anything, however, my husband seemed to understand what I was thinking and assured me that we would not abandon my venerable mother. We thanked Mr. Rosenberg for his well-intentioned offer, but politely declined. We told my mother that at the last minute we changed our minds about joining the others in the bunker. We returned home feeling somewhat disappointed, but knowing we had made the right decision.

Later, my husband and I went back to the bunker to wish Mr. Rosenberg well and to supply his group with some gold and jewelry for use just in case they were discovered and needed a negotiating tool to save their lives. By the time we arrived, the bunker was already closed. Silently, we walked back and awaited our dim future.

As the slow days before deportation passed, we made our final preparations.

My husband went to a tailor and had him hide several diamonds in the soles of his shoes. Unfortunately, as my husband was to later find out, the tailor did a poor job in securing the diamonds.

Meanwhile, I managed to search for my beloved father's unpublished *"sefer."* I found some of the precious papers in my father's elegant handwriting. I hid the pages inside my jacket and brought them to my husband, who buried the *sefer* with other valuables, as previously described.

On the night before our deportation, Thursday, June 4th, my husband went to speak to his Chassidic followers. He later told us that many *Chassidim* privately confided that they were terrified, primarily for their families. My husband gently reassured them and reminded them that whatever was in store for us, we were Jews who believed in Heaven's rule. We still believed, however, that we were going to a work camp, and that we would not be separated.

Since I have already described most of our torturous journey towards the infamous gates of Birkenau, I will here only discuss some of the thoughts which crossed our minds during those few remaining hours on the train on Sunday morning, June 7th.

After my husband found out that we were on our way to an extermination camp, we recalled Mr. Rosenberg's offer to hide us in his bunker. I began to wonder whether, according to *halachah*, we had made the right decision in turning him down. We questioned what good it would do my mother if my husband and I were killed along with her. We spoke quietly, so as not to disturb my mother who was deep in meditation, silently reciting *Psalms*.

Our thoughts naturally turned to Mr. Rosenberg himself, and the others with him in the bunker. Where were they now? Were they still safely hidden, or had they been discovered by the gendarmes? We prayed for their safety.

Rabbi Moshe Isserles, known as the Rema, Av Beis Din of Cracow, Galitzia, Poland, was the great halachic codifier of Ashkenzic Jewry. The famous Rema Synagogue in Cracow and the old cemetery there are both still intact. R' Rubin, shown here praying at the Rema's tomb some years after the war, and myself are both descendants of the Rema.

I fretted about the whereabouts of my revered uncle, the Satmar Rebbe, and his Rebbetzin. My thoughts then turned to my dear father. I found some comfort in reminding myself of the various Chassidic stories where *tzaddikim* in Heaven remember their relatives on earth. I wondered if he was looking down at us at that moment from *Gan Eden*, and tried to imagine what words of *chizuk* he would offer if we could only hear him.

My husband worried about his own beloved family in Szaszregen. Would the gendarmes also come for his parents, brothers and sisters? What was to become of his married siblings, their spouses and children? Were they in as much danger as we? Had they been condemned to the same fate? Wherever our thoughts wandered during that dreadful journey to Birkenau, they always returned to one word: faith. We had to maintain our faith.

The remainder of our journey dragged on as we tensely awaited new developments.

The train made another stop. The sign indicating that we were in Cracow stared bleakly back at us through the cattle car's tiny window. Trying to make conversation, my husband commented that Cracow was the birthplace of the great *Rema*, R' Moshe Isserles, who annotated the text of the *Shulchan Aruch* (written by

The Aron Kodesh of the Rema's Shul

R' Yosef Caro, who followed the practices of the Sephardic communities) and thus made it the ultimate codex of Jewish law for Ashkenazic Jews as well. Cracow and Selish had something in common: the last Rav of Cracow, R' Yosef N. Kornizer, came from Selish.

Abruptly the whistle blew and the train pulled out of the station. I was suddenly overcome with a queasy, unsettled feeling and somehow knew that the next stop would be the end of the line for us — both literally and figuratively. Not wanting to frighten my husband or mother any further, I kept this uneasy feeling to myself.

CHAPTER 7
The Death Camps

ASHORT WHILE LATER, THE TRAIN SCREECHED UNEXPECTEDLY to a sharp halt, causing its bewildered passengers to collapse against each other. This abrupt stop felt different

Our First View of Birkenau from the other routine ones we had made along the way. Fear permeated the stilted silence which filled every corner of our boxcar. It was easy to figure out that we had been deceived and were not going to a "family labor camp" as the Germans had promised.

We turned to one another — spouses, neighbors, mothers, fathers, *zeides*, *bubbes*, sons, daughters, brothers, sisters, aunts, uncles, rebbes, teachers, friends — our eyes silently communicating our terror. We realized that these might be the last few moments we would see our dear ones alive. There was so much we wanted to say to one another, but the words wouldn't come.

The cars were crammed with men, women and children, who were given no food and no water. Our journey from the ghetto of Selish to Birkenau was two-and-a-half days of sheer, inhuman torture. I cannot to this day understand how I am, please the A-mighty, here to tell my story.

Before we had time to think, or find words to express our thoughts and feelings, violent and noisy blows began to rain against the car doors, shaking us up and frightening us further. We heard men screaming angrily, *"Raus! Raus! (Out! Out!)."* Suddenly, to our shock, the freight car door was forced open by skeletal men dressed in striped clothing and caps. We later learned that these men were Jewish prisoners forced to unload valises and dead bodies from the cattle cars.

Just as the German SS was trained in sadism and viciousness, so they indoctrinated and forced such helpless prisoners to perform their assigned duties. Some were even appointed as *"kapos"* — overseers whose job it was to keep their fellow prisoners docile and obedient by any means necessary, not excluding brute physical force. After many years of humiliation and psychological torment these unfortunates followed their SS captors. It is no wonder that some of them, so brutalized for several years, had lost most of their human characteristics, and had taken on the attributes of German sadism.[1]

Our eyes had become accustomed to the darkness of the boxcars. As the bright morning sunshine poured in, we squinted at the sud-

---

1. It must be mentioned, however, that there were some Jewish and non-Jewish *kapos* who displayed kindness and mercy toward the prisoners and who "looked the other way." I firmly believe that some of these *kapos* were among the true heroes of the Holocaust.

den rush of light, and stared at our immediate surroundings in bewilderment. Many from our transport began to weep piteously as the SS continued their harsh, guttural shouting. I saw their wild hands and those of the inmates reaching up roughly to grab people. Everyone — including the pregnant, the elderly, the sick and

The system the Germans used to transport people to the concentration camps was terribly cruel – even subhuman. These are pictures of the type of boxcars we were transported in. There was little air and no sanitary facilities.

the blind — was mercilessly dragged out through the doorway.

I trembled at the prospect of being handled by those men. As insufferable as conditions had been inside the boxcar, I felt safer inside, and momentarily wished that I could remain hidden somehow — but, of course, there was no place to hide.

I felt the inmates grabbing and pulling me roughly forward, and saw and heard the Nazis behind them, maniacally screaming at us. Before I knew it, I lay sprawled on the rough pavement, momentarily winded by the impact of being thrown out of the car.

Catching sight of my husband and fragile mother nearby, I struggled to my feet, then helped my mother to hers. Surveying my new surroundings, I tried to catch my breath and absorb the reality of the unimaginable. I turned to my husband, and his saddened gaze met mine.

"Will there be another day for us?" we asked each other with our eyes.

Our nonverbal exchange was cut short as my husband was seized by cold-blooded German soldiers and dragged away with the other men. Within seconds he was swallowed up in a sea of unknown people. Suddenly I discovered that my mother had also disappeared, and I was standing alone among thousands of strangers!

Behind me, I heard a snarling SS soldier shout, "You're in Auschwitz now!" as he proceeded to nearly beat the life out of a helpless new arrival. My heart sank as I realized that everything the sneering Hungarian guard had told my husband just a few short hours earlier, at the Nove-Sacz train station, was indeed true. We were now in a Nazi extermination plant!

Auschwitz/Birkenau was located just outside the small Polish village of Oswiencim. Before World War II, Oswiencim was a town with a fine religious Jewish community. During the course of the war, however, Oswiencim would become the international symbol of the worst subhuman crimes imaginable to the human mind, as well as of nightmares which had not yet been imagined. The name Oswiencim is not widely recognized today, but nearly everybody has heard of its Germanicized equivalent — Auschwitz — the infamous site of the incomprehensible, cruel, unprecedented mass murder of infants, children, and adults — the elderly, the young — mothers, fathers, intellectuals, peasants, war heroes and criminals. The modern, scientific technology of the Germans, the systematic, sceintific, deadly efficient plants of the Nazis, were responsible for torturing and killing them all.

When Himmler was showing Commandant Hoess the site in Auschwitz before the camp was erected, Hoess asked, "Where will you get the manpower to build this camp?" Himmler answered that the prisoners will erect the camp themselves! And so it was that Jewish and Polish prisoners, as well as those from other nations, built that extermination factory! This tactic of the Germans was not very different from forcing other prisoners elsewhere, such as my father, *H"yd*, to dig their own graves!

The generic name "Auschwitz" actually encompasses three adjoining concentration camps: the original Auschwitz I; Auschwitz II, or Birkenau — the main killing center of the complex; and Auschwitz III, or Buna. Buna provided slave labor for a nearby chemical factory operated by the infamous German industrial cartel, I.G. Farben.

We later found out that it was to Birkenau's unloading platform that our train had pulled up on that sunny Sunday morning. Little did we know then that approximately 12,000 innocent people, mostly Jews, were being murdered daily at this site. By this stage of the war, the Germans had realized that as a result of Hitler's strategic blunders, they were losing the war. Urgent orders from Berlin expedited the mass murder of Jews before the final German defeat.

The Germans were also determined to liquidate the Russian and Polish intelligentsia as well as other "inferior" masses in order to make room for their own "Aryan race." To this end, Birkenau became the site of the bloodbath of innocent victims of other nationalities as well.

A firing squad of task-force commandos adds to the pile of corpses in a clearing near the Polish town of Bydgoszcz

My eyes turned toward the cold, metallic train tracks extending beyond an ominous brick guardhouse. I later learned that these tracks, which led our train directly into Birkenau, had only recently been extended by orders from Berlin. Previously the tracks had ended at Auschwitz I, approximately a mile away from Birkenau. Victims selected in Auschwitz I for the gas chambers were herded into trucks to be taken there.

In the normal world, railroad tracks are extended to make it more convenient for passengers to disembark. In the twisted, sick logic of the Third Reich, however, the distance between Auschwitz I and Birkenau was a problem because it slowed down the process of "handling" the new transports of victims. Practically overnight, it was accomplished, with the help of the best engineering minds the Germans could find. New tracks were quickly built to go directly into Birkenau, near the gas chambers, and to thus speed up the killing process

I was sickened by the sights and smells of the camp. Black smoke and bright red flames shot heavenward from a nearby chimney, and a terrible stench, with a bizarre sweetness to it, filled the smoky air. Dust particles and embers invaded my lungs and made me cough uncontrollably. We later learned that thousands of bodies were burned daily in the four huge crematoria, and the putrid smell was the burning human flesh of our Jewish brethren, even of our closest relatives. The stench did not reach the nostrils of the Pope in the Vatican, it did little to awaken Winston Churchill at 10 Downing Street in London, nor did it disturb the slumber of President Franklin Delano Roosevelt in the White House in Washington. And what about the Jewry of the Free World and of Palestine?

Small particles of ashes — all that remained of what had been living human beings just a short while ago — swirled around in the wind and blew into our faces. When I revisited Auschwitz-Birkenau in 1953, I was to relive that awful experience. As I stood by the ruins of Crematorium IV, a powerful gust of wind blew some stray ashes into my face. Remembering that there was a pit next to Crematorium IV which was filled with human ashes, I wondered whose ashes had grazed my face. Could they have been those of my revered relatives?

Using clubs and canes, the SS continued to chase the bewildered and helpless people. Many of the Germans were accompanied by fierce, snarling dogs straining at their leashes, ready to tear into the flesh of anyone who resisted. What frightened me more than the clubs or the dogs, however, were the machine guns and bayonets, and I shuddered at the possibility of the SS pumping bullets into us on a whim.

THE ORDERLIES LINED US UP IN GROUPS OF FIVE. AS OUR LINE advanced, I observed that each person was forced to stop before a

Mass Murder by the Flick of a Finger

tall, youthful German who was immaculately dressed from his death's-head insignia cap right down to his shiny black jackboots. I saw him glance, steely-eyed, at each person, then flick his wrist, pointing his thumb either to the left or to the right. The orderlies would enforce his decisions, pushing each person to the left or right as ordered.

Finally it was my turn to stand in front of him. My mind froze as I looked into his piercing eyes, my heart pounding wildly in fearful anticipation. Even though I had never met this man before, I sensed that I was in great danger. He acted as one who had the power and authority to determine everyone's fate and position in Auschwitz. I later found out that this man was the subhuman Josef Mengele, who had obtained a medical degree in Berlin and brought shame to the title of "doctor." Besides sending more than 400,000 men, women and children to their deaths, Mengele was responsible for conducting cruel and inhuman "medical experiments" on many Jewish and non-Jewish prisoners with unprecedented sadism.

Mengele motioned me to the right with his thumb. Later we found out that Mengele selected people still capable of working, such as myself, for hard labor, and sent the others, including my saintly mother, to die in the gas chambers. I saw the line of women standing on the left side, some yards away from us. Most of the women carried babies or held the hands of small children. Sobbing youngsters fearfully clung for the last time to their mother's skirts, piteously weary and soiled from the uncomfortable cattle-car journey. Many of these sweet children stared about them with glazed eyes, not knowing that civilization, humanity and mercy vanished right there. Parched beyond human comprehension, they cried, *"Vasser* (water), Mamma, *vasser!"* Pain and anguish lined their mothers' faces. How could they find a merciful way to explain to their thirsty offspring what kind of danger they were in?

As I turned my head, I saw lines of men in the distance and wondered whether my husband was among them. For a brief moment, I felt as if I did not want to go on without my husband and mother by my side.

Just when the situation seemed to be incredibly hopeless, I perceived a tiny ray of light. Near my position on line, I spotted four close girlfriends from home. They were the ones I had seen but could not approach in my boxcar, because it had simply been too crowded for anyone to move.

Still unmarried and living at home, they had come with their parents and siblings. The four girls were Perel, 20 years old, whom everybody called Parry for short; Perel's older sister, Rita, who was 22; Miriam, also 20; and Rivka, Perel's niece, only 16 but tall for her age. Because of Rivka's height, she had managed to pass Mengele's selection; usually, the death-doctor automatically consigned girls under the age of 18 straight to the gas chambers. As if in a groggy dream, I ran over to them as quickly as possible and they, upon spotting me, grabbed me by the shoulders and hastily positioned me as the fifth in their line. The five of us huddled closely together, trying to avoid more blows and slaps from the Germans. The horrified expressions in my friends' eyes must have mirrored my own; I could see that they were as frightened as I. Our teary silence was broken by shouts in German.

"You're going to the showers for delousing! *Schnell! Schnell!"* the SS cried.

The SS quickly led us into a nearby red brick building and ordered us to remove our garments. Many women, especially those raised in *frum* circles, almost collapsed from shock. Most of us began to weep in sheer terror. In a matter of moments, however, our clothing was piled everywhere. After the war, we learned that the Germans had sorted through our garments and taken whatever they wanted for their girlfriends or wives. The remaining items were distributed via Berlin among German civilians throughout Germany.

The opportunity to steal from the victims proved to be as strong a motivation for the actions of the German officers and soldiers as simple hatred of the Jews. During the time of Queen Esther, a similar phenomenon occurred. Haman's request, which was granted by King Ahasuerus, was for permission to annihilate the Jews. Yet, when he ordered his underlings to effect the genocide, Haman added that they could loot the belongings of the victims as well.

From the first room we were chased into a second one, stumbling and tripping over each other as we tried to push our way through the narrow stone passageway. Once inside, *K.Z. (Konzentrationslager)* male inmates shaved our heads and scraped off all our body hair. Not only was the ordeal humiliating, it was also painful. Since there were enormous numbers of people arriving daily, the scissors and clippers used by the inmates were already rusty, their blades dull. Supplies of fresh blades were scarce. Some girls screamed in pain, but this did not elicit any sympathy from the *K.Z.* inmates, who continued chopping off the hair. The lives of these inmates were also on the line, and they had to continue cutting quickly, or face the ovens themselves.

Hills of beautiful, soft hair — brown, black, blond, red, gray, silver and white — curly, straight, and braids still intact — began mounting by the minute as the *K.Z.* inmates continued clipping at a fast pace.

Many young girls wept in shame from the humiliation of having their heads shaved and seeing their beautiful hair on the floor. The experience was not quite as shocking for me since, as a *kallah*, my head had been shaved after the *chasunah* and I had seen my own hair in a pile. Then, however, I submitted to the shaving willingly, as it was done for religious reasons; now, however, it was done maliciously, to shame us. I began to cry, not only for my own pain, but also for the pain of the other branded women. We were now women whose heads were either starkly bald or peppered with short tufts of hair. We stared at one another in shock: we had been transformed into carbon copies of one another! This was a key tactic in the Nazis' efforts to break our spirits and to discourage us from resisting.[2]

In a frenzied panic, my girlfriends and I tried to locate one another in that room of chaos and despair. Once together again, we tightly clasped one another's trembling, cold hands to ensure that we would not be separated again. All of us were weeping forlornly by then, and we simply concerned ourselves with remaining together for as long as possible. The veteran inmates, already hardened from their stay in the camp, wondered how we — the new inmates — could still feel shame and have tears in our eyes. They told us that soon we would harden too, once we realized where we were.

We were next herded through another doorway into a white, tiled room with shower heads built into the ceiling. Each of us was given a tiny piece of yellow soap. Crammed in with barely enough room to move and breathe, we were suddenly inundated by powerful, shocking streams of ice-cold water from the shower heads. Some of the women and girls were knocked back by the force of the high-powered streams of water — but there was no escape. We instinctively raised our arms and hands to protect our shaven, raw heads, now stinging and throbbing from the jet streams of water.

Minutes later, the water was shut off as quickly as it had been turned on. Soaking wet and stumbling on the slippery stone floor, we were pushed through yet another door which led outside to a dingy courtyard. We were each handed an ill-fitting, threadbare, gray prison dress, reeking strongly of chlorine.

---

2. Our hair was carefully collected and sold to German industries. The Third Reich kept a meticulous accounting of these transactions. After the war, the Allies seized voluminous records, listing shipments figured out to the last kilogram of hair, and anticipated payments calculated almost down to the last pfennig.

To our dismay, we were not given undergarments, stockings or socks, but we were given shoes. I was grateful to the A-mighty for this small favor because I later saw other prisoners limping around the camp with ill-fitting wooden clogs.

The SS laughed at us as we stumbled about the courtyard in a daze. Even today, over half a century later, I cannot forget or describe the special brand of sadism the Germans possessed. No matter how hard I try, my words will never adequately convey the humiliation and degradation my fellow victims and I suffered on our first day in Birkenau.

My friends and I were spared the painful indignity of having a number carved into our arms. We later found out that the SS had classified us as possible transport prisoners. Instead of being tattooed, we were ordered to glue prison numbers on our prison garb. Therefore, unlike my husband and many other former inmates, I have no tattooed number on my arm.

After we had been issued our "uniforms," we wondered when we would be given water, or perhaps something to eat. We had eaten very little in the cattle car, and had even less to drink. Our mouths and throats were parched, and I could hear my own empty stomach groaning. But on our first day at Birkenau, the SS did not grant us a drop of water or a smidgen of food. This was yet another form of German sadism. Instead of feeding us, the SS made a motion with their trigger-hungry fingers and ordered us to march. Escorted by their vicious dogs, they led us through one section of the camp after another. We dragged our tired feet through the muddy pathways and noticed how each section was fenced off with high, electrified barbed-wire fences.

Finally, we were ordered to stop in a bleak area filled with dilapidated huge wooden barracks surrounded by weeds and unkempt brownish-green grass. Except for small panes of glass atop the wooden structures, there were no windows. I surmised that it would be dark and bare inside.

The lines of barracks seemed to stretch unto eternity. As far as I could see, there were electrified barbed-wire fences and heavily guarded watchtowers everywhere. And off in the distance, I once again saw the fierce flames. One thing was always constant in Auschwitz: the steady red flame, extending upward to a thick and overcast sky. A sense of doom gripped me, and I broke into a cold sweat. Would any of us ever get out alive?

Instead of allowing us to use the latrines, the SS ordered us to stand for *zeilappel* (roll call). The Germans continued to take head counts while we were forced to stand motionless. This *zeilappel* lasted a few hours, as would others that followed, and we watched the transition of day into night. Once the sun had set, the air became more frigid, and I began to shiver. Never in my life had I ever trembled so much from the cold, not even during the bleakest and darkest winters back home. I am sure that my fears played a major role in my trembling.

As dusk mercifully brought our first day in this hellish place to a close, we were strangely relieved. In the dark we would not be able to see as much of the horror around us, and we would be somewhat hidden from the cruel eyes of the SS. Isn't it ironic how, under normal circumstances, we look forward to the sun rising in the morning? Sunshine and daytime are symbols of happiness — but in this inferno, we actually looked forward to twilight.[3]

Our relief proved short-lived. As soon as the sky grew dark, the entire camp was lit up by high-intensity spotlights. We could even hear the electric juices zapping through the wires strung above our heads. What amazed me was how incredibly bright those lights were. I had to squint in order to protect my eyes from the glare. This artificial sun lit up the camp, creating the illusion of daylight.

---

3. This wasn't the case in Ebensee where my husband, R' Rubin, was. There, Commandant Ganz and Lord, his vicious, biting dog, tortured the inmates as they returned from work.

This was just another German tactic to torture us and to keep us under surveillance at the same time.

Finally, our female *kapo* ordered us inside the barracks. Hundreds of us filed into a stuffy, almost airless room, and were dismayed to find no bunks to sleep on. Our "bed" was to be the bare dirt floor. The *kapo* ordered us to sit down (in lines of five, of course) and once seated, to put our knees up so that the girl in front could lean back onto them. Following these orders seemed impossible, because we were already cramped for space and we were literally on top of one another. But threatened by the whip, we quickly scrambled to the floor. Somehow, my girlfriends and I managed to remain together as a fivesome.

The lights went out and the doors were locked behind us. One could hear agonized cries of *Shema Yisrael* coming from various directions. When I came to the *pasuk* (verse), "*V'chara af Hashem bachem* (And the A-mighty's anger will be aroused against you)," I stopped to think, What does this mean to us, interned in Birkenau?

But today, as I remember and write this, I would like to draw the attention of the reader to another verse several lines later, "*L'maan yirbu yemeichem v'yemei vneichem* (that your days may be multiplied, as will be those of your children)...*" [One of my main motives in writing this book is to emphasize the idea of "*L'maan yirbu* ... "]

The first night in Birkenau went on like an endless nightmare punctuated by snatches of fitful sleep.

Before dawn, the door to the barrack was abruptly flung open and the *kapo* ordered us out for *zeilappel*. Dazed and aching though we were, we practically flew out to avoid the sharp blows of her truncheon. Our thin dresses offered little in the way of warmth or protection from the chilly pre-dawn air as we stood outside shivering, watching the fiery red sun rise in a smoke-filled sky.

After *zeilappel*, a couple of *kapos* brought in filthy barrels of foul-smelling liquid they called soup. A piece of dark bread, which tasted like straw, was handed out to each woman. The *kapo* gave each group of five women a tin bowl to share. Without spoons, we were forced to take turns sipping the "soup" out of the communal bowl. It was a very degrading experience, another form of torture by the Germans. If not for the fact that my friends and I were close, we would have fought for that larger sip as others did.

During one meal we received a thin slice of liverwurst, but my friends and I did not touch the meat because it was obviously *treif*. While we still had strength from home, we were able to turn down the *treif* meat and sometimes even trade it for a piece of bread or soup.

We weren't assigned any work during those first days in Birkenau. When we were not standing on line for hours at *zeilappel*, we were inside the barrack trying to comfort one another by recollecting, imagining and philosophizing. Although we knew that the odds were against us, my friends and I continued our attempts to boost one another's morale.

Life experience has taught me that by occasionally allowing the mind to slip away from reality into a daydream, one can, at least temporarily, alleviate the emotional and physical agony of a seemingly impossible situation. In the concentration camps, daydreaming helped us to "escape" from our imprisonment and enabled us to better cope with our dreadful situation.

A FEW DAYS AFTER OUR ARRIVAL IN BIRKENAU, THE SS BARGED INTO our barrack in the middle of the night, screaming, *"Alle raus! Alle raus! Schnell!"*

Work Factory Under the Wehrmacht

Startled and groggy, we stumbled over one another into the cold night air. As I looked around, I noticed that none of the women from the other barracks had been called outside. I wondered why we were the only barrack to be summoned, and whether these would be our final moments alive. Gazing at the huge flame reaching towards Heaven, I feared that we would be its next fuel.

I was jolted back to reality by the sound of the SS officer's voice ringing through the cold night air.

"Who knows how to sew?"

Weak with relief that we were not about to be summarily killed, I followed my instincts and stepped forward. Parry, Rita, Miriam and Rivka followed my lead. Soon others stepped out, and once five hundred heads were counted, the German sent the remaining girls back to the barrack.

The volunteers were ordered to march into the darkness. A few moments later, we reached some train tracks where a freight train awaited us. Silhouetted in the background was the ominous guardhouse we had seen upon our arrival in Birkenau. It was then that I realized we were standing at the arrival ramp, at the very place where I had been separated from my esteemed mother and husband.

The Germans wasted no time in packing us inside the freight train. A whistle blew and the freight train slowly pulled out of Birkenau. Despite the fact that we were wedged into the cars with standing room only, we were relieved to be moving away from this place of horrors. Of course, we had no way of knowing where we were headed. Could we be going to a place worse than Auschwitz-Birkenau?

About a day later, our transport arrived at Krotingen, a town near Riga, Latvia. The SS ordered us off the train and we had to stand for *zeilappel*. Some soldiers dressed in regular German army uniforms approached the SS and began speaking to them. Then the unexpected happened. The SS handed us over to the *Wehrmacht* soldiers and left. As we saw the SS leave, our morale improved. We had already been transported out of Birkenau, and now we were no longer directly under the thumb of the SS! We anxiously waited to see what would transpire next.

The head officer introduced himself to us as our new *Stabzahlmeister* (the head officer of a factory), and announced that we would be working for the *Wehrmacht*, sewing uniforms for the German army. Apparently, the SS officials at Auschwitz had

A groups of female camp inmates on their way to work detail. But for the dresses, you would never know they were women.

"rented" us out to the German army. After the *Stabzahlmeister* spoke, some of the other soldiers pulled him aside and whispered something.

Returning to us, the officer said, "I don't understand. We asked for women and the SS sent you instead. We didn't ask for men."

"But we are women!" we shot back in amazement.

Their mouths dropped. "How can this be?" they asked. "All of you have shaven heads, and … "

"They shaved our heads in Auschwitz," we explained.

We couldn't blame them for being shocked. With our shaven heads, baggy clothing and skinny figures, we really did look like men. It was heart-wrenching for us to recall that we were once healthy, attractive women before undergoing the brutal metamorphosis in Birkenau. The soldiers nodded in assent and without shouting or pushing, ordered us to follow them to the factory. We didn't yet understand this new, less cruel German tone.

The factory building was huge and dusty, with a minimal amount of light trickling in through dirty windows. Even though the windows were open, there was not much ventilation inside.

Torn uniforms needing mending, spools of thread and sewing machines littered the room from one end to the other. Small pieces of material, probably discarded from the garments being sewn, lay all over the hard wooden floor, and huge bins of garbage were lined up in the back.

The tailors and seamstresses — both men and women — did not even glance up as our group walked by. We later learned that many of them were local Jewish citizens of Latvia who were forced to work there. Some workers had been there for years and it was they who held the most "prestigious" positions of all: working in the office. I noticed many empty sewing machines and assumed that we would be assigned to operate them.

But first we had to be oriented into our new "home." We were filthy and our uniforms were shabby from the grueling ride in the freight car. Fearing that we might be infested with body lice — which, at the time, was not yet the case — the soldiers took us for disinfection. Of course they made it clear that the disinfection was not for our benefit; they only wanted to protect their uniforms from lice infestation. We didn't complain, however. The soap they gave us easily washed away the dirt and filth in which we were covered — and the shower water was warm! I almost felt like a human being again.

The uniforms issued to us were also a welcome change. Instead of the shapeless gray prison dresses we had worn in Birkenau, we were each given a pair of comfortable military pants and a matching jacket. We still had our shoes and were given scarves to cover our heads.

Once clean and dressed, we were led into a dining hall where we were served a bowl of nourishing soup and a piece of bread. After lunch, the soldiers took us to our work stations. My friends were assigned to their sewing machines, and a soldier led me to a separate table. There were several other women already working there.

My job, the officer informed me, would entail sewing felt boots for the soldiers. I felt my face turn pale: I had not the slightest idea how to make boots! Trying to appear calm, I began to handle the felt material, huge needle, and heavy thread. With an armed soldier standing behind me and observing, it was amazing how quickly I learned how to make boots! Within a matter of hours, I was quite proficient at this new skill of sewing with double needles.

I was assigned to the day shift, and worked from sunup to sundown. The labor was backbreaking, the workroom sweltering; yet despite the difficulty and discomfort, we were expected to fill a daily quota. When long shadows appeared and the light from outside began to dim, I knew that my shift was almost over.

Following my evening meal, I collapsed, exhausted, into bed. I was grateful to have a real bed to sleep in, even though the covered straw was hard and the blankets were made of rough, regulation army material.

My friends were assigned to the same barrack, and fell into a similar daily routine.

What impressed me most about the *Wehrmacht* soldiers was that they treated us more like human beings. Even *zeilappel* was not as strenuous — the soldiers dismissed us right after the first head count. There was a catch, however. All of the time we were working in the factory, we were still under the control of the SS. Every night, the SS showed up at the factory for inspection. The *Wehrmacht* officials would warn us of the SS's impending arrival. We stiffened to attention as we saw the privileged SS officers pulling up in their fancy automobiles. [The soldiers of the *Wehrmacht* were not informed about the concentration camps. Only their generals knew.]

The Russians Are Coming

DURING THE MOURNFUL DAYS BEFORE TISHAH B'AV, WE HEARD shelling in the far distance. We sensed that the Russian front was nearing. One bleak day, the *Stabzahlmeister* assembled us outside and with a grim expression on his stern face, said, "The Russian army is advancing and all of us have to vacate this area immediately. We have no choice but to hand you back to the SS."

Groans welled from throats up and down the line. Instead of being freed by the Russians as we had begun to hope we might soon be, we were being reclaimed by the SS! When I looked at the other women, their facial expressions mirrored mine. They, too, were in a state of panic; unadulterated terror glazed their eyes. Little did we know that this was only the beginning of a torturous journey through a hellish jungle; it also marked the beginning of the end of Nazi Germany.

Soon we were assembled for *zeilappel*, where we were confronted by the hated SS. One of the SS men began shouting at us.

"Your easy days with the *Wehrmacht* are now over. You are back with us now! We are taking you on a long march, and anyone not able to keep up will be shot.

"And by the way," he added with a smirk, "it won't do you any good to try to run away and look for the Red Army. One woman already tried and we found her hiding in a field. Our soldiers dragged her out, cut up her body and left the pieces there to rot. The last time we looked, the hawks were hovering over her, pecking away." We cringed in fear as we listened to their wild laughter.

The SS took back our shoes and handed us wooden clogs to wear. This was the first time that I had to wear the inflexible clogs, and I experienced immediate discomfort. I wondered how I would manage to walk in them.

We were lined up and led away from the factory — a place which had provided us with some semblance of tranquility for a while. Soon we found ourselves on the side roads which ultimately led into the deep woods. The SS probably chose to take this route in order to stay out of the way of the retreating Germans on the main roads, and because they wanted to camouflage their barbarism from the population.

On the march, the clogs made it difficult for me to maintain the running pace set by the SS. To add to our agony, the Germans did not give us any food or water from the moment we set out. They could have murdered us outright, but the order from Berlin was to get as much use out of the victims as possible: make them work until they dropped dead.

Bombs were exploding everywhere. We ran for cover into the ditches, where we vied for space with the dead and broken bodies of martyrs from previous marches. The Germans had us covered with their high-powered machine-guns and pistols, and their vicious dogs, trained to tear us limb from limb upon command, snarled and snapped at our heels. We knew that the bombs had the potential to wipe us all out in a split second, or we could be shot, or we could die of exhaustion and starvation. Yet we kept on moving.

We actually hoped for rain so that we could tilt our heads back, open our parched mouths and let the water drip in — but the skies remained clear. Our swollen feet began to bleed: the hard wooden clogs were cutting our feet, rubbing off tender skin, and splinters made it nearly impossible to put our weight on the affected areas. Some of the girls even tossed the clogs aside, believing that the walk would be less painful without the added torture of the terrible wooden shoes. This was a disastrous mistake, however, because their bare feet were now completely unprotected from the filthy ground littered with thorns and small pieces of wood, which penetrated their arches and heels.

Hundreds of women died every day. Their bloody bodies were piled high in surrounding ditches. Parry, Rita, Rivka, Miriam and I somehow managed to stay together despite the chaos around us. Sometimes when one of the girls began to falter, the rest of us would support her on our shoulders.

Soon our throats and mouths were so dry that we could not speak. We had to conserve whatever strength remained for the arduous run through the woods. All I could think about was moving forward; I forced myself not to look back at the bodies of people I knew, lying in the ditches.

We marched for a number of days. Since the Germans did not have enough men to change guards for the night, they had to find places to stop for a few hours' sleep. They would find abandoned buildings or a concentration camp along the road, and order us to go along with them.

One evening, we stopped in a small concentration camp. Upon entering the camp, we were assailed by a putrid smell and a sight which shocked even us, who thought we had seen everything in the subhuman world of the SS. We realized we were wrong, however, as we were confronted by the sight of about one hundred emaciated girls sprawled on a bare floor, lying in their own excrement and vomit. Some, near death, lay hopelessly still while others continued to moan in pain.

These women must have been suffering from dysentery, or some other contagious disease, and we were afraid to go near them. As we gazed at the pitiful, half-dead women — the poor innocents — our hearts and souls bled for them, and for ourselves. We felt so helpless, knowing there was nothing we could do to alleviate their suffering. Taking one last look at the young women before turning away, we wondered yet again: What would ultimately happen to us?

We were told that there were empty rooms in other parts of the abandoned concentration camp, and we could sleep in any of them — on the floor, of course. In the meantime, the SS stayed in large quarters elsewhere in the camp, and had the use of a full kitchen. They ate well — even their dogs had generous portions of food — but our stomachs continued to grumble from hunger.

Late at night, we noticed several garbage pails behind the SS quarters. Knowing full well that we were risking our lives, we sneaked over to the pails to see if we could find anything remotely edible. We found mounds of dirty potato peels and, with trembling hands, stole the garbage and nourished ourselves. We were so hungry that those potato peels actually seemed appetizing! We then managed to sneak back to the barrack, unnoticed.

At daybreak, we awoke to harsh cries: *"Raus! Zeilappel!"* Ordered outside, none of us dared hide inside the barrack or run away. After *zeilappel*, the grueling march continued.

What did they gain by taking us? What would they have lost by leaving us there?

The support that my friends and I gave one another provided us with the courage — if not necessarily the physical strength — to survive the formidable SS obstacle course. Finally the Germans ordered us to halt in front of another concentration camp. The death march was over.

So many victims did not survive that death march. I still look back and wonder how I did.

AS I GAZED UPON THE ENTRANCE TO THIS NEW CAMP, MY HEART sank. We had hoped the Red Army would catch up with us, but
Stutthof
once again the SS had kept one step ahead of the Russians, while continuing to slaughter us in the process. Now here we stood, still under control of the SS, waiting to enter yet another of Hitler's death camps. What new hardships and tortures awaited us here?

Two German officials opened the gates and ordered us to march inside. As other Germans shoved us through the gates, I read: *KZ Stutthof*. Our new surroundings bore many similarities to Birkenau, such as the guarded watchtowers and the barbed-wire fences.

Once again we had to line up for *zeilappel*. Behind me, one of the terrified girls was softly sobbing. A German SS soldier dragged her out of line and pounded her viciously with kicks and blows until, within seconds, she lay still in a pool of blood. This was obviously a warning from the SS that the same could happen to any of us who angered them even in the slightest degree. Something as trivial as a sneeze or a yawn could bring on a beating or instant death.

After *zeilappel*, we were once again given gray prison dresses with numbers on them, but no shoes — we continued to wear the wooden clogs we had worn on the march.

The barrack to which we were assigned resembled the one we had occupied in Birkenau, except this one had wooden planks for us to sleep on. There were three tiers of planks in each row, and three of us were crammed onto each plank. Not only did the hard wooden surfaces hurt our backs, we all had to sleep in a curled-up position to make room for the others. Parry, Miriam, and I shared one of the "beds" and we each tried to accommodate the other as best we could.

Our first night there was harrowing. There was no air in the overcrowded barrack and we sweated profusely. But even worse: we were suddenly inundated with body lice! The vermin seemed to crawl out of the woodwork and were soon creeping all over us in the darkness. No matter how hard we tried, we simply could not rid ourselves of them. For each one that we picked off, several others latched onto our skin, even through the thin clothing. The itching was unbearable, and soon our skin was covered with open sores caused by incessant scratching. During the first few days at Stutthof we spent hours standing on our feet for *zeilappel*. One morning I witnessed a desperate young woman fling her frail body against the electrified barbed wire surrounding our block. I watched her struggling in the throes of death until her body gave one last, violent convulsion, and her limp frame slumped over the fence. Her bulging eyes remained wide-open, staring blindly Heavenward. May she rest in peace, I thought, as tears flooded my eyes.

I later learned that this latest victim was a young woman from Szaszregen, a talented singer from a wealthy family. I knew her from the barrack. Sometimes, when our captors were not around, we used to sit on the floor and she would sing for us. She entertained us with different Hungarian songs, which strengthened our morale. Some girls, impressed by her talent, affectionately nicknamed her Karady Ketelyn, the name of a well-known popular singer of the time. But pampered and delicate as she was, she was unable to cope with her new surroundings at Stutthof and committed suicide.

I wished that the victim had not been someone from Szaszregen. Just hearing the name of this town reminded me of my newlywed husband. Where was he at that moment? Was he still alive?

As the days passed, more and more miserable girls claimed to envy the girl who had electrocuted herself. I observed that most of the girls from less advantaged families were able to withstand the horrendous living conditions of the camp more easily than most of the girls from wealthier families. Those who were accustomed to tough times, to struggling, to hard work and difficulty, seemed better prepared than the inmates from more sheltered backgounds to deal with the blows, the slave labor and the unsanitary living conditions of our captivity. The daughters of the Torah way were also able to better endure the horrid conditions. Their *bitachon* (faith) gave them inner strength.

Days of Awe in Stutthof

SINCE WE ARRIVED AT THE CAMP ONLY A FEW DAYS BEFORE Rosh Hashanah, we were not forced to work on Yom Tov; new prisoners did not receive work orders for the first few weeks.

How did we know it was Rosh Hashanah? After all, we did not possess a Jewish calendar, and in our state of mental and physical exhaustion we had very little concept of time.

Actually, a series of small miracles occurred to help us observe the *Yamim Nora'im* (Days of Awe) that year.

It began one day when a woman in my *Lager* (sub-division of a concentration camp) excitedly rushed into the barrack. She proudly held up a Jewish calendar and told us how she had managed to smuggle it in. We were thrilled; now we would know the dates of the upcoming Days of Awe, and could prepare for them as well as possible, living as we did under the thumb of the SS.

The timing of our arrival and the acquisition of our new Jewish calendar were Heaven-ordained. We could now concentrate on our *tefillos* without worrying about having to go to work.

Another unusual event occurred right before Rosh Hashanah. One of the girls found a *siddur* — left behind from a previous transport — which contained the Rosh Hashanah prayers. We considered this to be a good sign from Heaven and felt relieved, even happy to be able to pray from a *siddur* in this forsaken place. As we watched the sun set over the horizon of our world at Stutthof on *erev* Rosh Hashanah, we were grateful to have the holy book in our hands.

One of the most common prayers on the High Holy Days is *"Zachreinu l'chaim,"* when we ask Hashem to inscribe our names into the Book of Life. It would be hard to find any individual at any time or any place who recited that prayer more sincerely and more wholeheartedly than we did that Rosh Hashanah. We asked the A-mighty to show infinite mercy toward us for another year. We handled our precious *siddur* carefully, and passed it around as if it were an irreplaceable, breakable piece of Waterford crystal.

The SS selected a tall, robust Jewish Hungarian woman from Munkach to be the *kapo* of our block. She was supplied with a club, a comfortable bed, better clothing, substantial food, whiskey, cigarettes — and even an occasional piece of chocolate. In return, her job was to make our lives miserable.

As Yom Kippur approached, the *kapo* seemed highly agitated. Yet instead of behaving in a manner indicating she was doing *teshuvah* (repenting), as is the Jewish way at this time of year, her actions were more intolerable than usual.

On Yom Kippur we stood at *zeilappel* under the tranquil sky and took turns davening from the *siddur*. When it was my turn, I opened the *siddur* to the *Shemoneh Esrei* and started to pray. Suddenly I felt sharp blows raining down on my back and shoulders. I whirled around and came face to face with the *kapo*, who then struck me so severely that I lost my balance, fell down and dropped the *siddur*. The other women gasped helplessly, but were afraid to move. I gathered courage, regained my composure, retrieved the *siddur* from the ground, kissed it gently, and stood back in line for *zeilappel*. The *kapo* angrily stared at me and waved her rubber stick first in front of me, and then near the *siddur* in my hand. As she walked away in a huff, I noticed the comfortable leather shoes that she was wearing.

Why did she hit me? Was her action simply an expression of German sadistic brainwashing, causing her to lose control of what normally passes for civilized behavior, or was she venting the guilt of a non-observant Jewess on Yom Kippur? I strongly believe that both answers apply in this situation. Yet despite her outrage, the *kapo* did not confiscate the *siddur*. Could it be that underneath the layers of complicity and anger, a *Yiddishe* heart still beat within her chest?

(Generally, however, this *kapo's* behavior was unabashedly cruel. Some of the women in our *Lager* even talked about seeking revenge on her after liberation.)

SOMETIME AFTER THE *YAMIM TOVIM, WEHRMACHT* SOLDIERS CAME to the camp, requesting the return of the women who had worked

Hard Labor and Starvation

for them previously. My girlfriends and I were included in this group. Once we were assembled, the soldiers informed us that they had work for us and ordered us to follow them. Would we once again be repairing their tattered army uniforms? If so, we would be doing a familiar job. Perhaps conditions would not be so bad in Stutthof after all, I thought.

I could not have been more wrong.

After about half an hour we arrived at a building and were ordered inside. Sheets of the leather and cork materials used in the manufacture of shoe soles were stacked up to the ceiling. I looked around, wondering where the sewing machines and fabrics were.

"Do you see those sheets over there?" shouted one of the soldiers.

We nodded.

"You are to carry them in bundles to a transport train about a kilometer from here. Form a line and follow me!" he shouted.

We looked at one another in amazement. How could we — relatively small women to begin with, now emaciated from starvation — carry those weighty bundles? These soldiers were demanding the impossible. Why didn't they assign male prisoners to perform such arduous labor?

Under the unblinking gaze of the soldiers, we each stooped down, picked up a heavy bundle and strapped it to our backs. Carrying our burdens, we followed the soldiers to the transport trains. At the station, we lugged the heavy sheets onto the freight cars. We repeated the same strenuous procedure over and over again until evening, when the workday was done and we were marched back to camp.

This was how we were to spend our days at Stutthof. We knew that we would have to get accustomed to harder labor — or else. Now we were sure of the reason we were not sent to the left in the Auschwitz selection: the Nazis needed us to be their slaves.

Those who worked in the vegetable fields were more fortunate than the rest of us, and managed to benefit from some extra nutrition. Whenever the SS looked the other way, the workers grabbed raw carrots or potatoes and wolfed them down. Even though gobbling the raw vegetables meant eating the dirt in which they were covered as well, the field workers forced themselves to ignore the foul taste of the soil and were thus able to receive a fair amount of vitamins from the garden. Our new daily routine was to rise before dawn, stand at *zeilappel* for a few hours, have a cup of muddy water called coffee, and march to work. At night, "soup" was dished out by the *kapo*. Unlike in Birkenau, each woman received her own bowl and the *kapo* dished out two ladles of the "soup" to each of us every night.

The "soup" we received was actually a watery substance with a few grains of barley in it. We noticed that the deeper the ladle was dipped, the thicker the "soup" became. When the soup barrel was finally emptied, some barley and vegetables remained stuck to the sides and bottom. I saw women, crazed with hunger, throw their bony bodies into the barrel and scoop out the remaining soup with their fingers.

The *kapos* enjoyed watching this, and once in a while, just for laughs, they would flip the can over the poor woman who was still inside, causing the remaining food contents to drip down over her head, onto her dress, and all over her body. Between the forced hard labor — which consumed a great deal of energy — and the lack of nourishment, we began to lose weight very rapidly.

The Hanging

LATE ONE AFTERNOON WE HEARD AN ANNOUNCEMENT OVER the loudspeaker, ordering us to assemble for an "extraordinary" *zeilappel*. We quickly lined up, exchanging frightened glances. A "special" *zeilappel* in the late afternoon meant something serious. Through the barbed-wire fences, we saw the entire camp standing at attention. The Germans were up to something. Was this a "selection"?

We didn't have long to wait for an answer. A German approached the microphone and in enraged tones informed us that one of the male inmates had tried to escape, had been caught, and was now to be hanged for his efforts. This hanging was to be an "object lesson" for the rest of us, should anyone be harboring intentions of flight. Whoever would be caught not watching the hanging, the Nazi concluded, would be blinded.

The unfortunate victim was brought out by a guard and forced up a few steps to the gallows. Many thousands of us watched as a noose was placed around his neck and the platform was quickly removed from beneath his feet. He struggled for a few seconds, then hung limp and lifeless.

Who was this young man who had just been victimized? All we could see was that he was very frightened and didn't utter a word before the hanging. Our eyes remained focused on the limp hanging body for a few seconds, then *zeilappel* was over. We returned to our barracks in deep silence.

IT WAS BY HEAVENLY DECREE THAT MY FRIENDS AND I WERE STILL alive and together as winter arrived. The frigid winters in Stutthof

My Father's Presence were just as brutal as the scorching summers. The chilling wind and gusting snow bit through our emaciated, shivering bodies which were clothed in the same dresses we had worn in the summer. Wasn't it a sad irony that we were no longer clothed in the *Wehrmacht* uniform which could have better protected us from the cold and wet? We had no stockings or socks to protect our legs and feet from the elements; all that separated the soles of our feet from the frozen ground, the ice and snow, were our wooden clogs.

We suffered from severe frostbite and frozen extremities. The sickly pallor of our cheeks was now camouflaged by bright red windburn. To keep our blood circulating, we literally had to keep our hands and feet in constant motion; otherwise we would have frozen to death. This exposure to the elements was the cause of the severe infection I soon acquired.

Upon awakening one frigid morning, I felt pain in my left heel. I examined the affected area and noticed a red circle, tender to the touch. I rubbed the spot gently, worried because I could not do anything more for the inflammation. I opted not go to the dangerous *revere* (camp hospital) and reported to work as usual, trying to keep my weight off the swollen heel. After standing at *zeilappel* and trudging through the ice and snow that day, however, my heel froze and filled with pus. Every time I put my weight on it, I felt a pinching pain, as if the skin was stretching beyond its capacity.

By nightfall the agony was excruciating, and I could hardly walk. My head throbbed and I was shivering violently. During *zeilappel*, standing under the floodlights, I ventured a quick look at my foot. The sight made me gasp. One section of the heel was beet-red, and huge pus pockets were forming in several places.

I had no appetite for that evening's "soup," and by curfew time I could barely climb into my bunk. That night, I was so relieved to be off the inflamed heel that I didn't mind lying down on the lice-infested, rotting board.

During the night I broke into a sweat, even though the room was so cold that icicles clung to the interior walls. Moaning in my sleep, I tried to touch my heel but was unable to do so because I was wedged so tightly into my spot between two other sleeping girls. The pain was unbearable and my tormented body was burning with fever. The others awoke, alarmed by my grunts of pain. Parry asked what was troubling me and I told her about the heel. One of the others touched my forehead and commented on how hot it was. My friends cuddled closer to me in an attempt to keep me warm.

Through a feverish haze I heard my girlfriends whispering, frantically attempting to figure out how to save my life. When I heard one of them suggest that I be taken to the *revere*, I forced myself out of my cocoon of fever and pain for long enough to explain that the *revere* was the last place I wanted to go. Selections in the *revere* were held any time, at random, and those unfortunate enough to be there when the selections occurred were marched off, never to return. My life would be in greater danger there.

Morning arrived very soon, and the *kapo* stormed in and ordered us outside for *zeilappel*. With my inflamed foot, how would I be able to walk fast enough to avoid her blows?

Two of my friends acted quickly. They grabbed me and managed to help me off my plank and down to the floor, supporting me on their shoulders. I tried not to flinch as we filed past the *kapo*. She noticed the girls holding me up, and could have sent me to the *revere*, or whacked me with her club, but instead she simply motioned me out the door with the others.

The biting air smacked our faces as soon as we were out the door. Needless to say, the last place I wanted to be at that moment was outside, standing at attention in the brutal wind and snow — but not to do so would have meant certain death.

As it began to get lighter outside, I managed to sneak a quick peek at my foot. It was worse; the inflamed circle was larger and the pus pockets were enormous! Just the mere sight of them made me feel faint. I was almost grateful for the freezing winds, which helped control my nausea. Of course there was no way that I could protect my heel area, and it throbbed more with each hour that I was on my feet. The stinging arctic winds intensified the agony.

When it was time to march to work, the women supported me as I walked, thus allowing me to somewhat ease the pressure and pain inflicted on my wound by each step. We realized that we would have to do something soon — otherwise the infection would worsen and my fever would climb.

But then something wonderful happened! While bringing her daily quota of fresh clothing to the train for the German soldiers, my dear friend Rita stumbled across a strange-looking, small, flat packet filled with sand and chemicals. Not knowing what it was, Rita examined it, turned it this way and that, and finally shook it. Much to her surprise, it became hot. It was a heat pack, probably used to treat the German soldiers' minor war wounds and other injuries. She later told me that its resemblance to a hot water bottle caused her to wonder if the heat from inside could possibly break the pus pockets in my inflamed heel. This clever reasoning on her part would save my life.

Rita went to great pains to smuggle the packet into camp. To this very day I do not know how she managed to outsmart the eagle-eyed SS. That night, eyes glowing with anticipation, Rita showed me the packet. She shook it and then gently placed it on my heel. Almost immediately the warmth soothed the swollen, inflamed area. When the warmth wore off, I shook the packet again.

A couple of hours later, a miracle happened! The mysterious packet began to combat the infection. As pus began to ooze from my foot, the thought came to me that my dear father in *Gan Eden* had somehow sent the packet to me through a *shaliach* (messenger), Rita, to save my life. I confided my conviction to Rita — no other explanation could justify this extraordinary miracle.

The following morning I discovered that some of the pus pockets had indeed opened, yet one or two still remained intact. I knew I would need the aid of additional packets because the one I had been using was beginning to lose its warmth. But how could I get any others?

Before going to work, I insisted that Rita not take any more chances; that the A-mighty would heal my infection over time. In spite of my reservations, Rita told me she would attempt to bring back more heat packs. She assured me that she would be careful. Despite her fragile physical state, she was (and still is) a strong person, one of great inner strength and determination. Once she sets a goal for herself, she will practically shake the foundations of the earth to achieve it.

That evening Rita excitedly handed me a fresh heat pack, and that night more pus flowed from my heel. About a week later, the pus was completely gone, my chills and body aches went away, and the sores were drying up. Deep gaps pocked my skin, marking the areas which had contained the pus pockets. I knew it would take a long time for fresh skin to grow over them.

Eventually the pain began to diminish and I did not limp quite as badly as before. However, for quite a while after the infection was gone, I would return to the barrack in excruciating pain after a full day on my feet. After some more time elapsed, the pain completely subsided, and the heel looked better.

The kind of heroism and *mesiras nefesh* that Rita exhibited is rarely mentioned in Holocaust literature. Today my friend resides in *Eretz Yisrael*; may the A-mighty bless her.

Our Final March

WINTER FINALLY CAME TO AN END. THE WARMER WINDS AND gentle, refreshing spring rains rejuvenated us physically and emotionally. By this time we were extremely emaciated and dehydrated, almost to the point of death.

Once again rumors circulated that the Russian army was approaching, and once again we hoped that we would soon be liberated. Unfortunately, our eager anticipation was short-lived. One grim, chilly morning, the SS marched us out of camp in a hurry and suddenly, without explanation, we were on another death march!

By that time we were walking human skeletons, so weak that we could barely stumble along. How would any of us be able to keep up with the brisk pace of the SS? Trying to settle my fears and remain sane, I continually resolved to focus on the positive: Thank G-d we were still alive, and our victory and freedom were literally footsteps away. I was determined not to give up. That is when I began to understand how determination to survive, and refusal to give up are important factors in the survival of the Jewish people over the ages.

As in the previous death march, the sounds of gunfire were everywhere and we had to duck the sprays of stray bullets. Every passing moment was a tug of war between life and death. As we continued to flee along the back roads in the woods, horrifying images flashed before my eyes. I envisioned myself slowing down, unable to take another step, falling, and thousands of desperate girls trampling my inert body into the dust of the road. Would I, too, be tossed into a ditch to lie, unburied, with the decomposing bodies?

As the days dragged on, I began to notice that the SS officers were behaving in a panic-stricken manner. Evidently the Red Army was just hours behind us, and the Germans were frantically trying to stay ahead of them. It would be just a matter of time before the gap between us and our liberators would begin to close. If we could simply survive for a few more days — hours, even — we might actually see freedom, please G-d!

Until now the Germans had gotten away with everything — from conquering Europe to cruelly slaughtering millions of innocent people who did not fit their Aryan mold. Now the tide of history was about to turn. The Germans had lost the war, and it was simply a matter of time before the Russian Army would capture our SS tormentors, set us free and take revenge. I held on to this thought for days, and it became my beacon of light.

As each night approached, the SS looked for shelter. Either they steered us into small labor camps or into abandoned barns along the roads. We slept on scratchy hay or on cold barrack floors, always uncomfortable and miserable.

The latrines became our "information center." There we had a modicum of privacy, where we could communicate with one another. Rumors flew like wildfire. One day we heard that the Russians were on our heels, but on another day we learned that they were far behind and that the SS would liquidate us before the Russians caught up with us!

As a result of being on the run, the SS began to run short on food supplies. Of course, they kept most of what was available for themselves. On some days we received one slice of bread and a cup of hot water; on other days we received nothing at all.

An Unexpected Surprise

ON THIS MARCH WE MET UP WITH A LARGE NUMBER OF NON-JEWISH female Russian prisoners. It was evident that the SS was treating them better than they were treating us. These captives appeared healthier and were allowed to carry and consume their own supply of food. They even had suitcases or satchels which contained several changes of clothing.

One night, I noticed a Russian girl wearing a familiar garment — my jacket! I looked again and again, just to make sure. Yes, the garment appeared old and worn, but I was convinced that it was my jacket — the one into whose buttons I had sewn some of my precious jewels, and which had been taken from me, along with my other clothes, before our disinfection at Birkenau. Who knows how many hundreds of garments with treasures hidden inside were thrown away by our conquerors!

I wondered how I could get my jacket back. This woman was a complete stranger. How would she react if I asked her to remove the jacket from her back and return it to me?

It so happened that in Selish Parry had learned Russian in school and could speak the language. I asked her to approach the Russian woman on my behalf and explain that I was the owner of the jacket she was wearing. My friend complied and a few moments later returned with the response that the Russian woman would return my jacket in exchange for my entire bread ration.

Soon my precious jacket was in my hands again, and I tearfully put it on. I was amazed to find that three of its five buttons were still attached to the jacket. I did not check inside them for the jewels until I had a moment of privacy later that evening when, to my joy and amazement, I found a ring and two earrings!

Having been reunited with my jacket and some jewelry — tangible symbols of my former life before this nightmare — I felt renewed hope. I assured myself that I would soon be reunited with my husband and mother as well.

A Crowded Journey on the Vistula

BY THEN, ONLY ABOUT ONE HUNDRED OF US REMAINED. WE MARCHED for a few days and approached a fairly large body of water which I later learned was the Zaluka Gdanska, a bay coming off the Baltic Sea on the northern coast of what is now Poland. The port city of Danzig, now known by its Polish name of Gdansk, is located on this bay, and the Vistula River, which runs through much of Central Europe — and which, ironically, flows past Oswiencim, not far from the death camp of Auschwitz — empties into it near Danzig.

After his liberation, Miklos Nyiszli, a Jewish doctor from Budapest selected by Mengele to perform autopsies on selected prisoners before their bodies were burned, wrote a book detailing the atrocities he had witnessed firsthand in Auschwitz. In it, he mentioned that when the Auschwitz ditches were too full to accommodate the ashes from the crematoria, the ashes were dumped into the Vistula River.

In the *Selichos* prayers, a Jewish *churban* (destruction) is described as *"Damim b'damim naga* (Blood met blood)." In the waters of the Vistula, too, during the *Churban* of European Jewry, the ashes of murdered victims were reunited with the ashes of their loved ones ...

Standing at the edge of the Zaluka Gdanska, we noticed a small, dilapidated raft bobbing in the choppy, dark waters. Pointing in its direction, the SS ordered us onto it. All at once, everyone made a mad dash for the shabby wooden raft. Fights erupted as the desperate women struggled to gain a foothold. Soon more rafts arrived for the remaining women, and after they had all clambered aboard, the SS and their dogs followed. We were wedged tightly into a small space in order to make room for the guards and their canines. The girls nearest to them cringed in fear and crowded back even further, trying to shy away from the vicious jaws of the snarling animals.

Other SS men untied the mooring rope and pushed us off. Words cannot describe the terror which engulfed each one of us at that fateful moment. There we were, alone with the SS on a makeshift wooden raft in the middle of a desolate body of water, on our way to parts unknown. The puny raft creaked ominously, but we were sure it would not collapse under our weight since the SS guards, as well as their precious dogs, were aboard with us. The Russian girls remained behind.

We finally docked near Danzig, Poland and were ordered off the raft and into marching lines. In order to make their point, a few soldiers shot their guns into the air, causing many women to scream and run.

Laughter broke out among our captors as they heard our panicky screams. My legs, still wobbly from the sea journey, hardly held me up, but I found myself running, too.

The Final Days of the Journey

ONCE AGAIN WE FOUND OURSELVES TRAMPING OVER BACK ROADS, and marching in and out of small towns. We stretched our hands out to the onlooking citizens, pleading, "Bread! Bread!" — but to no avail. Captives unable to keep up with the fast pace set by the Germans continued to die in the roads and ditches. The Germans no longer needed bullets to kill us on these marches. They made jokes about the tortured victims dying on their own. Many prisoners developed dysentery. Doubled over with severe cramps, they tried to keep running. Ultimately those people simply wasted away, collapsed and died.

In the days that followed we encountered lines of male prisoners marching in separate lines. We did not know where they were from, but their appearance suggested a recent stay in concentration camps. Pale and emaciated, the men also tried their best to maintain the grueling pace set by the merciless Germans.

In normal times, the countryside we traversed would have made a delightful backdrop for a leisurely afternoon stroll. But now, as we urged our broken shells forward, sweat poured down our backs and our dehydrated bodies cried for water. Prisoners continued to collapse and were either shot by the guards or trampled.

Finally we reached Danzig. By this time, the Russian soldiers and tanks were catching up with the Germans. We sensed the nervousness of our captors; more shots rang out, more screams were heard, and the marching tempo quickened noticeably.

Breathless and panting, we continued our struggle for life. From snippets of conversation overheard among the guards we understood that if we could only hang on long enough, we would see liberation.

Locked in a Burning Barn

AS DUSK FELL ONE EVENING, WE APPROACHED AN ABANDONED, ransacked barn standing at the side of the road. The Germans forced us and the marching men inside, hitting us with the butts of their rifles. We fell over one another to avoid their painful blows as we ran into the barn. The stable doors slammed shut behind us and we breathed a sigh of relief; the stillness of that dusty, wooden space was a welcome comfort, if only for a short while. We found piles of thick straw and settled ourselves for the night, assuming that we'd be in the barn overnight, and back on our weary feet by dawn. The Germans did not supply us with food or water, but we were too overcome with exhaustion to be concerned about anything. All we wanted to do was rest our weary bones.

As we expected to be awakened by the Germans in a few hours, we dropped off quickly. Little did we know at the time that we would never see those German guards again.

In the middle of the night we awoke with a start; somehow, it was too quiet. A few of the men checked the doors. They were locked! The Germans had locked us in! Smoke began wafting into our confined space, filling our weak lungs. The wooden doors started to burn. The men banded together and threw themselves against the doors. By a heavenly decree they succeeded in breaking the enclosure, and the wide doors were flung open. By then the barn was completely engulfed in flames! We raced out and ran away before we could be injured. But then something unusual happened.

From force of habit we looked over our shoulders as we ran — but nobody stopped us! There were no bullets whizzing in our direction. The shots we did hear came from the battlefield some distance away.

From our safe observation point we attempted to piece together what had just happened. It seemed that the Germans had decided to make a run for safety that night, but not without killing us first. To that end, they locked the barn doors and set the barn on fire when they thought we were sound asleep. It was our *mazal* that the men had been locked with us inside the barn, for it was they who first sensed that something was wrong and helped us all escape.

When we first saw that barn full of straw, I remembered what we had learned in the Bible about Pharaoh not giving the enslaved Jews any straw (*Exodus* 5:6-13); yet the SS gave us plenty of straw in the barn! After the fire, we understood why.

The Germans fled, assuming they had burned us all in the stables. The orders from Berlin to kill innocent victims even after there was no more hope of winning the war were based on the belief that by destroying the evidence and witnesses to their deeds, they would be able to deny the Holocaust. But a "Heavenly Final Solution" dictated that I survive to give an eyewitness account of the atrocities committed by the German-Nazi government, and a description of how the individual soldiers willingly complied. Those German cowards knew they were defeated — but even then, they blindly acted to destroy: here, in the slave labor camp at Ebensee, and elsewhere.

By the time others gazed at the ruins of the still burning barn — our intended funeral pyre — the German killers were probably miles away, dressed in civilian clothing, hoping not to be recognized by the Russian soldiers.

Liberation

FROM A DISTANCE, WE HEARD THE THUNDER OF MARCHING SOLDIERS and felt the vibrations of approaching tanks and jeeps. At dawn we saw figures moving in our direction. Our hearts stopped. Was this finally liberation, or would we be disappointed again?

The soldiers finally reached us, but against the headlights of the jeeps, we could not discern their uniforms. We heard them speaking in a strange tongue and breathed a sigh of relief. The language was not German! We knew then that these were the Russians. We were liberated — and we were still alive!

The skies brightened over our heads, and so did our hope and anticipation. As it grew lighter, we and our liberators had a chance to look each other over. The Russian soldiers appeared robust and healthy, while we looked like walking skeletons. Our liberators stared at us, but not with shock and wonder — they had already seen others like us as they crossed German-occupied territory. With our closely-cropped hair and emaciated figures, most of the women looked like boys, while the men appeared grisly with their short beards, uncombed hair and bulging eyes. All of us were dressed in filthy rags and were covered with dirt and sores from head to toe. I actually saw tears in the eyes of these strong men as they stared at us.

THE FIRST PRIORITY OF OUR RUSSIAN LIBERATORS WAS TO OFFER US
food. Smiling sympathetically, they handed us pieces of black

Freedom and a
Bout of Typhus

bread with jam and cups of strong black coffee. Many in our group were too weak to
stand any longer and chose to sit on the
damp ground, sipping the steaming coffee and taking tiny bites of
the bread. Some men and women devoured the small meal as if
they were eating the only food left on earth.

For those of us in a more weakened state, eating and drinking
was a hardship. Even though I was eager to receive food, I did
not have the strength to eat. I could not even lift the piece of bread
to my mouth. Parry urged me to eat and raised the bread to my
mouth. I turned my head away. I did, however, with her help, take
slow sips of the hot coffee. Afterward, I curled up in the grass
and fell asleep near the ruins of the barn which had almost become
our death trap. Before I dozed off, I half-expected a German or a
kapo to summon us to *zeilappel*, so dominated were our minds
by the horrors we had experienced. I awoke a short time later.
From what I could surmise as I looked around, the first group of
Russian soldiers had gone on ahead and another occupation unit
had taken over. We went with its men to a small nearby township.
I do not remember the name of the town, but I do remember
seeing empty houses lining the streets. This was where we were
to settle temporarily, and we began to believe that our lot would
improve from that day on. Even though we were extremely weary
and thin, we looked to the future. We spoke about returning
home to look for our families. I was hopeful that my husband
might still be alive.

The following day, many of us suddenly became ill. We were
taken to makeshift hospitals, examined by Russian doctors and
informed that we had contracted typhus. For a few days I drifted
in and out of consciousness, burning with fever and wracked by
violent trembling. I recall lying in a pool of sweat on a narrow army
hospital cot in what was formerly a large home. My head lay flat
on a small, firm pillow. My eyes scanned the pattern of wooden

beams in the ceiling and the round light bulbs suspended by narrow strips of wire.

I was surrounded by the critically ill and dying. Hospital personnel were quietly carrying the dead to a designated spot for burial. Tears flowed down my cheeks. These poor innocents had fought so hard to see liberation, only to die so soon afterwards! Some of the female soldiers were talking amongst themselves, apparently making plans for those of us still clinging to life.

A dark-haired nurse dressed in army clothing and a white apron sat next to me, held my hand, and tried to talk to me. As I spoke no Russian, I could not understand what she was saying, but smiled weakly at her to acknowledge her kindness. She wiped beads of perspiration off my face with a cold white cloth which she dipped into a basin filled with ice and water. The cool fabric felt soothing against my feverish forehead. She pleaded with me to drink some water but I turned my head away. I was too weak to move. Even sipping water seemed an impossible task. As the days slowly passed, I was finally able to sip a little tea mixed with sugar.

Occasionally a man I presumed to be an army doctor made the rounds; I distinctly remember him checking my vital signs. He probably wanted to make sure I was still alive, as I was lying so still. Many of the patients in the army hospital suffered from the same illness. Moans, sobs and gagging sounds were heard throughout the rooms, and I sadly watched the orderlies carry bodies out to be buried.

Sometimes in the middle of the night I cried out in my sleep for my revered father and mother. The room was dark except for a dim light hanging from the ceiling; the darkness scared me. The daylight helped drive away the nightmares about what I had seen and endured over the past year.

One day a nurse offered me some thin potato soup. She fed me the tasty liquid and I was able to digest it with little difficulty. When I had the strength to move my arm, I placed it over my shrunken belly and felt my protruding rib cage. There was no fat left, only bones and skin. I removed my hand from my skeletal body as if it had been burned, turned my head to the side and wept silently. What had become of me? Would I ever get out of this hospital alive, or would I become another statistic of the war?

One morning I awoke and felt somewhat better. The headache was gone and my body had stopped convulsing with chills. The nurse came by and looked relieved after taking my temperature: my fever had broken.

I was hoping to find my girlfriends alive and close by. Sighing with happiness and relief, I saw two of them not too far from my bed. Later I was to find out that the other two were alive as well.

The following day I got out of bed for the first time, supported by one of the nurses. Initially I felt wobbly and weak on my feet, but as the weeks passed, I began to regain some strength. We remained in the same quarters for a few weeks, then, as we continued to recover, we were moved to another building for convalescents. At that point we were hopeful that we would actually undergo a full recovery.

Another Escape

WHILE WE WERE CONVALESCING, OUR RUSSIAN LIBERATORS WERE making plans for us. They wanted to take us back with them to Russia once we were well enough to travel. They told us that as we no longer had homes to which we could return, it would be to our benefit to go with them. To this day, I have no idea why it meant so much to the Russians to take us back with them.

We, of course, had no way of knowing at the time what fate lay ahead for Jews or others who would be taken behind what would later be called the "Iron Curtain." Some of us knew vaguely that atheism was the official "religion" in the U.S.S.R., or had heard stories about the persecution of religious Jews, but these, of course, had paled in comparison with what we had all experienced at the hands of Hitler and his cohorts. Only later did the world learn the full details of Stalin's own demented efforts to do away with Jews and Judaism. (Who would triumph in the contest of behaving sub-humanly, Hitler or Stalin? I find this an interesting question.) I strongly feel that G-d had saved me from the fate of those Jews who fell into Stalin's hands.

I am reminded of the case of Raoul Wallenberg, the courageous Swedish diplomat who managed to save thousands of Jews from under the very noses of the Germans in Budapest. While his diplomatic status was strong enough to protect him from the *Gestapo* — who surely knew full well what he had been doing — it could not save him from the Stalinist conquerors after the Hungarian capital fell to them. Wallenberg was seized and hustled off to the Soviet Union and reportedly died in prison there.

Even though we would be forever indebted to our Russian liberators for saving us from the SS, we knew we could not and would not return to Russia with them. We wanted to return to Hungary to search for our relatives.

One evening, my friends and I devised an escape plan. We knew the Russians observed May 1, or "May Day," as a national holiday to commemorate the 1917 Bolshevik Revolution, and they were in the midst of arranging a huge celebration. The day's festivities were to be held outdoors, and everyone from the hospital was invited. My friends and I decided that this would be a perfect opportunity to slip out unnoticed by the Russians. Several other women asked if they could join us and, of course, we included them in our plans.

The first of May finally arrived. The hospital staff handed us clothing, shoes and stockings to wear to the festival. I also put on my cherished old jacket with the jewel-filled buttons. Taking one another by the hand, the five of us walked outside to join the others in the May Day celebration.

In the courtyard, we met the other seven girls as well as a young Czech former political prisoner who had learned of our plans and now offered to accompany us. A tall, well-mannered man, he was to assume the role of protector and look after us all.

Tables were set up with desserts, strong coffee and vodka. Before long, the Russian soldiers and officers were laughing, singing and pouring themselves more glasses of vodka. They were celebrating not only the traditional Soviet holiday, but the final defeat of their enemy, as word had come that Soviet troops were in full control of Berlin and that Hitler had fallen.

We waited for the right moment to leave. Finally, during the height of the festivities, we seized our opportunity and quietly slipped away. We moved toward the trees surrounding the area, all the while glancing nervously over our shoulders. When we reached the perimeter, we dashed out of the Soviet camp unobserved, with nothing but the clothes on our backs.

Those who remained behind eventually went with the Russians, and who knows where the Stalinists stationed them! I know a man who spent five years in Siberia before he was able to return home.

BECAUSE OF OUR WEAKENED STATE, WE WERE UNABLE TO RUN very far. Once out of the confines of the Russian grounds, we

"Free" Train Ride stopped to catch our breath. We sat for a while, shared the little bread we had taken with us, and began walking.

A while later we found ourselves in the middle of the town, hoping to find a train station. We finally located some train tracks and followed them to an almost empty station house. Other scraggly victims of war were milling about the platform, also waiting for a train headed for Poland. We asked some of the people if they knew when the next train was coming, and they laughed at us. In the postwar chaos, there were no train schedules. A train could arrive in 5 minutes, in 2 hours, or in 24 hours. And once a train arrived, nobody knew where it was headed.

As a result of the inconvenience and confusion, no fares were collected. Everyone seemed as eager as we were to return home and see what they could find in the ruins. Many of the people waiting were in situations similar to ours — victims of Hitler's death camps eager to find their families.

I found myself constantly looking over my shoulder. Would anyone back at the Russian camp notice our disappearance? Would the

Russians decide to search for us and deduce that the train station would be our first destination? At last we saw a train coming around the bend and we breathed a sigh of relief. The train screeched to a halt and we hastily climbed aboard one of the two passenger cars. Gratefully sinking into our seats, we sought comfort in the knowledge that we were finally on our way as free civilians. How different from a year ago in Selish, when we were herded into cattle cars like animals!

Many of the other train passengers were soldiers returning home, some of them lightly wounded. I dozed off, lulled by the monotonous rolling of the train. Towards evening the train halted. It was obvious that we had reached the end of the line, but we did not know where we were. We also had no idea when the next train would arrive.

We decided to spend the night nearby, in one of the vacant ruined houses, and to wait for another train the following morning. We got water at the station's pump, and the Czech (as we had taken to calling the young Czech ex-prisoner who accompanied us) found an empty building for us to sleep in. As soon as he felt we were safe, he walked into the heart of town and begged some of the local Poles for food. Many obliged, giving him bread, apples and raw vegetables.

The following morning we returned to the train station to wait for another train. After many long, lonely hours, a freight train rolled into the station. This time we were the only ones waiting, and we boarded quickly.

The train reached the Praga outskirts of Warsaw. After we disembarked, we asked around and learned about a Jewish organization set up in Warsaw, most likely financed by the Joint Distribution Committee. By then it was nightfall and we had no place to go, so we slept in the railroad station.

In hopeful anticipation that the officials of the Jewish organization would be able to somehow help us find our way back to Budapest, we eagerly set out for Warsaw the following morning. We met many other refugees and they gave us directions to the Jewish organization. Once we found the address, we were greeted warmly at the door and offered a hot kosher meal. When we met with the Jewish officials, however, we were dismayed when they advised us that the only way to get back to Budapest would be through the Russian transit camp set up in Praga. They apologized and sadly said there was nothing more they could do for us at the moment. Where were the British and American Jews? Why weren't they looking for survivors like us?

We had to decide what to do next. Having just taken pains to escape from the Soviet Army, we certainly did not want to return to another Russian camp. Our decision was unanimous — we would find our way home on our own. We were still left with several dilemmas, however. Penniless as we were, how would we be able to accomplish our goal? How would we eat? How could we continue to move on without resting first?

While we were pondering what our next move should be, the Czech came forward and revealed that he was carrying some hidden pieces of jewelry. He offered to sell one piece to pay for a few days' lodging for our group, but did not wish to offer any more of his wordly possessions — namely the jewelry — toward food expenses. The issue of food would be up to us.

One of my girlfriends then whispered to me, "Chana, now is the time to reveal your secret."

Convinced that this man was trustworthy, I decided to follow my friend's advice. Not wanting the entire group to find out my secret, I called the young man over.

"I have a small fortune hidden inside my jacket," I confided. Pulling off one of the buttons, I showed him the ring. I then went on to explain the astonishing story of my jacket. With amazement and interest, the young man listened to my story. I then told him that I would be willing to barter the ring for food. We began making arrangements right away.

First the Czech rented a few rooms in a private home. Then he sold my ring, but much to his (and our) disappointment, he didn't receive much cash for it. We would have to budget carefully.

Our next problem was to find a food market. Very few people

were buying directly from vendors, and finding one would not be an easy task. We had to walk quite a distance before we found a store. Our eyes scanned the scantily laden shelves. Only a limited amount of food was available — bread, milk, butter, cream and eggs. The grocer did not have any fruits or vegetables. We would have to settle for dairy meals, and purchased enough to last us a few days. The others in our group were appreciative and thankful to the Czech and to me for supplying shelter and food.

People in the street and in the house where we lodged stared at us and whispered to one another. We emaciated concentration camp survivors — the freed remnants of the Holocaust, snatched from the clutches of the "Final Solutionists" — must have looked frightening and strange to them. Yet we received no assistance, recognition or even compassion from the local townspeople. Given their history of pogroms against the Jews, could it be that the Poles were sorry that we had returned, alive? Through it all, we tried not to let our embarrassment show, and strove to maintain our dignity.

As soon as we reached our lodgings, we designated who would share which room. Parry, Rita, Miriam, Rivka and I bunked together. There was one bathroom down the hall for all the boarders on the floor to share.

In the privacy of our quarters we sat down to eat. Although the food looked appetizing, I warned the others to eat only a few bites at each meal, reminding them that our stomachs were shrunken and weakened from the many months of food deprivation. I had already seen too many starved people become ill with uncontrollable diarrhea, both in the Russian camps and in the hospital, from overeating.

The next few days passed quickly. Except for short walks in the sunshine and fresh air, we spent most of our time trying to find a solution to our problem. Soon — all too soon — our funds ran out and we had to leave. We were, however, grateful for the short respite. We felt more ready — both physically and spiritually — to move on. But the big problem still faced us. How could we return to Budapest on our own? We had no choice but to turn to the Russian transit camp in Praga.

THE RUSSIANS, SURPRISINGLY, WELCOMED US WARMLY WHEN WE arrived and placed us in the camp. We found that they had no

The Russians Send Us Home way of knowing that we had escaped from the Soviet encampment in Danzig, so we would not be punished. With the exception of my four girlfriends and myself, our large group had broken up. Even the Czech, who had accompanied us this far, had gone his own way.

There was not much for us to do in the camp except to rest while waiting to move on. Often the others and I wandered around the camp grounds for a little exercise and fresh air. There were many trees beneath which to rest when we were tired. We were amazed by the huge numbers of released prisoners of other nationalities within the camp.

Sometimes I chose to be alone with my thoughts. I wondered if I would ever see my husband again. When I had seen him last, he was going off with the men after we had been forcibly separated at Auschwitz. I knew from the camp grapevine at Birkenau that young men who appeared to be in good health were sometimes forced to do labor rather than being killed outright, so there was some hope. However, I also knew that even being chosen to be a laborer was no guarantee of safety and survival. I prayed that we would find one another amidst the thousands of uprooted people wandering around Europe at the time.

By word of mouth at Birkenau, I also knew that my mother had perished. My dear, sweet, gentle mother — what would I do without her now? She and I were still adjusting to my father's loss when we were taken away to the ghetto. I would never forget the look on her face just before the doors to our cattle car opened in Birkenau. She took my hand and told me not to lose faith, no matter how rough life became in the camp. Perhaps Mother thought our faith was being tested by the A-Mighty, or perhaps she believed that He had a plan for us which only He understood. She never had the chance to tell me. I wondered about my beloved uncle and aunt, the Satmar Rebbe and Rebbetzin. My uncle had been like a second father to me, and for that I would always be grateful. I prayed that my uncle and aunt were still alive and that I would somehow find them.

The staple of our diet in the Russian camp was a grainy cereal called grits. It resembled thick, watered-down rice. Although it did not look terribly appetizing, it was surprisingly tasty and satisfying. We tried our best to finish our portions, but tasty as the food was, our stomachs were still sensitive and could handle only a small amount of nourishment at one time. The day would come when we would again be able to consume full portions, but that would happen gradually.

Eventually we all started to gain back a few pounds, but the weight returned slowly. Looking in the mirror was a ghastly experience. Even though we felt somewhat stronger and healthier, our cheeks remained shriveled and pale, and our arms and legs still appeared bony in our oversized clothing.

We remained in the Russians' Displaced Persons camp for a few weeks, waiting eagerly to leave. One day the Russians announced that they were going to send the displaced prisoners back to their homes by train, and asked us where we wanted to go. My friends and I were given the choice of going to Budapest or Prague. We chose to go to Budapest. The camp leaders made the arrangements and started to send transports. Our turn came in July.

On the designated day, fortified with a supply of food, we boarded a train. After a relaxing journey of approximately 10 hours we arrived in Budapest. From my window seat, in every direction I looked, I saw desolate ruins where homes and buildings — including synagogues —had once stood. Most of Europe — places we had once called home — was in ruins.

Budapest, too, had been badly bombed during the war and was

in ruins. When we arrived, the station was filled with *"Heftlinges,"* the German name for displaced people. People from the Joint Committee and UNRA were there to direct us to the Joint offices in the city. People always came to meet the train, hoping to finding lost relatives.

As I walked around the platform, I surprisingly found my cousin, Suri Ganz. (Later, she would marry Mr. Abe Hartmann and move to the United States. Today, they live in Boro Park.) My girlfriends also met relatives at the platform. My cousin brought me back to her family's apartment, and I remained there for the duration of my stay in Budapest.

It was time for my girlfriends and me to go our separate ways. Each of us had found some surviving relatives or friends, and had a place to go. For the time being, I chose to remain in Budapest. The others were worried about leaving me alone, but I assured them that I would be fine.

It had been slightly over a year since all of us had been torn away from our families at the Auschwitz-Birkenau platform. By Hashem's hand, the five of us — Parry, Rivka, Rita, Miriam and I — had found one another there, and had managed to stay together until the day we parted in Budapest.

We decided to have one last luncheon together and met at the community kosher kitchen. This kitchen was operated by a small group of refugees who were helping homeless fellow Jews while trying to pick up the pieces of their own lives.

Long after we had completed our meal, we continued to sit quietly at the table. Finally it was time to say good-bye. It was an emotional moment for all of us as we parted. We hoped we would be able to rebuild our lives and have cheerful, or at least encouraging, news to impart the next time we spoke or wrote to one another.

Days passed. I began going to the train station daily, hoping to meet a relative or a friend getting off an incoming train. Even if I didn't meet anyone I knew, I hoped to at least encounter someone who would have information about my husband.

Baruch Hashem, my search was not in vain. Several people in the streets recognized me and told me that they were sure they had seen my husband after liberation.

Much to my surprise, there were several different rumors circulating about my husband. Among those who claimed to have seen him after the war were some *Chassidim* who had once studied with my revered father, R' Horowitz, *ztk"l*. Their stories varied. Some people claimed to have seen my husband alive and well in Auschwitz; some said a Jewish chaplain had taken him to America; and still others told me that he was on his way to *Eretz Yisrael*.

My head was spinning. Were any of these stories true? If so, which one? Was my husband looking for me at that exact moment? It did not make sense that he would leave Europe without looking for me first. On the other hand, maybe he tried and simply couldn't find me, just as I couldn't find him. If only I knew what to believe!

If I were to search for him, believing the rumors that he was still alive, where would I begin?

One day, I met a member of a friend's family from Satmar. She told me that the Satmar Rebbe and Rebbetzin were, indeed, alive and in *Eretz Yisrael*! I then learned that another uncle had also survived, and was living in the United States. For the first time in days, I actually smiled. I felt a small spark of hope — if the Teitelbaums and my other uncle were alive, perhaps I would find my husband and other family members among the survivors, too!

After jotting down the information I had just learned, I needed to take a walk and clear my head. I was suddenly confronted with a major decision — the first one I would ever make on my own. Should I stay in Europe and continue looking for my husband — who may or may not have been alive at the time — or should I make arrangements to go to *Eretz Yisrael* and stay with my uncle the Satmar Rebbe, and my aunt, with whom I was so close? At the time it was not possible for me to travel to the United States to join my other uncle. I knew that I, a young woman alone in a large city, could not remain in Budapest without emotional support from my loved ones.

I resolved to go to *Eretz Yisrael*. I would search for my husband there, and if he were not there, I would return to Europe to look for him. Of course I would have to wait until it was safer to travel. Perhaps by then the Teitelbaums would accompany me back to Europe.

I learned that in order to go to *Eretz Yisrael* I would have to travel to Italy, and from one of the port cities I could be smuggled onto a boat that would attempt to run the British blockade around Palestine. This sounded risky, but I decided to take the chance.

With help from Jewish agencies I managed to make arrangements to travel to Italy, from where I would contact my uncle and let him know of my plans.

Before leaving for Italy, I traveled to Selish in the hopes of reclaiming my father's *sefer* along with the jewels which had been buried in the cellar of my mother's house. In Selish I stayed with a Jewish family who had also survived the Holocaust and had just found their way home.

At the first possible opportunity I returned to our former home. Much to my disappointment, the apartment was empty and the cellar had been dug up. All of our precious possessions were gone!

The only remnant of the Jewish community was the cemetery. Many of our friends had been buried there, along with a number of *rabbanim* and *tzaddikim*, including the father of the founder of the Chabad movement, R' Shneur Zalman of Liadi. The cemetery was peaceful and quiet. I stayed a while and said a prayer.

Upon returning to Budapest, I registered to emigrate to *Eretz Yisrael*. Before leaving, however, I had one final trip to make in Europe. Rumors were circulating that the Romanian king had spared the Jews. Since Alba Iulia, the hometown of my sister-in-law Chana, was in Romania, she and her family living there had been spared. I gathered my few possessions and boarded a train to Romania to say good-bye to them.

I ARRIVED AT REBBETZIN CHANA KAHANA'S HOUSE EARLY ON A Thursday evening. We fell into each other's arms and cried broken-

Family Reunion at Alba Iulia

heartedly for all we had lost, for all the uncertainty that remained and because we had found each other. When our tears were spent we entered the house, where a pleasant surprise awaited me. Two of my brothers-in-law, R' Shmuel Shmelka and R' Mordechai David, were there. I was extremely disappointed, though, when I realized that my husband was not there with them. My new relatives offered me *chizuk*, telling me that they had also heard vague rumors that my husband was alive, although they knew nothing definitive about his whereabouts.

I also learned that my husband's uncle, the Rebbe of Tomashov, Poland, R' Moishe Frisherman, was also alive and had arrived at Alba Iulia. He had survived Auschwitz, but tragically, his beloved wife, Rebbetzin Mindel (my father-in-law's sister), and his five dear children, *zk"l*, died as martyrs, *al Kiddush Hashem*.

We talked briefly about what had happened to us over the past year. My brothers-in-law told me the tragic news about the deaths of their — and my husband's — parents. Although I barely had a chance to get to know them, I had nothing but the utmost esteem and respect for my revered father- and mother-in-law, *H"yd* My husband and I had been looking forward to seeing them often throughout the years and, G-d willing, making them grandparents. Now they were gone. If my husband were alive, I wondered if he knew.

I was later to learn about the deaths of the other family members.

My brothers-in-law told me that they wanted to search for my husband in Germany, and asked if I wished to join them. It was then that I informed them of my plans to travel to *Eretz Yisrael* to be with the Teitelbaums. Surprised, they attempted to convince me not to go until we had confirmed my husband's whereabouts. I explained why this trip was so important to me, that I longed to be reunited with my aunt and uncle. Finally, they nodded in reluctant approval.

My brother-in-law R' Shmuel Shmelka, and R' Frisherman decided to accompany me to Italy, and from there to *Eretz Yisrael*. I appreciated their kind offer and accepted, relieved that I wouldn't have to travel alone. It was decided that my other brother-in-law, R' Mordechai David, would stay behind just in case my husband did show up.

I was so weary from traveling and from the overall emotional strain I had been under that I retired to the guest room after we ate. Despite my state of mind, I fell asleep the second my head hit the pillow. With the help of my sister-in-law and her husband, Grand Rabbi Nachman Kahana, *shlita*, preparations were made for our long trip.

Our Shabbos in Alba Iulia was delightful and peaceful. We learned that a group of Jewish refugees was leaving to *Eretz Yisrael* from the neighboring town of Temes-Var. We decided to join the group and set out for Italy the following night.

Such a journey normally would have required a great deal of luggage, but I didn't have many belongings. All I took was one small valise. We traveled on regular passenger trains, which were sometimes very crowded. The organizers of the trip, the *"brichah"* from Palestine, were responsible for obtaining the tickets, supplying some food, and making arrangements for border crossings.

Italy A FEW DAYS LATER WE REACHED PADUA, A CITY NEAR MILAN, ITALY. We arrived in the evening and were placed in an existing local Jewish camp. One of the leading Jewish officials of the camp took us to the barracks in which we would be staying. These barracks brought back unpleasant memories of those at the Russian camp.

Although the kitchen at the camp was fully kosher, my brother-in-law did not rely on its *kashrus*. I cooked him fish, stewed fruit, potatoes and fresh vegetables on a handmade outdoor grill put together with bricks.

The following morning, my brother-in-law and my husband's uncle took me into town and we sent a wire to my uncle in *Eretz*

Yisrael. As the days passed, we waited eagerly for his reply, checking with the telegraph office daily.

The next few days were tense. We went to the telegraph office, but there was no word from my uncle. At the camp, we asked around and heard horror stories about Jews being arrested on their way to *Eretz Yisrael*.

Traveling to Palestine was a dangerous undertaking at the time. In 1939, Great Britain, seeking to appease the Arabs, had issued its infamous White Paper halting all Jewish immigration to Palestine. How bitter it was that just when the Jews most needed a refuge, the door to one of the most logical havens had been slammed in our faces!

The war interrupted most *aliyah* activities and made it difficult, if not impossible, for immigration ships to sail the Mediterranean. Once the fighting ended, the British went back to strict enforcement of the White Paper. British policy called for the interception of all refugee ships and incarceration of all passengers and crews in detention camps on the island of Cyprus. Once again Jews were living behind barbed wire, sleeping in tents and getting precious little to eat. This time, however, they were there as prisoners of the British, not the Germans. It could take months — even years — before they were released.

We were also told that the journey itself was treacherous. Passengers were squeezed onto the boats with little breathing space, reminiscent of the way we had been crammed into the cattle cars. Many people became violently ill from the severe rocking motion of the ship; some even died along the way.

On the bright side, however, there were a few boats that managed to slip past the watchful eye of the British fleet and make it to *Eretz Yisrael*.

Finally, on a dreary, rainy morning we received discouraging news. A message was waiting for me in the telegraph office:

Palestine, Eretz Yisrael, Elul 5706
CHANA: BARUCH HASHEM YOU'RE ALIVE. (STOP)
WOULD LIKE VERY MUCH TO SEE YOU (STOP)
BUT TRIP WOULD BE TOO DANGEROUS (STOP)
PLEASE DON'T COME AT THIS TIME (STOP)
WE WILL FIND ONE ANOTHER LATER ON.
— RABBI YOEL TEITELBAUM

A sinking feeling came over me, and I dropped the telegram from my hand. Seeing my pallor, R' Shmuel Shmelka asked me what was wrong. He picked up the paper and read the message.

"We must be grateful that your uncle sent us this warning," he said. "We must heed his advice and not go. It is too risky. I do understand your disappointment, but your uncle is right." The Tomashover Rebbe nodded in agreement and said that according to the Torah, one must not knowingly put oneself in a dangerous situation. Traveling to *Eretz Yisrael* would put us in such a situation.

I folded the telegram and tucked it away, then the three of us despondently left the telegraph office. We headed back to the D.P. camp. What should we do now?

We had a long, serious discussion later that day. "I still have hopes of finding R' Mendel in Europe," said my brother-in-law. "Perhaps it was *bashert* (ordained) that we did not make the trip to Palestine. Maybe we can consider this a sign from the A-mighty that R' Mendel is still on this continent, searching for you at this very moment."

R' Shmuel Shmelka's words touched my heart and, after thinking things over, I agreed with him.

"What shall we do now?" I asked.

"We must return to Germany and look for him," he answered.

"But … how? We had help getting to Italy. How can we return safely to Germany? We still don't have passports or official papers."

"Don't worry. I will make the arrangements," my brother-in-law assured me.

And so he did. A few days later, all arrangements had been

made. However, since the *yamim tovim* were nearly upon us, we would remain in Italy until after Succos.

We *davened* in the *beis midrash* set up in the Padua D.P. Camp for Rosh Hashanah, 1945. Yom Kippur was more somber, especially when it was time to say *Yizkor*. My sobs joined those of the other women around me, and the cries and wails from the men's section were unbearable. As I memorialized my dear parents, *ztk"l*, our venerable relatives, the Selisher *kehillah* — all martyrs who died *al kiddush Hashem* — every nerve in my body shivered and my heart pounded at twice its normal rate. Saying *Yizkor* remains difficult and continues to shake the foundations of my *neshamah* even today, 50 years later. As I remembered those who had died, I also thought of those who were still missing.

Our only comfort was in the knowledge that this year we were *davening* quietly and uninterrupted in a *beis midrash* as free persons — quite a contrast from Yom Kippur of just one year ago! I remembered the tall Jewish *kapo* in Stutthof beating me with a stick after she caught me holding the *siddur* on Yom Kippur. I was grateful to Hashem for having inscribed and sealed me in the Book of Life last year, even as I stood in the midst of Stutthof's death mill. Did He do the same for my husband? The suspense of not knowing whether or not he was still alive was agonizing.

As Succos approached, we faced the problem of securing and building a kosher *succah*, but the camp officials managed to provide us with the necessary materials to build one. The huge community *succah* was built on the camp grounds, and we had a festive time. Eating outside even enhanced my poor appetite. Although in the past we traditionally ate stuffed cabbage on Simchas Torah, this year our stomachs could only handle simple fare like boiled chicken and baked potatoes.

Simchas Torah brought out every possible emotion, including elation that we were celebrating our holy Torah in freedom.

After the *yamim tovim* were over, it was time to set out for Germany. In the interim, the Tomashover Rebbe, much to our surprise, decided to stay in Italy. He explained that he was getting on in years and wasn't up to making the trip back to Germany. We asked him where he would go and what he would do, alone in a strange country.

He responded that through the grapevine he had heard that R' Ephraim Oshry,[4] had started a new yeshivah in Rome. This rabbi was a survivor of the Kovno Ghetto of Lithuania and many survivors had followed him there. The Tomashover Rebbe decided to join R' Oshry's following at the yeshivah. He assured us that with the A-mighty's help he would be all right, and that we shouldn't worry about him. But when the time came for us to say good-bye, it was an emotional moment for all of us, especially after what we had been through together.

WE PACKED VERY FEW THINGS FOR OUR JOURNEY. MY BROTHER-IN-LAW took a small bag which carried a *siddur*, a *Sefer Tehillim*, his *tefillin*

A Perilous Journey to Germany

and a couple of changes of clothing. I also packed clothing and some food which would, we hoped, last until we had safely crossed the border into Germany.

Finally the hour of departure arrived. It was late at night, and we slipped out of the camp quietly to meet a couple of Polish guides whom R' Shmuel Shmelka had hired to get us back to Germany safely. We found a group of six men standing in a dark courtyard, waiting tensely for the same two guides to take them over the border as well.

The instructions our guides gave us were explicit, and were to be followed to the letter. We would begin walking through some back streets, which would eventually lead us into a wooded area. Once in the woods, we would pick our way over dark and treacherous paths. The guides warned us not to panic, even if we couldn't see

---

4. Rabbi Oshry, the Tomashover Rebbe, came to America and settled in the Lower East Side and continued the Tomashover dynasty.

where we were headed. They assured us that they knew the routes well and would get us over the border safely. Nobody was to speak and no questions were to be asked. We had to remain as quiet and inconspicuous as possible to avoid risk of capture.

Silently, carefully, the men opened the courtyard gates. In single file, hearts hammering wildly, we proceeded through the gates. For a panicked moment I almost wanted to run back to the safety of the camp, but it was too late. We were on our way.

Exercising extreme caution, we hiked through the thickets for a few hours. The following night we reached a train station near Padua. A freight train heading toward Munich, Germany, pulled into the station, and our two guides pried open the doors of a freight car. They hurried us in, motioned for us to lie down on the floor, and covered us with blankets. *Baruch Hashem*, our car was not opened for inspection at the Italian- German border, and sometime the following morning we arrived in Munich.

Large as Munich's train station was, we didn't recognize anyone on the platform. We immediately headed for Fehrenwald D.P. Camp. Arriving there in the afternoon, we found that the camp was badly overcrowded. The Americans did not confiscate large German houses for the convalescing survivors, only old army bar-racks, and there was no place for us to stay in the camp. A camp official arranged for me to stay with a Miss Miryam (who is Mrs. Waldman today) and her family for the interim. My brother-in-law was placed in the men's dormitory.

We were ecstatic to learn from people in Fehrenwald that my husband was, indeed, alive, and that immediately after the *yamim tovim* he had left the camp to look for me! Although initially the news was exciting, I was devastated by the knowledge that my husband and I had just missed one another by a few days. I had a nightmare vision of the two of us individually crisscrossing Europe, continuing to miss one another. How long would it take until we got back together?

My brother-in-law advised against trying to catch up with my husband. The best thing we could do now was to remain where we were and trust the A-mighty to send him back to us. All we could do was sit and wait.

Little did we know as we observed our first Shabbos in Fehrenwald that my husband was spending Shabbos not far away, in D.P. Camp Parsh, near Salzburg, just over the Austrian-German border, where he had stopped on his way to Italy to find me.

A FEW DAYS LATER, I WAS SURPRISED WHEN R' SHMUEL SHMELKA, accompanied by my other brother-in-law, R' Mordechai David,

Reunion With My Husband
came to see me. The last time I had seen R' Mordechai David was at Rebbetzin Chana's house in Alba Iulia. Before I had a chance to say anything, my two brothers-in-law told me the happy news: my husband had finally returned to Germany! He would be coming to meet me at the apartment in which I was staying later in the afternoon — around 5 o'clock.

I was ecstatic. There was so much I wanted to ask; so much I wanted to know. My first question, however, was about his general state of health. They assured me that my husband was well — albeit walking with a slight limp, due to an accident in the Ebensee slave and labor camp and a subsequent operation in Salzburg after liberation — and was resting from his trip.

Tears of relief flooded my eyes. The search was finally over. The fact that my husband and I were both still alive after having been slated for death by the Nazi war criminals was nothing short of a miracle.

After my brothers-in-law left, I prepared for my reunion with my husband. All I had to wear was a tattered but clean dress, and a *tichel*. Even my shoes were worn out and my stockings were ragged, but in the overall scheme of things, did that really matter? The important thing was that we would soon be back together, ready to begin rebuilding our lives. We were, indeed, a very fortunate couple.

By 4:30 that afternoon I was dressed and ready for our meeting. It had been well over a year since my new *chassan* and

I were brutally pulled apart at the Auschwitz platform. Now my legs felt like jelly as I stood up to greet him, and my heart pounded from both joy and nervousness. We stared at one another for a few seconds without uttering a single word, in a state of near disbelief.

I saw before me a very thin, very pale young Chassidic man. His face was nearly free of facial hair, although he had regrown a small beard on the lower sides of his cheeks and chin. Pools of anguish lay in the depths of his large brown eyes and, as my brothers-in-law had warned me, he was limping; his injured leg had not yet healed. Was this gentleman, this stranger standing before me, the tall, handsome, bearded young *chassan* whom I had married not so long ago? His physical deterioration came as a great shock to me. It took me a few moments to convince myself that this young man was, indeed, my husband.

I was sure that he was thinking along similar lines; I did not look like the radiant young *kallah* who had stood beside him under the *chuppah*; the pale young woman before him was thin and bone-weary. Neither of us spoke until we were absolutely sure that we recognized one another. Not quite knowing what to say first, we communicated through our tears. We would both be eternally grateful to the A-mighty for leading us back together once again!

WE NEEDED TIME TO RECOVER FROM THE INITIAL SHOCK AND excitement of seeing one another again. We did not recount our

Recovering From Our Shocking Experiences experiences initially; we were simply not ready emotionally to bring back such raw and painful memories. Our first concern was for each other's health and well-being. We also had to make plans for the future, starting with finding a place to live. Since D.P. Camp Fehrenwald did not have accommodations for married couples, we had to find an apartment. Finally, the camp administrators found a small living space for us.

It was in that apartment that my husband and I had our first discussions about our experiences after we were torn apart at the Birkenau ramp, often talking late into the night. As time went on, all the gruesome details of our suffering emerged.

My husband waited for what he felt was the right time to inform me that he had witnessed my dear mother marching to her death. Although I had known that my dear mother had perished, my husband's words reopened the wound in my heart. I was in shock for days and cried hysterically in my sleep. I had not yet recovered from the loss of my father, and was forced to deal with the loss of my innocent, holy mother, who was also stolen from us by the German-Austrian murderers in SS uniforms. My husband tried his best to console me, as I did him, but how could words ease the pain of losing our families?

As my husband recounted the particulars of his own horrifying experiences to me, I shivered with each detail, able to relate to the atrocities that had been inflicted upon him by his captors by remembering the harrowing things that had happened to me ...

CHAPTER 8
The Survival Story of My Husband, R' Menachem Rubin

AT THE BIRKENAU PLATFORM, ALONG WITH EVERYONE ELSE, my husband was dragged out of the railroad car by other camp inmates. Once on the ground, he scrambled

First Hours in Birkenau

unsteadily to his feet, astonished by everything going on around him.

As the Germans pushed the men to one side and the women and children to another, my husband managed a last, long look at my petrified face and saw the terror in my eyes. What he didn't see was his own bewildered expression.

In a state of confusion, my husband heard the SS barking orders in German, and cringed as those who were unable to comprehend

The terrible selection process at Birkenau. Josef Mengele and other S.S. officers sent people to the left (the gas chamber) or to the right (slave labor) with a flick of the thumb. The line of people at the top has already been marked for death and is unknowingly headed for the gas chamber.

Doomed Jewish women and children on their way to the gas chamber. I can imagine that this was the way my mother and my mother-in-law looked after their selection.

them were beaten mercilessly. He noticed the high barbed-wire fences, and an appalling brick guardhouse which stood in the distance, with its many windows and an immense watchtower. The ramp on which everyone stood seemed to stretch on for miles. Before him was the long train of cattle cars from which we had just disembarked. The line of Jews, young and old, healthy and sick, seemed endless. His mind froze as he gazed on a world previously unknown to mankind — a place which defied all logic.

My husband saw some elderly men sitting on the train platform, silently awaiting new orders. For that brief moment they seemed content to sit quietly and catch their breath outside the boxcar.

With thoughts of miracles and salvation in mind, my husband suddenly found himself face-to-face with the notorious "Dr." Josef Mengele, who gazed at him in cold triumph, then jerked his thumb sharply to the right. SS guards obediently made sure he moved in that direction.

He saw Mengele motion all the elderly men to the left. Initially, rumors circulated that the elderly would be taken to a rest camp within the compound. My husband noticed other inmates "escorting" those too feeble to walk on their own. Little did the newcomers know that these elderly men would soon be reduced to ashes by the German-Austrian Nazi murderers.

Not far from the pit of ashes near the ruins of Crematorium No. 5 there was another large pit of ashes where someone put 4 small marble markers. Each is inscribed – one in Hebrew, one in Yiddish, one in English and one in Polish – "Here are the ashes of the victims of the crematorium."

Organized into groups of five, the men on the right were next ordered to wait in a long line before a brick building which they were to enter for delousing. Volvi Kahan, a young, frightened man from Selish, was among the men in the group. He knew my husband from back home and managed to approach him with a question.

"Rabbi Rubin, what is written in the Scriptures about life after death?" he stammered.

My husband can still recall the terror of death in the young man's eyes as he told him a little about *Olam Haba* with a quote about Jews who died *al Kiddush Hashem*. (Volvi Kahan, *a"h*, survived and ultimately moved

In Birkenau, the ashes of the victims at first were buried in pits by the crematoria and later dumped into the nearby Vistula River. One such pit was located near Crematorium No. 5, whose ruins are seen in this photo taken recently by Mr. Meir Rosen-Rosenberg. My husband saw my venerable mother disappear forever into this building and we consider the pit of ashes near these ruins to be the kever of my mother z"l.

to America, settling in Los Angeles, California.)

As the men quietly stood in line, waiting to move on, they watched as the SS directed a long line of hysterical women and

The memorial marker for my mother is near the tombs of her father, Rabbi Yom Tov Horowitz, zt"l, Grand Rabbi of Sighet and author of Kedushas Yom Tov (right), and his Rebbetzin, Chana, after whom I am named (center). At left is the tomb of Rochel, the daughter of R' Yoel Teitelbaum of Satmar.

We considered putting a tombstone for my mother at the Crematorium No. 5 ash pit, but decided that putting it there would be too complicated, and it might be removed. We therefore decided to place the marker next to the tombs of my grandparents in my mother's hometown of Sighet.

terrified young children toward a red brick building, which we later learned was one of the four gas chambers in Birkenau. Suddenly my husband caught sight of my dear mother, the *tzaddekes*, among the others walking briskly toward the building. For a split second their eyes met, and she nodded at him with her usual gentle smile. Feeling his heart pounding uncontrollably, my husband returned her greeting with his eyes and head, and remained still as he watched her move away and enter the building. He did not see me near my mother, and wondered frantically where I was. Had I been lost among the sea of women entering the building, or was I somewhere else in the camp?

R' Rubin stands near the tombs of my mother's parents

Once the group of women and children was shoved inside, an SS man emerged from the building and slammed the heavy iron door shut. Following several moments of eerie silence, my husband and the other men heard screams and pitiful wails coming from inside the building. Minutes passed, the screams rose to a crescendo and then — silence once more. Some of the men tried to approach the brick building, but an angry *kapo* immediately descended upon them and ordered them back into line, his long rubber hose flailing left and right. My husband did not know it at the time, but he and the other men had just witnessed the murder of my venerable mother, gassed together with the other holy martyrs, *H"yd* Before entering the delousing building, my husband was branded with an Auschwitz tattoo number on his forearm by a young Slovak inmate. (In the hellish, upside-down world of Auschwitz there were no people, only numbers. My husband's number was *A-13352*. It is still on his arm.) He asked the boy when he would see his wife and mother-in-law again. Pointing to the high flames spewing upwards, the boy raised his hand toward an angry sky, inundated by red and black flames, and answered coldly, "Up there! Soon you will join them!"

The boy's response was so outlandish and bizarre that my husband did not know quite what to make of it, although he was convinced that the boy could not have literally meant what he said. Later he was to find out otherwise. The numbers of *kedoshim* (holy martyrs) were so extensive that the huge crematoria couldn't accommodate them all, even though they were functioning 24 hours a day, seven days a week. As a result, the SS established an enormous pit of fire into which victims were tossed and burned around the clock. Often these innocents — especially the babies — were still alive when they were thrown into the open pits.

After being stripped of their clothing and possessions, the men were shoved into the delousing building where they were greeted by barbers who shaved their hair, sometimes with dull clippers and razors. After a brief shower, they were issued striped prison uniforms. Aside from their shoes, which they were permitted to keep, everything was gone. Of special import to my husband was the fact that his *tallis* and *tefillin* had been held back in the cattle car.

After the delousing ordeal, the men were marched, always in lines of five, to another part of the camp. After entering and exiting one section of the camp after another, they were finally commanded to halt. The SS ordered them into a wooden barrack, similar to the one I stayed in while in Birkenau. The structure was long and narrow — certainly not designed to fit the huge numbers of men crammed inside.

Before they entered the barrack, SS barbarians shouted at them to hand over any remaining jewels or valuables in their possession — or face severe punishment.

While we were still in the ghetto, my husband had hidden some diamonds in the soles of his shoes. During the journey to Auschwitz the soles had become loose, and the hidden gems were visible to anyone who held the shoes in his hand. Fearing punishment, my husband humbly removed his shoes and surrendered them to the SS. Much to his astonishment, the SS man laughed, while everybody else on line glared at my husband, silently condemning him for his gullibility. As we were later to find out, the Germans relied on the naivete and fear of the newcomers when ordering them to surrender their hidden valuables or risk serious consequences.

Early the following morning, in the predawn darkness, my husband found himself scurrying out the door with his barrack-mates for early morning *zeilappel*, where he recited *Shema* while standing. Wearing only the thin cotton striped uniform he had been issued the previous day, my husband shivered in the cold. In the dark, the skies appeared angry; a heavy haze blocked the stars and the moon from view.

Soon the sun rose over the forsaken camp and the sky turned beet-red and gray. It was a new dawn at Auschwitz-Birkenau. No *tefillin*, no *tzitzis*, no *chavrusa*... My husband remembers standing in one position for hours, longing to close his eyes and wake up somewhere — anywhere — else. What kind of place was this? Who would have dreamed that the formerly civilized Germans would design such an inhuman place of torture?

My husband and the others were to remain in the same barracks for a couple of weeks during a period known in the camp as "quarantine." Each day at *zeilappel*, the cruel *kapo* would call out a list of occupations — such as painter, plumber, carpenter — and ask who in line was skilled in those fields. Men would step out, and they would be led away. Eventually the men began to raise their hands in response to queries regarding just about any skill, hoping to be taken away to something better. My husband tells the story of how, one day, the *kapo* mockingly called out, *"Wir suchen zizi beissers?* (Are there *tzitzis*-biters here?)"* Not realizing what the sarcastic *kapo* had actually said, many raised their hands, only to realize they were being ridiculed.

A friend finally convinced my husband to volunteer, as a means of getting out of Birkenau. That day, after making his little joke at the prisoners' expense, the *kapo* called for carpenters to step forward. My husband was among those who did, even though he had never held a hammer — or any other tool, for that matter — in his life.

He realized that he was taking a chance. The alternative was to remain in Birkenau, living in a barn with several hundred other inmates, never knowing whether the next moment might be his last. He joined the other "carpenters" on line, and was marched through a series of gates which led out of Birkenau.

Close to an hour later, he and the others approached a bizarre looking gate with the words, *"Arbeit Macht Frei"* ("Work Makes You Free!", the ironic German motto found like some kind of corporate slogan at the entrance to many concentration camps, including Auschwitz) inscribed in an ironwork design above the gate. The entire Nazi system was based on misleading lies; this was one among thousands. The German guards opened the gate and counted the men as they walked through. The doors slammed shut behind them.

IS THERE ANYONE TODAY WHO DOESN'T KNOW ABOUT AUSCHWITZ? Fifty years ago, only a handful of people knew.

Auschwitz   The learned Wolf family, now members of our congregation in Brooklyn, tell the story of a relative named Chayim Wolf. During the war the Wolf family lived in Csop, Hungary, but they were originally from a Polish town named Aushpizin (in Yiddish), Oswiecim (in Polish), or Auschwitz (in German). After being interned in the Csop ghetto, the Wolf family and hundreds of other Jews were placed on a transport to Auschwitz. When they arrived at the Auschwitz train station, Chayim remembers saying, "Well, what do you know? We're home! We've returned to our hometown of Aushpizin!" What he, his family and the others on that train didn't know was that because of its geographic situation, their hometown had been chosen by Berlin to become a murder facility for millions.

My husband recalls that, superficially, Auschwitz-1 looked more aesthetically attractive than it had any right to. There were flowers by the gate, neat patches of green grass bordered by stones, and lines of trees along paved blocks and streets. The brick buildings with their red-tiled roofs did not appear as dilapidated and sinister as the barracks of Birkenau. However, the watchtowers, electrified barbed-wire fences, and bright lights surrounding the camp were all there, reminding the men that they were prisoners and that their lives were still very much in danger.

The stench of burning flesh was not as pervasive as it was in Birkenau, due to the increased distance from the crematoria. But a foggy thicket of haze was everpresent, and at night, one could see the high flames. In the *Beis HaMikdash*, the Holy Temple, a fire had to burn on the Altar at all times, a fire of holiness. In Auschwitz, the constant flame was nurtured by evil and sin.

My husband's group was assigned to a brick building. One positive aspect about this new "home" was that each inmate was assigned his own bunk bed. After what he had endured in Birkenau — being wedged in among several men — having his own bunk actually made my husband think of his comfortable bed in Selish.

When he had time to think about it, my husband wondered why his group was more fortunate than the wretched souls in Birkenau. He later discovered the answer: the barracks in Auschwitz were to be shown to the Red Cross. Just as the Nazis had lied to the Jews to bring us to Auschwitz with a minimum of trouble by telling us we were merely going to a "resettlement" camp, so they were now lying to everybody else about the treatment they were extending us. [The entire murderous Nazi Germany regime was based on lies, again and again. Lies to Chamberlain, to Moscow, to Roosevelt … the list is endless.]

While the accommodations were somewhat better in Auschwitz-1 than they had been in Birkenau, the food was the same in both camps: a piece of thick, moldy, tasteless bread and thin, weak "coffee" for breakfast; watery, ersatz "soup" (containing anything from a few grains of barley to a couple of rotten potatoes) for lunch, and more "coffee" or "soup" at night. Many men, repulsed by the foulness of these brews, and already nauseated by the revolting smells of the camp, spat it out or threw it up.

A camp street in Auschwitz in late 1944

Auschwitz as it looks today

The men may have lived in brick buildings, but they still had to report to *zeilappel* twice a day, once before the crack of dawn, and then again at dusk. And always, always, the SS guards, as well as the *kapos* and veteran inmates, did their best to make the lives of the newcomers totally miserable.

One example of this sadism remains vivid in husband's mind to this day. The wooden clogs he was given to wear were causing his feet to ache and blister, and my husband was suffering terribly from the pain. One morning, a veteran inmate of his barrack, a Polish fellow, noticed his discomfort and beckoned him over. Appearing friendly, he advised my husband to ask the *Blockaeltester* (the overseer of a barrack), a fat German inmate, for a regular pair of shoes if the wooden ones were bothering him so much.

Naively, my husband heeded the man's advice. As he and the others entered the block one by one, he approached the *Blockaeltester* and asked him for a pair of shoes. The *Blockaeltester*, appalled by my husband's audacity in making such a request — let alone the impertinence displayed in addressing him at all — raised his hand and gave my husband two sharp blows across the face. From the corner of his eye, my husband saw the Polish man laugh. The *Blockaeltester* began laughing, too.

My husband told me that the Pole's betrayal hurt him more than the slaps. He learned a very painful lesson that day, and was relieved to get off simply with blows. But could he fault the Polish inmate completely? Not really. After all, the man had already been subjected to years of brutality and dehumanization by the SS. Additionally, the Poles resented the fact that the Hungarians had been free until April 1944, and their jealousy sometimes caused them to torment their fellow inmates in revenge.

Newly arrived, my husband was not yet affected by the system of Auschwitz. Even though he was dressed in a striped prison uniform and was in a strange place, he still remembered that he was a young Chassidic rabbi, the son of a famous *Admor*, and a part of the golden chain of various Chassidic dynasties.

One element of heroism is missing from much of the literature and stories of the Holocaust. The *mesiras nefesh* of many religious Jewish individuals, whether living under the iron thumb of the Nazi mass murderers or subjected to the rule of Stalin's Communists, needs to be discussed and documented. These heroic Jews, including my husband and others interned in Auschwitz, managed to overcome the obstacles of their circumstances and find ways and means to *daven*.

My husband relates how sometimes, while saying *"Ma tov chelkeinu u'ma na'im goraleinu* (How good is our portion, how pleasant is our lot ...)," he would stop and question whether he should say those words in such a place as Auschwitz. He found his answer in the *pasuk* which followed soon after: *"Kadesh es shimcha al makdishei sh'mecha* (Your Holy Name is sanctified through Jews who do sanctify it),"* so my husband concluded that it was proper to say, "My lot is good" — even in Auschwitz. No force was stronger than *tefillah*; it surpassed the barbed-wire fences, the watchtowers and the irate German-Nazi SS with their machine guns.

After settling in at Auschwitz-1, the members of my husband's group were assigned by SS officers to work details. My husband was assigned to a department called *Deutsche Ausrustungswerke* (DAW), or German Armaments Works, Ltd., an SS commercial enterprise that also had plants in other camps outside Auschwitz-Birkenau. It cannot be emphasized strongly enough that the German industrial complex worked hand-in-hand with Germany's military establishment, and shared the murderous goals of the SS, *Gestapo* and the entire Nazi government structure.

My husband's days at Auschwitz quickly fell into an established routine — up before dawn for *zeilappel*, followed by a breakfast of "coffee" and stale bread, off to work at DAW early in the morning, a short break for lunch at midday, *zeilappel* at dusk, ersatz soup with sausage (which my husband traded for bread) for dinner, and back to the barracks for the night. In the summer, it was still light outside when they returned.

One of my husband's most unpleasant memories of Auschwitz was of the line-up and march to and from the factory. The walk was long, about a half-hour each way. Of course, the prisoners were not supposed to converse with one another enroute to work or back to the barracks, but they managed to do so anyhow. The *kapos* were at the head of the line, and the SS men with their vicious dogs surrounded them on all sides. The subhuman SS did not refrain from laughing, insulting and cursing the wretched humans as they hobbled past in pain. If someone collapsed or died on the way, the other prisoners were responsible for dragging the corpse to *zeilappel*. Woe to all if the exact number of live prisoners and corpses did not match the official SS figures down to the last person!

The DAW workshop was a large gray room with long rows of worktables and benches. Dim light threaded its way through the foggy, grimy windows. In the section that my husband was assigned to, huge piles of metal boxes, damaged on the front, were stacked against the walls, and tools were provided to fix them. My husband's assignment was to repair broken metal bullet boxes that were sent back from the front. He had to learn his craft quickly or face severe consequences.

A German civilian represented the firm and was in charge of overseeing the work. An SS man and several *kapos* watched the men like hawks to ensure they delivered their maximum output, resulting, of course, in their extreme exhaustion as well.

The work and daily routine were incredibly tedious, but at least some of the men could sit while working. Those laboring inside the workshop were also protected from constant exposure to the elements. Luckily, my husband was not forced to take any of the harder, more backbreaking assignments there, such as dragging heavy wagons, digging ditches or laying hot tar for roads. He was also grateful for not having been assigned to the *Sonderkommando* unit, which had to remove the clothing left behind by the men and women led to the gas chambers, and — even more

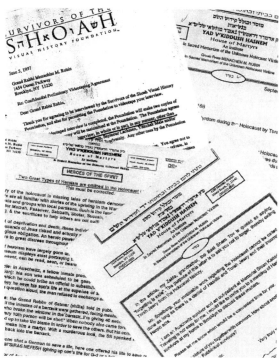

R' Rubin has long fought to have the heroism of Torah Jewry highlighted in Holocaust studies

horrible — was forced to shove the bodies of the gassed victims into the ovens. My husband knew someone who had been assigned to the *Sonderkommando*, R' Wertzberger, *z"l*, from Orshiva, a township located in the vicinity of Muzsay-Beregszaz-Munkach. From time to time, R' Wertzberger threw little notes over the barbed wire, detailing what was going on inside the walls of the crematorium and what his own role was there. (R' Wertzberger's son survived the war and now lives in Williamsburg.)

A YOUNG MAN, A REFORM JEW FROM BUDAPEST, WAS MY HUSBAND'S *Vorarbeiter*, or foreman, in the DAW compound. Noticing the fum-

A Brave Vorarbeiter

bling way my husband handled the tools, the foreman immediately realized that this worker was not as nimble with his hands as he had been led to believe. He asked my husband who he was, and what he really did for a living. After my husband told him the truth, the foreman did not waste any time. He immediately handed my husband a hammer, followed in turn by the other necessary tools, and quickly showed him what to do. Learning to solder with the blowtorch was a little more difficult, but soon R' Rubin became rather efficient at it, and his hands even looked like those of a workman: dirty and sweaty from fingernails to palms. Not only did the foreman teach my husband how to use a hammer and a blowtorch, but he also made it possible for him on Shabbos to avoid doing *melachah* (any of thirty-nine types of labor forbidden on the Sabbath). One might ask how in Auschwitz, a human extermination factory where anyone caught performing an act of "sabotage" —i.e., observing the Torah — was instantly beaten, or worse, could this incredible human being allow my husband, a Chassidic Jew, to observe Shabbos? This man's acts of *tzedakah* went way above and beyond the call of duty, and my husband will never forget what he did on his behalf.

As far as the SS was concerned, it was work as usual in

Auschwitz-Birkenau on Saturdays. The official day of rest was Sunday. My husband still remembers shedding bitter tears that first Shabbos morning as he walked into the workplace, anguished by the prospect of being forced to desecrate the Shabbos. Other workers felt as he did: one repeated the laws of Shabbos in the Torah, citing how one should not do a craft nor light a fire, while another questioned whether he was in his current terrible predicament because he had not observed Shabbos properly in the past. My husband broke out in a cold sweat as he sank down on the workbench and feverishly tried to come up with the proper solution to his problem.

The foreman immediately noticed his distress. After carefully looking around the room to make sure nobody would catch them conversing, he asked my husband what was wrong. As my husband explained the situation, compassion and warmth surfaced in the foreman's eyes, and he nodded his head in understanding. He assured my husband that he would not force him to work on Shabbos, even though they would be taking a big risk. My husband was astonished. Could it be that someone in that forsaken place was actually interested in looking out for him? But at what cost?

Placing a hammer into one hand and a damaged box into the other, the foreman ordered my husband to sit quietly and go through the motions of hammering the box — without actually repairing it. This way, my husband technically would not be working. The foreman promised to be on the lookout and, if anyone was to enter, he would alert my husband. Upon his signal, my husband would begin to straighten a bump in the box, but would be allowed to discontinue his work once the officer left. The foreman also did not require my husband to turn on the blowtorch, thus allowing him to avoid transgressing the Shabbos by lighting a fire.

A story is told about some young Jewish boys who were captured by the Russian Czar and sent to Siberia as soldiers for life. On Yom Kippur, one lad turned to the group and said, "Comrades, what shall we do? We don't have a *machzor* (holiday prayerbook) and we cannot pray properly if we don't know the *tefillos* by heart.

Perhaps we should instead whistle the melody from home." The famous Berditchever Chassidic leader said that the tune whistled by the boys on that particular Yom Kippur made a greater impression in Heaven than many prayers at home.

We feel the same is true of that Shabbos in Auschwitz. At home, my revered father-in-law, the Rebbe, sang *"Keil Adon"* every Shabbos. In DAW, the rhythm of the hammer hitting the box without *chillul* Shabbos (desecration of the Sabbath) was just as inspiring. Possibly the sound of the hammer on that holy Shabbos was exceptionally remarkable in Heaven. In *"Keil Adon,"* we say, "You are the Master over all that is happening ..." We truly believe this includes what happened there in Auschwitz.

Helping him avoid transgressing the Shabbos was not the only deed of righteousness the foreman extended to my husband. After he saw how hard my husband tried not to eat *treif* in the camp, he often smuggled in a potato for him. To this day, my husband does not know where he found the potatoes, although he recalls marching past a potato supply area on his way to and from work. How the foreman managed to smuggle the potatoes into the factory also remains a mystery.

A ripe potato in Auschwitz was as precious as a sparkling diamond, but how could it be eaten? How could my husband and the foreman divide a potato without word somehow getting back to the *kapos*? My husband assumed that he would be sharing the potato with the others or, at the very least, with the foreman who had risked his own life to smuggle in the precious vegetable. Great was his astonishment when he found out that this would not be the case. The treasure was for him alone! My husband's eyes filled with tears. He did not know how to thank this kind man, who was obviously jeopardizing his own safety to perform this act of *chesed*.

The foreman told my husband he would show him how to cook the potato. Quickly he bent down, pulled the raw potato out of his pocket and handed it to my husband, whose hands were trembling so violently that he dropped it. The potato made a very soft thud as it landed on the hard wooden floor, but to my frightened husband's ears, it sounded like a cannon shot. Without panic or hesitation, he picked up the incriminating spud and stuffed it into his shirt. Looking warily around the shop, he was mildly surprised to see that nobody was looking in their direction. Everyone continued working; nobody was even paying attention to his conversation with the foreman. Just to be on the safe side, though, the foreman moved slightly so that he stood between my husband and the others, blocking their view of him holding the potato in his shirt.

"You have to be more careful," the foreman whispered, wiping the sweat off his brow. My husband was not alone in fearing that a mere potato could threaten his very life; the foreman, too, dreaded the idea that somebody else might see them and decide to turn informer.

The foreman then proceeded to show my husband how to cook the potato. There was water available in the room, needed for repairing the boxes. The foreman poured some water into a metal box and placed the potato inside. He showed my husband how to prepare "potato soup" by lighting the blowtorch and holding it under the metal box. It wouldn't take long for the heat to soften the potato. Since it would appear to the others that he was simply repairing the box, nobody would notice that my husband was actually cooking a potato inside.

How clumsy he felt the first time he tried to cook the potato! Praying that he would neither get caught, nor burned by the blowtorch, he was amazed to see how quickly the potato cooked over the fire as his eyes and nose watered from the hot steam.

Holding the hot, soft potato in his bare hands, he hunched over the steaming "soup" and bit into the precious vegetable, savoring its delectable taste. Never in his life, in all the years before or since, had he ever eaten such delicious potato soup — even though this particular batch did not have salt or fat or anything else added to enhance its flavor. Of course he could not fully enjoy his meal; he had to practically wolf it down so that he wouldn't get caught.

As the days at DAW dragged on, my husband's new friend and protector continued to bring him a potato from time to time. These precious potatoes helped to satisfy my husband's hunger, thus enabling him to sometimes turn down the undesirable "soup" served to the men back in the barracks. On those evenings when the camp soup was prepared with pieces of horse meat, regardless of whether my husband had a potato to eat that day or not, he did not consume the meat.

There is a concept in Jewish law known as *pikuach nefesh*; loosely translated, it means that one does what one has to in order to save a life, even if it means violating the strictures of *halachah*. For the prisoners in the concentration camps, eating the *treif* soup was necessary in order to give their bodies the nourishment needed to go on living. However, my husband was sometimes spared from having to eat it, thanks to his courageous young foreman.

The weeks and months in DAW fell into a routine until January 1945, when Berlin ordered the camp liquidated. Those of the men still able to walk were forced into a Death March to areas still unconquered by the approaching Red Army.

As my husband set out with his ragged comrades, he searched all around him, trying to find the foreman, hoping to acknowledge his kindness once again. But he could not locate him in the vast crowd of men. Much to my husband's everlasting regret, the two men had never exchanged names; thus, they could not seek each other out after liberation. Did this kind man survive the war? Is he alive today?

In later years I was to hear many harrowing stories of foremen who were so thoroughly brainwashed and dehumanized by the Germans that they served as mere puppets of the SS. Having lost their own identities, they were only interested in currying favor with their SS masters, and this sometimes resulted in their behaving with exceptional cruelty to their subordinates. Luckily, my husband's foreman was just the opposite.[1]

Our mothers used to say, *"A Yiddishe neshamah ken men nisht shatzen.* (The value of the Jewish soul is inestimable.)" May the A-Mighty reward this anonymous man for the great deeds he performed for my husband in the *Gehinnom* that was Auschwitz and its DAW.

GRATEFUL AS HE HAS ALWAYS BEEN FOR THE PHYSICAL SUSTENANCE he was granted in Auschwitz by his anonymous young foreman,

R' Jacob Zeligfeld my husband feels everlasting gratitude as well for the spiritual sustenance he received from another man: R' Jacob Zeligfeld, who lives today in Williamsburg. As a result of the efforts of this very special person, my husband and other religious inmates had the chance to put on *tefillin* on Sundays in Auschwitz.

R' Zeligfeld, a courageous, religious young man from Poland, had somehow managed to smuggle *tefillin* into the camp. He hid them carefully and on Sunday, the day the Germans allowed the men to remain in the barrack and rest, R' Zeligfeld ran from block to block to give each man a chance to put them on, even if for only a few precious moments. Since time was always working against the men in this death plant, each one only had enough time to say *Shema Yisrael* while wearing the *tefillin*. In this way, everybody was able to do the *mitzvah* of putting on *tefillin* with, at the very least, a short *berachah*.

R' Zeligfeld also smuggled in a small electric shaver, which turned out to be a spiritual lifesaver. On Sundays, the men were ordered to go to a barber to have their week's stubble shaved with a razor. Instead of going to the barber, who would shave the men with a straight razor, which violates *halachah*, they were able to use R' Zeligfeld's shaver. Not only did this brave man give up his day of rest to help his fellow inmates, but he actually put himself in

---

1. Our worthy friend, the venerable Kashover Rav, *shlita*, wrote in his book, *Tal HaShamayim,* that a non-observant Jew helped him as well while he was in the camps.

constant danger as he ran from block to block with the *tefillin* and shaver. How lamentable it is that such acts of heroism are so often overlooked or eliminated from historical accounts of the Holocaust!

Whether one should be shaven with a razor or a knife, whether one could put on *tefillin* and say a *berachah* — these may seem like trivial matters to some, particularly when viewed against the life-and-death backdrop of Auschwitz. But it must be stressed that for my husband the Rebbe, and others like him, these issues were no small matters at all. So scrupulous was my husband's upbringing by his revered father, *ztk"l*, that being forced to transgress the Commandments of G-d, even under extreme duress in a place where one had to scramble just to survive, let alone live an observant life, brought him profound anguish. This was true for any religious Jew — I felt the same way when I was confronted with situations in which I had to consider the possibility of disobeying the Law.

Therefore, on those occasions when my husband was able to observe a positive precept, such as the putting on of *tefillin*, or was spared the necessity of violating a negative precept, such as the injunctions against cutting the beard with a straight razor or doing work on Shabbos — it was a big accomplishment indeed, a victory over the barbarians in a place of madness specifically designed to prevent a Jew from winning any kind of victory at all.

IN DAW, A BRAVE SOUL HID A PAIR OF *TEFILLIN* IN THE MIDDLE OF THE courtyard, under a pile of lumber near the garbage bins. Soon word

Bitachon Conquers All

about the *tefillin* got out and, despite the risk to life and limb, several men immediately set out to devise clever ways of getting to the courtyard. My husband's method of getting to the *tefillin* was to volunteer for garbage duty every morning so that he would have an excuse to be around the garbage bins. His devoted foreman understood his motive and appointed him to the garbage detail.

It was a long walk to the lumberyard, and the large can of refuse he dragged was heavy, but the reward was well worth the effort. After emptying the garbage, my husband sneaked behind the piles of lumber. Hurriedly, he put on the *tefillin*, then gently returned them to the hiding place, near a high stack of boards. After looking around to make sure the coast was clear, he would race back to the DAW barrack.

One day my husband panicked as he got ready to run to the lumberyard to don the *tefillin*. Why was he risking his life? If he were caught by a *kapo* or an SS guard, he would be tortured brutally. But then he remembered his roots, his *yichus* and the teachings of his revered father, the Szaszregener Rebbe, and the feelings of anxiety started to melt away. As my husband confidently reached for the *tefillin* and prepared to put them on, he said to himself, "I am doing this, knowing the danger, knowing where I am, but also knowing who I am."

To this day, my husband cherishes the memory of that moment. The well-publicized picture of the Polish Jew wearing *tefillin* on his head and wrapped in a *tallis*, knowing that he is about to be shot any second by an SS soldier, very well illustrates the heroism of religious Jews prepared to risk all for the preservation of Torah.

IN 5705/1944, ROSH HASHANAH FELL ON SEPTEMBER 18TH AND 19TH, a Monday and a Tuesday. This was the first Rosh Hashanah since

Surgery in Auschwitz our marriage, and instead of spending the Yom Tov with his new wife and family, my husband would spend it in Auschwitz. Finding a way to avoid going out to work on Rosh Hashanah in Auschwitz would take nothing less than a miracle.

It so happened that a cyst developed on his arm. After showing it to one of his colleagues, my husband was told that he could go to the *revere*. The idea of finding an infirmary in a place where people were routinely killed en masse might seem strange, but the Germans had indeed set them up in most camps. This way they were perhaps able to prolong the lives of their slave laborers so that they could squeeze more work out of them before they finally collapsed.

In Auschwitz, if a prisoner needed surgery and either had the right "connections" or was simply lucky enough, he was operated on and given about a week in the barrack to recover. However, it must be noted that having an operation of any sort there was always dangerous — and not just because of the primitive medical facilities. The Germans conscientiously strove to keep the gas chambers filled to capacity at all times. Therefore, when the SS had extra time available, plus room to fit more victims in the gas chambers, a "selection" would take place in the *revere*. None of the patients survived those selections, not even the healthier ones scheduled for release. The quota of murder victims simply had to be filled. This was a perfect example of German "efficiency."

As a newcomer, my husband did not fully realize the dangerous situation he was putting himself into by going to the *revere*, and he took his chances. The infirmary was in a tiny barrack, with white-washed walls and a few closets containing meager amounts of bandages (actually white paper) and other primitive medical supplies.

The Polish doctor examined the arm and decided to remove the cyst. My husband was instructed to lie down on an "operating table." He was administered a little anesthesia (an unusual occurrence in Auschwitz), and began to feel woozy. As he went under, he heard the doctor ask, *"Ist er Jude?"* ("Is he a Jew?") My husband was still able to hear the question and answered, *"Ich bin Jude."* It was too late to turn back. He was completely in "their" hands.[2]

When my husband woke up after the surgery, he was drowning in pain. At first he didn't know where he was, but when the anesthesia began to wear off, he came up with an interesting question:

---

2. Normally there were selections in the *revere* for the gas chambers. At the time my husband was there, the Lodz ghetto had just been liquidated and the crematoria were filled to capacity. For that reason, a selection in the *revere* may not have been made that time and my husband was spared.

Was it proper or necessary, he wondered, to recite the *Bircas Gomel* — a blessing in which one thanks G-d for sparing one's life — in Auschwitz, where one's life was in danger 24 hours a day? The blessing praises G-d "Who has granted me all good." What was good in Auschwitz?

His arm, wrapped in makeshift bandages and tissue paper, was throbbing and inflamed. As soon as my husband was able to sit up, the doctor told him to leave the *revere*, and excused him from work for five days so that his arm could heal properly. This meant that he would not have to work on Rosh Hashanah!

THERE WERE MORE MIRACLES IN STORE FOR MY HUSBAND AFTER he returned to his barrack. Somehow, a man newly arrived with the

Rosh Hashanah in Auschwitz

transport from the Lodz ghetto had managed to smuggle in a few pages from a *siddur*. Also, since Auschwitz-1 had formerly been an army camp, the brick buildings had cellers. As a result, the men managed to secretly form a *minyan* in the clammy dark cellar of their barrack building. The *davening* took place after the men returned from work and *zeilappel*.

Although a *shofar* circulated secretly in the camp, it did not reach the DAW block. Nevertheless, my husband and the others were grateful just to be able say the *Shemoneh Esrei* of Rosh Hashanah in Auschwitz! While the Nazis sat in Berlin swigging beer and shouting, "It's all over for the Jews!" my husband's plea, "*Zachreinu l'chaim!*" was heard in Heaven, and we were granted life.

R' Landau of Zawiercie, the son-in-law of the Radomsker Rebbe of Poland, led the *tefillos*. My husband led the early *Shacharis* service, and R' Landau was in charge of *Mussaf*. R' Shmuel Ber Layos, the *shochet* of Szaszregen, also participated in the *tefillos*. The Zawiercer Rav even delivered a few words of *mussar* and offered *chizuk*, heartfelt words of encouragement, in lieu of blowing the *shofar*. He interpreted *Psalms* 118:18 where King David says, "The A-mighty punished me and to death did [He] not put me."

When applied to inmate life in Auschwitz, it should have read "but" instead of "and." Although their days and nights in the camp were filled with suffering and anguish, they were still alive. When one is still alive, there is hope; as we say before hearing *shofar*, "*Min hameitzar karasi … anani bamerchav…* (I begged you from a dangerous place; answer my prayers!)" Some prayers truly were answered, including my husband's prayer for his and my survival!

Yom Kippur in Auschwitz

ON ROSH HASHANAH, WE SAY THAT ON THAT DAY HASHEM decides whether or not to inscribe in the Book of Life the name of each individual and the fate of each gentile country. On Yom Kippur, we say, those fates are being sealed. On Yom Kippur 5705, (Wednesday Sept. 27, 1994) my husband's life and my own, as well as those of the other Holocaust survivors, were granted to us. We were destined to live and bear witness. Another great decision was sealed, also — the fall of the Third Reich.

My husband and the other workmen returned from work on *erev* Yom Kippur and watched the sun slowly set over the horizon. They began their fast and silently recited the *Kol Nidrei* prayers from memory. R' Landau led the *minyan* as he had done on Rosh Hashanah. Even though the heartrending *Kol Nidrei* of the Zawiercer *tzaddik* was powerful enough to split the Heavens, the tears rolling down my husband's face were evoked mainly by the memory of his holy father reciting the *Kol Nidrei* back home. The atmosphere in his father's *beis midrash* was one of fear based on *emunah* (faith) and *kedushah* (holiness). *Chassidim* came to hear and enjoy my father-in-law's *tefillos,* sometimes traveling miles from home in order to do so. (Some of them are still alive in the United States and in *Eretz Yisrael.*)

Not remembering all the *tefillos* by heart, my husband thought back to the previous Yom Kippur in his father's *beis midrash,* and silently recalled the words of his father's *derashah* that had preceded the *Ne'ilah* service.

I once asked my husband how we could say, *"Ashamnu mi'kol am* (We are greater sinners than the other nations),"* in front of the SS. My husband answered with a fable: A mother punished her 12-year-old son for misbehaving. The boy protested that his younger brother had misbehaved also, yet wasn't being punished. He wanted to know why. The mother replied that because of his age, the younger boy did not know better. Finer behavior was expected from her older son, however, who was but a year short of his *bar mitzvah*, and therefore only the 12-year-old was being punished. Applying this concept to the *klal*: we, the Jews, were privileged to get the Torah at Sinai. Others nations were not. Therefore, our code of pious and moral behavior must be a cut above those of other nations and people.

ONE OF THE INCREDIBLE STORIES MY HUSBAND RELATED TO ME WAS of a public hanging in Auschwitz on October 10, 1944. On that day,

The Hanging: A Tribute to Three Brave Men

the SS forced every prisoner in camp to witness the hanging of three young, courageous Jews in Auschwitz III (Buna Camp). The three men, Nathan Weissmann, Janek Grossfelf, and Leo Yehuda Diament, conspired with a group of Polish partisans from outside the camp, along with some other Auschwitz-Birkenau prisoners, to organize a mass breakout from the camp. This plan was a desperate attempt to save as many Jewish lives as possible: word had gotten out that Himmler, facing Germany's likely defeat by the Russian army, had ordered the liquidation of every Jew in Auschwitz-Birkenau.

The escape plans were proceeding smoothly when, somehow, a Polish prisoner discovered what was going on and learned that Weissmann, Grossfelf and Diament were involved. He reported the three men to the SS.

Furious that anyone would dare try to outsmart them, the SS searched the camp until they found three of the plotters. The doomed men were tortured SS-style and dragged to the infamous Block 10 (a building in which torture and pseudo-medical "experiments" were carried out), where the SS brutally tortured and beat them some more. Despite the severe bruises, internal injuries and broken bones they sustained, the three heroes did not disclose the names of any of the others involved in the escape plan, nor did they reveal any other information which might have compromised the operation.

Nathan Weissmann, Janek Grossfelf, and Leo Yehuda Diament survived this ordeal — only to be sentenced to die on the gallows.

The hangings took place after work on a bone-chilling, rainy night. Instead of being allowed to return to their barracks, the thousands of inmates were ordered to the *Appelplatz,* a huge parade ground in the camp. An elevated platform had been constructed there — a gallows from which three nooses were suspended.

Night had fallen and the rain continued to beat down. The SS turned on three giant searchlights, pointing the bright beams directly at the gallows to ensure that the inmates would see every detail of the drama about to unfold. The thunderous sound of jack-booted, goose-stepping SS soldiers filled the air, and the inmates were soon encircled by SS troopers who strategically set up five heavy machine guns to make sure that no one could escape.

A fancy, heated limousine pulled up, carrying the obese *Sturmbannfuhrer* (Colonel) Schwartz, one of the most sadistic creatures ever to walk the muddy pathways of Auschwitz. The order, *"Muetzen ab! (Caps off!)"* was shouted, signaling the beginning of the "show." (How ironic that gentiles view the removing of one's head-covering as a sign of respect and subordination, whereas religious Jews cover their heads to indicate subservience to the A-mighty!)

The *Lageraelteste* and two SS guards brought out the victims and led them to the gallows. Their hands were tied behind their backs, and their faces appeared pale under the bright lights of the "stage." For those prisoners who didn't know who the men were, the SS announced that they belonged to the Buna underground and were involved in sabotage.

"In the name of the German people," and "by order of SS *Reichs-führer* Himmler," the sentence was pronounced: death by hanging!

Complete silence followed. Then a loud voice was heard from the gallows, *"Kopf hoch Kameraden! Wir sind die Letzten!* (Heads up, comrades! We are the last [victims]!)" My husband's heart beat with pride upon hearing those words. The SS froze in surprise, shock, and then outrage: how dare a Jew spoil their ceremony by mocking the SS and, by extension, the German army, the "master race," and *der Fuhrer* himself, by hurling these defiant words like a hand grenade at his executioners just before he was about to die!

"LOS!" shouted the furious, red-faced SS Colonel Schwartz to the hangmen, bidding them to hurry before any of the Jews said anything further.

Nathan was hanged first. Everyone was ordered to look directly at the wretched young man as the noose was draped around his neck. The trap door beneath him was sprung with an awful clatter, and he dropped through it, stretching the rope to its full length. The terrified prisoners heard the sickening crunch of Nathan's neck snapping, and then there was no sound at all as his body hung, jerking and writhing convulsively. After what seemed an interminable interval the movement stopped and he was still, his brave soul finally at peace.

Next came Janek, who remained silent before the hanging. A silent voice can have more effect than the noise of the loudest drum, and eyes can convey a deeper message than the most eloquent speech. He, too, died bravely, *al Kiddush Hashem.*

As Leo was about to be hanged, he shouted, *"Es lebe die Freiheit!* (Long live liberty!)," knowing that with certain death just seconds away, there was nothing further that the SS could do to punish him for this final show of defiance. These great heroes did not think and cry out about the murderous acts of the SS, but about the welfare of their comrades.

Enraged by the fact that the three Jews had been brave and defiant to the end, the SS forced all the prisoners to file past the three dangling corpses, hoping thereby to further break the spirit of the inmates and to discourage them from further rebelliousness. This morbid display had exactly the opposite effect upon the morale of the prisoners. The fighting spirit of these young, strong Jews who resisted until the very end, served as an inspiration to all not to surrender their fight for life and liberty.

To this day people ask my husband if he actually watched the hangings, or did he turn his eyes away? The answer is, he looked straight ahead, noticing everything, suffering along with the victims. All of the details are still before his eyes, especially the faces of the doomed men.

The Miracle of Chanukah: "There" and "Here"

CHANUKAH, THE FESTIVAL OF LIGHTS, WAS APPROACHING, AND MY husband and his comrades had to figure out how to make something resembling a *menorah*. With great effort, the men "organized" a candle and one match. On the first night of Chanukah, they gathered around one of the beds and secretly lit the candle for a few seconds, shielding the glow with their bodies. There was some discussion about whether or not to say a *berachah* before lighting the candle, since they would have to blow it out immediately.

The men *davened* and recited *Hallel* from memory. That winter, their *latkes* (potato pancakes) would be mere figments of their imagination. As they sat in their frigid, dreary Auschwitz barrack, they relied on recollections of previous celebrations back home with their families to get them through this bleak Chanukah.

I remember as a child always viewing the coming of Chanukah with anticipation tempered with dread — anticipation, of course, because of the joyous celebration of a great Jewish miracle, but dread because Chanukah usually coincides with the dates of the Christian festivals. In Szaszregen and Selish around that time of year, the local priests would frequently whip up hatred of the Jews among their mostly unlearned congregants with the accusation that the Jews had killed their "god" nearly 2,000 years ago. Some of their ardent followers would take the priests' words to heart and act upon them, and consequently this was always a time of fear and danger for us.

It is my feeling that this element of the populace played a big role in the existence of the Holocaust. Hitler, a Catholic by birth and upbringing, claimed not to believe in G-d; in fact, he killed thousands of German priests in an effort to turn the Church into a puppet of his Nazi regime. However, many of the Germans and Austrians who eagerly followed him were believers, and many, many of them felt that by persecuting Jews, they were "avenging" their god and doing his work. Even the Nazi arch-criminal Goering combined Christianity with Nazism in this way, claiming he believed "in one G-d and one Fuhrer."

But seasonal anti-Semitism aside, Chanukah was something that, on balance, we looked forward to. Back home, before the war, one of the most eagerly anticipated things about Chanukah was the family gathering around the table to play *dreidel*. I still have warm childhood memories of playing this game with my beloved parents, and my husband has told me of the great pleasure he had as a child playing *dreidel* with his father, brothers and sisters.

The four sides of the little *dreidel* are inscribed with the Hebrew letters, *nun, gimel, hei* and *shin* — an abbreviation for the Hebrew phrase, "A Great Miracle Was There." Nobody at home ever asked, What about a miracle "here" — in modern Europe — instead of "there," in ancient *Eretz Yisrael*?

But in Auschwitz and in the other filthy concentration camps, amidst the death and destruction of our people, we saw a miracle "here" every day: the continued survival of *Klal Yisrael*.

The story is told that one day, the infamous butcher, Mengele, caught a young rabbi from the Gerer dynasty with a very small Torah in his pocket. As he sent him to the gas chamber, he sneered, "Go to your G-d and pray."

My husband and the other men lit a Chanukah candle almost literally under the noses of this phony "doctor" and the rest of the SS killers; they "went to our great G-d" and prayed. They were not caught. In fact, a number of those men are still alive today. Therefore, we can say that a great miracle occurred "here." Heaven's Final Solution decreed that we should live to tell and write about Mengele's crimes, while he has been internationally convicted as a traitor to humanity, one who brought shame and dishonor to his profession.

I HAVE ALREADY WRITTEN ABOUT HOW TERRIBLE THE WINTER OF 1944-45 was in Stutthof. The brutality of the weather that winter in

Winter: the Rescuer

Auschwitz remains vivid in my husband's mind as well. Standing at *zeilappel* in the blustery winds and subzero temperatures was unbearable, and the unheated barracks in which the men slept at night offered absolutely no relief. During the workday at DAW, the chill was alleviated somewhat by the blowtorches used for soldering the broken boxes. The men also heated the iron boxes and hovered over them to warm their shivering bodies, yet they continued to freeze throughout that miserable winter.

Outside, the trees were stark against the ominous skies, their branches buffeted by the fierce winds. Crystal clear icicles formed on the roofs of the brick barracks and sometimes broke off, crashing down to the ground below. The Germans laughed at the inmates shivering on line in their thin striped uniforms. Not only did the Nazis cold-bloodedly continue to murder the Jews in their attempt to achieve a *Judenrein* Europe, but they indulged their sadistic need to torment their victims in the cruelest ways imaginable before killing them.

Although we didn't realize it at the time, the unbearably frigid winter of 1944-45 which made our lives miserable was also the cause of the collapse of the mighty German army at the Russian front. It was the bitter winter that caused General Paulus, with his hundreds of thousands of German soldiers, to capitulate to the Russians. The Fuhrer's plan was to achieve a speedy victory before the winter, but Heaven's own "Final Solution" was to unleash its own secret weapon, *"die geheime waffe,"* (namely, the record cold spell) to destroy Hitler and his evil minions. In retrospect I can regard that arctic winter as a gift from Heaven. In Stutthof, in Auschwitz — winter was terrible for us; but winter in Moscow — that's what ultimately aided in the destruction of the Third Reich.

AS 1944 DREW TO A CLOSE, THE SS SAW DEFEAT BEFORE THEIR EYES and began the futile attempt to eradicate all traces of their barbar-

Liquidation of Auschwitz

ic inhumanity to man. On orders from Berlin, they started to shut down the gas chambers and dismantle the crematoria at Auschwitz and various other death factories. As the Red Army came ever closer, the Germans began to blow up the remains of many of the camps and burn their files, vainly trying to get rid of the incriminating evidence.

The SS had also routinely been murdering the members of the *Sonderkommando* unit every three months or so, with typical German precision and efficiency. The men chosen for this gruesome work detail were eyewitnesses to everything that occurred in the gas chambers and crematoria.

The *Sonderkommando* witnessed countless innocent men, women and children entering the gas chambers alive; later, when they opened the steel doors, those people were dead. It was their job to collect the clothing which had been left behind by the victims, to remove the bodies from the gas chambers and to scrub the walls and floors of the chambers once the bodies were removed. They also had to shove the corpses into the ovens or outdoor fire pits, and remove the human ashes from the ovens. It was not uncommon for them to discover close family members or friends among the victims. The holy ashes were thrown into five huge pits. Two of the pits are visible today; I saw them on my visit to Auschwitz-Birkenau. The pits, housing the ashes of our martyred bretheren, have sadly remained unkempt since the war.

The SS routinely shot or gassed, then cremated, the men of the

Sonderkommando so that they could not bear witness to what they had seen. To many, death was a welcome release, as they had lost the ability to function as normal human beings, and no longer had the will to live.

BY HEAVEN'S DECREE, THE SS FAILED TO LIQUIDATE ALL *SONDER-kommando* workers. One such survivor, a Budapest Jew by the

Dr. Miklos Nyiszli

name of Dr. Miklos Nyiszli, was a skilled forensic surgeon appointed by Mengele to perform autopsies on twins and other martyred victims. He managed to escape before the SS liquidated him. He recorded what he had seen and done, and served as a witness at the Nuremberg trial.

I strongly recommend that everyone reading these pages should read Dr. Nyiszli's account of what transpired in Auschwitz. One of the most incredible accounts in the book describes Mengele's depression a short time before the liquidation of Birkenau and Auschwitz. After performing thousands of cruel and inhumane experiments, Mengele arrived at the conclusion that Hitler's race theory was false and foolish.

ON JANUARY 21, 1945, THE RUSSIANS ENTERED CRACOW, LOCATED in the vicinity of Auschwitz, and liberated the inhabitants of the

The Death March

city. How ironic that this occurred on the same day that my husband and many others were marched out of Auschwitz in an attempt by the SS to liquidate the camp and thus cover their crimes. If only my husband and the others had known, they might have contrived to remain behind, in the camp. A few people, such as my husband's friend R' Yecheskel Eisderfer (now living in Williamsburg), and several others, did manage to hide behind the coals in the basement of a barrack and remain there until they were freed by the Russians.

My husband recalls that day vividly. On the afternoon of January 21, rumors circulated among the inmates that the camp might be liquidated soon. The inmates feared that the SS would slaughter everybody. However, although Berlin had resolved to make Europe completely *Judenrein*, Europe was then on the verge of becoming *"Nazirein"* instead.

In the middle of the night, my husband and the others were awakened by the SS loudly ordering everyone out of the barracks to the frozen *zeilappel* field. After the usual head count, the men were ordered to march out of the camp. SS guards prodded them roughly with their rifle butts, and vicious dogs barked and snapped at their feet. For the last time, my husband and the other men passed the gate bearing the infamous German inscription, *"Arbeit Macht Frei."*

The SS led the innocent captives deep into the woods, and anyone unable to keep up with the rest of the group was shot and tossed into the ditches alongside the road. As the men marched on, their wooden clogs did little to shield their frozen, swollen feet from the icy and slippery pathways — and sometimes they got stuck in the snow. If one of the men held up the line by struggling to pull his foot out, he was shot. It meant nothing to the SS barbarians to snuff out more innocent lives, and soon corpses were strewn on both sides of the roadways.

During the following interminable, bitterly cold days, the men continued to march; and during the equally long and freezing nights, they were locked by the Germans into barns along the road, where they slept on straw. Much as the men hoped and prayed for liberation, it did not happen. Instead there was marching, marching, endless marching, a desperate marathon in which the freezing, starving, sick men had to maintain the merciless pace set by the warmly dressed Germans, mostly *Wehrmacht* soldiers under the command of the SS.

Heavy snow continued to fall, and by opening their mouths and letting the moist snowflakes fall onto their parched tongues, the men were able to avoid dehydration. My husband lost all sensation in his feet as he marched through the frigid landscape, but the constant motion saved what little circulation he had left.

Men were collapsing on all sides and being trampled underfoot by those still struggling to keep on moving. Bodies were shoved aside like stones, but by that time, nothing the depraved and evil Germans did could surprise the prisoners.

Among the many men who did not survive this horrible march, the memory of the tragic case of Grand Rabbi Landau of Zawierice-Radomsk, *ztk"l*, still pains my husband to this day. The frail, elderly rabbi had been slated to die in the Auschwitz gas chambers, but some Polish Jewish inmates saved him by bribing the SS with jewelry that they had "organized" from a transport of new arrivals from the Lodz ghetto. R' Landau was spared the trip to the ovens — only to surrender his holy soul to Heaven later on the death march.

The old rabbi managed to maintain the requisite pace for a while, but as the fierce winds whipped his face, he found it increasingly difficult to breathe. Seeing him begin to stagger, my husband and some of the others immediately grabbed him before he could fall to the ground, and dragged his feeble body along as quickly as they could. Burning with fever and unable to go on, R' Landau begged the men to let him go. All attempts by his friends to encourage him, to urge him not to give up hope, were in vain. The rabbi's glazed eyes gazed Heavenward, as if to acknowledge that his soul would soon be there.

The men did not want to let the old rabbi die, and continued to support his shivering body on their own weakened backs as they continued to advance. My husband remembered R' Landau's last words on Rosh Hashanah. Explaining the phrase,*"V'lamaves lo nesananu,"* he had said, "Sometimes the A-mighty may punish by *not* letting a person die."

My husband saw the aged rabbi smile peacefully before he and the others let him slip to the ground. They heard shots ring out here and there but they did not look back. Perhaps the Germans pumped some of the bullets into R' Landau's already limp body, but my husband and the others will never know for sure. In all probability, R' Landau passed away seconds, if not minutes, after my husband and the others left him. R' Landau's holy *neshamah* rose to Heaven while his body was left among those of the other victims, to be picked up and buried by local laborers. The only solace that my husband and his fellows had regarding R' Landau's death was that he would be buried beneath the earth, as required by *halachah*. Had he died in Auschwitz, his body would have been burned and the ashes dumped into the Vistula River, along with the ashes of tens of thousands of other martyred victims.

The days dragged on, and more and more bodies were tossed into the deep snowdrifts and ditches. How anyone at all managed to live through conditions normally impossible for a human being to endure is hard to explain simply by laws of nature or science. It was only by a "Heavenly Final Solution" that they were able to survive. The endurance of my husband and his fellow survivors negates the theory eagerly advocated by Hitler and his gang, that "only the fittest survive." We survived — but Hitler and Himmler did not.

From Foot to Train

AFTER ENDLESS DAYS OF TREKKING THROUGH THE SNOW, THE MEN were led to a station somewhere in Austria where open freight cars awaited them. The Germans brutally herded them into the cars, and although weak from hunger, exhaustion and illness, the men stepped aboard quickly. The freight car was open to the harsh weather, there was no place to sit, and the men had no idea where they were being taken — but at least they could stop marching.

Hurtling through the icy Austrian countryside in open cars,

with neither food nor toilets available, the men were reduced to a mass of wet, shivering bones. Many of them, standing, slipped into a state of a semi-conscious slumber. Tragically, some of the men never woke up, and when the guard discovered the corpses, he coldly ordered them to be tossed out into the ditches alongside the tracks.

My husband longed for warmth: if only he could be bundled up in a *"tilip"* (fur coat worn by *Chassidim*) to protect him from the cold and wind! As he drifted in and out of semi-consciousness, he remembered how his dear mother used to light the stove every morning so that her sons could sit beside it and learn in comfort ...

Eventually the train arrived at a station in Austria and the men were ordered out for a brief stopover. The Germans had received orders to supply slave laborers to clear the ice off the streets in that small town, and these men had been selected to do the job. Handing my husband and the others picks and shovels, the SS commanded them to begin digging.

Out of nowhere, a woman (my husband didn't know whether she was German, Austrian or a hidden Jewess) passed by and quickly threw two pieces of bread in my husband's direction without looking back. Luckily no one noticed. Those pieces of bread shone like gold before his weary eyes and he eagerly lifted them up off the icy street, thankful to the A-mighty and this kind lady for providing him with sustenance.

Just as my husband picked up the bread, some of his emaciated comrades rushed over and begged him for a small piece. Unable to deny their desperate requests, my husband broke off half-pieces of bread and distributed them. One man criticized my husband for not giving away more, but another said his actions were extraordinary, considering the circumstances. My husband credits his behavior to the way he was brought up by his revered mother, may Hashem avenge her martyred soul, who taught him and his siblings never to deny help to a fellow Jew in distress.

As the men continued working, the townspeople came to stare. Along with the SS, they browbeat and tormented the unfortunate innocent captives who struggled so diligently to chip the ice off the streets. Some of the crueler onlookers threw rotten garbage at them.

After the SS had fulfilled their obligation to service the small Austrian township, the men were herded back into the open cattle cars — only to have this scenario repeated in another town where, unfortunately, nobody was kind enough to throw them pieces of bread.

ON JANUARY 27, 1945, AFTER MANY MISERABLE DAYS OF MARCHING and riding in the open cattle cars, my husband and his comrades **Mauthausen** arrived at the notorious Mauthausen concentration camp. This infamous place of human torture and misery was located in the heart of the treacherous Austrian Alps, whose wondrous natural beauty served as a vivid contrast to the horror of the camp.

Snow drifts were piled everywhere, and the winds blew with greater ferocity high up in the mountains. My husband and the other inmates wrapped their skinny arms around their shivering bodies, trying vainly to protect themselves from the harsh elements. When their SS tormentors looked the other way, the prisoners tried moving around to keep their blood circulating and to prevent their extremities from freezing. Thousands of men stood in this open area, exposed to the mountain gales. My husband says that he still feels the effects of that bitterly cold night, even to this day.

Just when it seemed that things couldn't get any worse, the sadistic SS forced the men to strip totally naked, leaving on only their shoes or clogs, and to run back and forth in the deep snow. Then they were ordered to march from one end of the open space to the other. At that point, the lowering winter skies dumped a load of fresh snow upon the hapless prisoners. Was this sudden burst of snow a tiny gift from Heaven? Those who turned their heads upward and let the snowflakes fall on their tongues greatly benefitted from the fluid provided to their dehydrated bodies.

Finally the SS ordered the men to stand at *zeilappel*. Throughout those long, tense hours, desperate declarations of *Viduy* and *Shema Yisrael* rang out, followed by echoing shots which pierced the thin mountain air. Thousands of bodies stiffened and dropped one by one into the deep snow, never to rise again.

This brutality which occurred in Mauthausen took place even as the Red Army was closing in. It was especially senseless and purely vicious and vindictive because it could neither change the course of the war, nor fulfill the Nazis' evil goal of destroying all of Jewry through a "Final Solution." The fact was that for the Nazis, the war was already lost. They were running for cover, and in four short months all would be over. Most of the concentration camps, including Auschwitz, Majdanek and Belzec, had already been liberated. But for my husband and the other men standing out in the freezing Austrian snow that night, the Germans' policy of subjugating others was still in full force.

After *zeilappel*, the Germans marched the straggling inmates to their unheated barracks, where they were given striped prison uniforms. A thousand men were crammed into a space meant to fit maybe two hundred people. Everyone was forced to sleep on the floor, just as my female comrades and I had been forced to sleep during our first night in Birkenau.

That night, my husband had an experience which even topped his earlier experience outside in the snow. Before the lights went out, he discovered that he was crammed among some prisoners from Budapest. Since my husband's parents came from Galicia, Poland, my husband grew up with a Polish-Jewish accent. His Hungarian neighbors noticed his accent and instantly resented his Polish identity. After lights out, my husband heard his neighbors buzzing in Hungarian, *"Hat ez Lengel!* (He is Polish!)." In the darkness, these men decided to eject my husband from their space and, with savage force, lifted him up and tossed him away. He crashed into some other men about two yards away. In a frenzied panic they pushed my husband away, and he was left to grope in the dark to find a spot for himself — but where? Mirthless laughter followed him as he tried to settle down for the night. Finally a kindhearted man grabbed my husband and squeezed him into the space in front of him.

One of the dubious achievements of the Germans was the diabolical way they psychologically manipulated their captives, turning man against man. This phenomenon was evident as the unfortunate prisoners fought among themselves for a little breathing space or a few morsels of rotten food.

Ebensee: A Historical Perspective

BY 1942 IT HAD BECOME CLEAR TO THE GERMANS THAT THE NAZI WAR effort was starting to run out of steam, and it was only a matter of time before they would lose the war. Their *blitzkrieg* strategy, used so successfully earlier in the war to wipe out their enemies, had failed. Massive air attacks had failed to bomb stubborn Britain into surrender. The invasion of Russia had stalled, and the Red Army had begun a fierce counterattack. Now America, with its great industrial power, had joined the Allied effort against the Nazis.

As his enemies began to close in on him, Hitler became more hysterical and desperate. He launched a campaign to create a new type of secret weapon which would turn the tide of war.

Holocaust researcher and author Florian Freund notes that at that time, after viewing the first successful firing of the A-4 rocket (later known as the V-2) on October 3, 1942, Hitler decided to go ahead with a German rocket program. Grasping at straws, Hitler thought that this was the "wonder weapon" he had been looking for to rain death on his enemies from the air. He would mass produce it and then destroy London and Moscow — and maybe, eventually, even Washington and New York, bringing his enemies to their knees.[3]

A new slave labor camp in the vicinity of the Austrian village of Ebensee, located in the Tyrolean mountain region, was quickly

---

3. *Konzentrationslager Ebensee — Ein Aufenlager des KZ Mauthausen* [Concentration Camp Ebensee: Subcamp of Mauthausen] (Vienna: Dokumentationsarchiv des Osterreichischen Widerstandes [the Austrian Resistance Archives], 1990, pp. 5-9.

erected for the purpose of building the rockets. Its gates were officially opened on November 18, 1943. This new camp was assigned the code name *"SS-Arbeitslager Zement"* (SS Labor Camp Cement) and was to become one of Mauthausen's forty subcamps, where prisoners were forced to work for the German war industry.

The inmates were put to work digging tunnels, called *stölenn*, through the Tyrolean mountains, a nearly impossible task. The stone of the mountains was harder than steel. Excavating the mammoth hollow cavities, which needed to be large enough to accommodate the huge rockets, then smoothing down the walls, was excruciatingly difficult work.

It is interesting to note that one of the original German rocket scientists who was at the Ebensee site during the war, Werner von Braun, later helped the Americans design the first rocket that would go to the moon in the late 1960's — slightly more than 20 years after the original "wonder weapon" (which, ultimately, didn't materialize) was to be produced in wartime Austria. This man, like other scientists, contributed to the mistreatment of many innocent concentration camp prisoners, but because of his scientific knowledge and talents, he was not classified as a war criminal by the Allies. Instead, he was praised as one of the original rocket pioneers![4]

Ebensee was not considered an extermination camp since the SS did not erect gas chambers on the premises. Nevertheless, thousands of prisoners died from sheer exhaustion. Approximately 27,000 prisoners were in Ebensee between November 18, 1943 and May 6, 1945 (the date of the camp's liberation by the U.S. Army). Of that figure, over 8,200 prisoners died, and countless others became ill and injured. It should be noted that the deaths of those who arrived in Ebensee during the last few weeks of its existence and died, most of them Jews, were not recorded.

If the prisoners did not die as a result of arduous work conditions or disease, they starved to death. Ebensee had a reputation of being a "starvation camp." After liberation, an "After Action

---

4. Ibid., pp. 10-11.

Report" (of which we have a copy) was written by the 3rd (U.S.) Cavalry. According to the report, "About 300 men died every day [in Ebensee] because of the rampant starvation and the neglected diseases ..."[5]

/ORD and OPINION

KZ EBENSEE

In the heart of the Alps in northwestern Austria, located by the lake of Ebensee, is a beautiful resort place named Ebensee. This area was blessed by the Creator with enormous natural beauty for the benefit of humanity, but had been converted by the infamous Nazis into a place to satisfy the sadistic desire of the Nazi S. S. officers.

A large Concentration Camp named "Ebensee Konsentrations Lager" had been erected there

The official report of the U.S. Army that gloriously liberated the camp reads as follows:
#SC 207999 5/8/45
"When the U.S. Third Army overran and liberated the large Nazi prison in Ebensee, Austria, they were confronted with a spectacle of 60,000 pitiable human wrecks of 25 nationalities, in various stages of starvation, malnutrition and diseases.

The Ebensee Camp

Even as they cut rock and loaded wagons, prisoners were required to doff their caps as their tormentors marched by

---

5. Ibid., pp. 42-3.

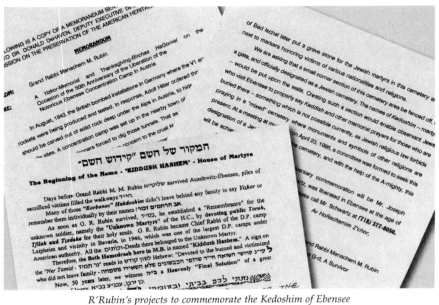

R'Rubin's projects to commemorate the Kedoshim of Ebensee

ON JANUARY 29, 1945 — TWO DAYS AFTER THEIR BRUTAL INITIATION into Mauthausen — my husband and approximately two thousand

Arrival in Ebensee

other prisoners were packed into trucks and taken to Ebensee. They arrived sometime around midnight. Images of the snow glistening near the lit entrance to the camp, and the cynical smiles and laughter of the SS as the men marched past, still remain before my husband's eyes today.

The half winter that my husband spent in Ebensee was brutal. Temperatures plummeted well below the freezing mark, and biting winds rarely seemed to abate. It snowed constantly, and the prisoners were almost blinded by the white glare of their surroundings. *Zeilappel* was absolute torture. The prisoners' lips cracked, their faces became red and raw from painful windburns and their unprotected feet swelled and bled from blisters and sores. Our brothers and sisters who had the misfortune of living in Communist Russia and running afoul of the authorities there tell stories about the bitter cold in Siberia. The survivors of Ebensee have their own stories about the arctic winter they endured in

The former Appelplatz in Ebensee. Today, the grounds are covered with grass, making it difficult to imagine the terrible crimes which took place there over 50 years ago.

1944-45. The U.S. report said that Ebensee was one of the most brutal of Hitler's death camps.

As if the cold and hunger were not enough, an outbreak of lice, resulting from poor hygiene, added to the agony of the inmates. Much to their frustration and pain, there was no way for the inmates to rid themselves of these tiny pests, who were seemingly immune to the subfreezing cold. Keeping clean was simply an impossible task.

My husband lived in a narrow wooden barrack into which approximately one thousand inmates were crammed. Not leaving out a single detail in their master plan to torment the innocents, the German-Austrians even figured out a way to make something as simple as climbing into bed a miserable experience. Decrepit and broken wooden shelves built in three tiers against the long rotting walls were their "beds," and each shelf was shared by several inmates. The prisoners constantly suffered from dust seeping out of their "mattresses," which consisted of a combination of straw and sawdust encased in rough burlap. Only a couple of feet of space separated one level from the next, so climbing in and out of the bunks was no easy task. The flimsy walls of the barrack were not insulated, and the men, malnourished and emaciated, shivered constantly in their thin clothing. Sometimes prisoners smuggled in coal — at great risk to their lives — to warm up the barrack.

R' YEKUSIEL HIRSH WERTZBERGER, WHO SURVIVED THE WAR AND lives in Williamsburg today, was one of the men who witnessed the following incident.

Hans the Kapo

One day, an inmate, an elderly man from Kashau-Kosice, accidentally spilled some of his "coffee" onto the floor of the barrack. Hans, the German *kapo*, discovered the drops of liquid on the floor and flew into a rage. He made it clear that the person who spilled the "coffee" would be severely punished for committing the crime of "sabotage": in this case, damaging a German floor! (At no time were Jewish prisoners merely hit or punished without a phony explanation to supposedly justify such mistreatment. This time the excuse was "sabotage." On other occasions, the men were punished for being *"blüt zaugers"* [blood suckers], *"shmutzig"* [dirty], and so on.)

Everyone in the barrack was silent. Hans demanded to know the identity of the culprit. Nobody answered. Hans then approached my husband and ordered him to respond. Not wanting to endanger the old man, my husband replied, "I do not know." Hans repeated the question and my husband remained silent, trying to avoid direct eye contact with the angry *kapo*. He did not want Hans to see how terrified he was.

Suddenly Hans turned around, as if to look for something. When he turned back he was holding a chair, which he then placed in the aisle between the two rows of bunks, and ordered my husband to sit down. Grinning from ear to ear, he circled my husband, the way a wolf circles his prey before attacking. He then stopped. As my husband sat frozen in the chair, Hans stood in front of him, then suddenly grabbed hold of two shelves, one on each side, and pulled himself off the ground, using his arms as a gymnast would to support his weight. He swung his legs back and then brought them forward, landing a powerful kick with both feet right on my husband's forehead. R' Rubin reeled from the impact and almost toppled backwards, but managed to remain silent.

Finally Hans let himself down. My husband feared that the man would torture him further, but he just turned and walked away. As he did so, he told my husband, *"Du bist ein braver kerl!* (You are a brave fellow!)"

My husband remained seated for a short time. The man he had protected looked directly at him, sorrow mingling with gratitude in his gaze.

A child emulates what he learns at home and carries these lessons with him on his journey through life. This enabled my husband to endure the beating he received to protect a fellow Jew. [6]

Deep Under a Tyrol Mountain

IN HOLOCAUST LITERATURE, ONE READS THAT THE SS MURDERED Jews and others by land, sea and air, but no mention is made of murder underground. At Ebensee, my husband was assigned the most dreaded task there: the "quarry" detail. His assignment was to dig out the underground *stölenn*. Besides cracking the stones in the tunnels, he had to fill lorries with the pieces of stone, empty them, then start the job all over again.

Since orders came from Berlin for the rockets to be completed swiftly, German and Austrian civilian workers were called upon to assist the SS in supervising the work of the concentration camp inmates. The lives of those captured men depended upon the temperaments of their respective supervisors. Some prisoners received milder treatment, while others were treated brutally.

The SS also appointed *kapos* to guard huge masses of prisoners. The *kapos* were under a great deal of pressure to please the SS. If they were caught falling down on the job or if they failed to fill their daily quotas, the SS would remove them from their position and severely punish them by torture or other means. As a result, the *kapos* forced the exhausted and ill concentration

---

6. In Williamsburg, R' E. Steinberger wrote a Yiddish book entitled *Netzach Kedoshim*, in which he gathered many special and interesting anecdotes about the Holocaust. The above incident was included in the chapter entitled, "Die Kinder Stube Geht Mit (The Childhood Home Goes Along)."

camp prisoners to work faster and faster, and saw to it that nobody stopped for even a moment's rest. Many men, too weak to endure the resulting beatings, died slowly and painfully on the hard ground.

At first, one might think that working in an underground tunnel is preferable to working outdoors in the winter, where one is exposed to the brutal gales. However, workers digging inside the stifling tunnels inhaled huge amounts of dust and foul air. They were also in danger of being trapped by an avalanche of rocks and stones tumbling down the mountains. Nobody — neither the SS, the private construction companies, nor the civilian supervisors — had any regard for the safety of the concentration-camp prisoners.

ONE DAY IN APRIL, SOMETHING EXTRAORDINARY HAPPENED. MY husband had an unusual "accident" — but in a strange way, it saved his life.

The "Accident" Which Saved My Husband's Life

It happened on a typical workday after the men had emptied their quota of stones into the wagons. My husband noticed that they were being watched by the SS and Ukrainian *kapos* who were conversing among themselves and repeatedly glancing in their direction, as if plotting something. As my husband and his co-workers were about to push the stone-laden wagons down the steep tracks, the *kapo* ordered my husband and another man to start pushing one full wagon, and told four other men behind them to push an equally heavy wagon. Of course, the four men pushing the second wagon would generate more force than the two men pushing the first wagon in front. Since all of them were going downhill, the wagon behind my husband would gain momentum more rapidly. My husband and his partner were overwhelmed by a feeling of dread, knowing that they were in imminent danger, but could do nothing to stop it.

It didn't take long for disaster to strike. The job did not so much involve actually pushing the wagons down the mountainside — gravity took care of that part — as it did holding them back and keeping them under control, applying just enough force to keep them moving but struggling to prevent them from getting away. Almost as soon as they began moving, the second wagon came crashing into the first. My husband's partner, positioned on the right-hand side, managed to jump out of the way of the colliding wagons. My husband, who was on the left-hand side, could not. His right leg got caught between the two colliding wagons. He screamed out in agony and tumbled to the ground, doubled over in pain.

Hearing the comments of his Jewish comrades standing a short distance away, my husband realized that his leg was already swollen and discolored (at the time, nobody knew that it had been broken in three places). Jagged pieces of bone were poking through the bloody, lacerated flesh.

Several Ukrainian guards working in the camp came running in his direction, carrying a narrow wooden stretcher. They were obviously going to transport him somewhere — but where? His comrades begged the *kapos* to be gentle with him. My husband's head was spinning, and he felt the strong hands of the Ukrainians grabbing and lifting his tormented body. They swung him into the air and down onto a stretcher held by two other Ukrainians. The louder my husband screamed, the harder they laughed. Just when he felt that the pain couldn't possibly get any worse, one of the brutes pushed my husband's broken leg off the stretcher and left it dangling over the side. One of the stretcher-bearers gave the order to head for the *revere* — the so-called prisoners' hospital. On the way, the Ukrainians made a point of maintaining a lively stride — almost a little dance — which caused the stretcher to bounce and shake even more. The pain shooting through my husband's dangling leg increased several times over. Some SS guards standing along the sidelines caught sight of the spectacle and erupted into uncontrollable laughter.

THE *REVERE* WAS A SHABBY-LOOKING, SMALL WOODEN BARRACK, located right next to the camp's crematorium. Surrounding bar- **The** racks were set aside for the patients, who were placed **Revere** according to their illness or injury. The prison doctors and nurses, prisoners themselves, were carefully watched by the SS. It was not in their power to determine which patients would remain in the *revere*; such decisions were made mainly by the SS, which included an SS head doctor (Dr. Willi Jobst was the head doctor when my husband was there), an SS sanitation corpsman and an SS overseer in the hospital. Some prisoners were sent to recovery barracks, while others were condemned to die. Some of the terminally ill or injured were placed naked on the floor of a barrack and left alone to die, while others were sent to the "sanitation camp" in Mauthausen where they were exterminated.[7]

It was not unusual for fellow inmates to grab the possessions of a helpless comrade near death. Mr. Yekusiel Bittman, *a"h*, who was a follower of my father-in-law in Szaszregen, was one such dying victim in a "death" barrack. Although he was not clothed, he was still wearing his shoes. At one point he was lying so still that some of the others assumed he was dead, and they started to remove his shoes. Although extremely weak, Mr. Bittman gathered what was left of his strength and weakly muttered, "I am still alive. Please don't take my shoes." The men left the shoes on Mr. Bittman's feet and helped revive him. Mr. Bittman survived to tell his story, and went on to rebuild a new life and family for himself. Today his son, Mr. Judah Bittman, is the *gabbai* in our *shul*.

Those who were considered to possess a chance of recovery were placed into different barracks. The hospital staff did what they could do to prolong the patients' stay. For those prisoners, there was a ray of hope. Even though they could not be treated with medicine (very little, if any at all, was available), they at least had a chance to rest. A small amount of food was distributed to the *revere* barracks as well.

---

7. Ibid., pp. 22-29.

The Ukrainians dumped my husband on the floor and left the building. Through a haze he surveyed his new surroundings and saw many other patients on all sides, moaning in pain. Waves of nausea overcame him and everything in the room seemed to sway. A grungy-looking man approached my husband, who looked up in terror, not knowing what this man was going to do to him. The man asked my husband who he was, but my husband almost passed out at that point. Before he lost consciousness, however, he did manage to mumble his name to the stranger, who then told my husband not to worry: the crematorium was right next door!

When my husband came to, the man was still leaning over him, examining the broken leg. Each touch caused excruciating pain, and my husband screamed out in agony. He felt more anxious when he saw the grim expression on the man's face. My husband later learned that this man was the *revere kapo*, a Jew from Kashau by the name of Mr. Hoffman. A small-town merchant by profession, Mr. Hoffman assumed the duties of both doctor and nurse in the *revere*, and tended to the sick and injured patients.

Mr. Hoffman advised my husband that he would be moving him into the next room. My husband was then placed on a flat wooden plank which served as a bed. He asked Mr. Hoffman what was to become of his leg. The man smiled — what a naive question to ask in this house of horrors! — but assured my husband that he would treat his leg as well as was possible under the circumstances.

My husband panicked. Was Mr. Hoffman going to operate on his leg, or worse still — amputate it? He was too weak to ask, and knew he would have no say whatsoever in this matter.

Mr. Hoffman began to carefully tear the pant leg, which was already bursting at the seams because of the extreme swelling. My husband heard the fabric rip and felt some of the pressure ease from his leg. Mr. Hoffman began to mumble to himself, then finally explained to my husband that the leg was broken in three places. He placed a cold rag on his patient's burning forehead before leaving him for a few moments.

In my husband's state of delirium, he lost track of how long he lay there, waiting either for the Angel of Death to collect him, or for Mr. Hoffman to return. Who would be first through the door? Soon he saw Mr. Hoffman come back in, holding something in his hand. My husband was too dizzy to see, or even care, what it was.

It turned out that Mr. Hoffman was carrying some type of plaster and told my husband that he was going to wrap it around the broken bones for support. Mr. Hoffman took my husband's leg and repositioned the three sections of bone. My husband said he actually heard the bone cracking under Mr. Hoffman's ministrations. Mr. Hoffman handled my husband gently (contrary to reports my husband heard later which claimed that he wasn't as caring in his handling of other patients), and gave him a rag to bite on for the pain while continuing to wrap the injured limb.

Finally Mr. Hoffman carefully lowered the throbbing leg. He wiped his patient's sweaty brow and waited to see if he would speak, but my husband simply continued to moan in pain. Jokingly, Mr. Hoffman told my husband that he was "not offering him a pain killer; in this place, people were painfully killed." He couldn't even supply a blanket to warm my husband's shivering body. In his traumatized state, it did not take long for R' Rubin to fall into a deep, albeit restless, slumber.

A dim light filtered through the *revere* and my husband guessed that it was early morning. An abominable stench pervaded the room — a mixture of the smells of rotting bodies, human waste, sweat and vomit. Moans and screams were heard from one end of the long room to another. Even though he was still feverish and suffering greatly, my husband somehow felt he might have a chance to survive, and so he said the morning prayers. He later told me that he did not know what caused his optimism, since he was not feeling any better physically. In fact, he was even weaker than he had been the day before when he was hovering between life and death.

His mouth and throat were parched, his lips were cracked.

Later, he mustered his strength and asked Mr. Hoffman the dreaded question: would he lose his leg? Mr. Hoffman was not able to answer one way or the other; only time would tell. As my husband grew accustomed to the pain, he attempted to keep a clear head. All he could do was wait and hope.

Over the next couple of days, Mr. Hoffman continued to make occasional visits to check his leg. As the days passed, however, my husband saw less and less of him. In time, my husband found out why. Mr. Hoffman had mistreated other inmates, and horror stories had been shared among the patients in the *revere*. Mr. Hoffman became aware of this and, worried that someone might try to hurt him in the *revere*, he avoided the inmates as much as possible. After liberation, he managed to escape to Australia to hide from those who had known him in Ebensee.

We will never know why Mr. Hoffman behaved in a more humane manner toward my husband than toward the others in the *revere*. Stronger and healthier patients than my husband had already been sent off to the crematorium.

The disgusting smells of the *revere* and the pain from his now-infected leg, filled with draining pus and sores, were constantly making him sick. My husband moaned silently, hoping that his *tefilos* would reach Heaven.

In retrospect, my husband and I believe that his "accident" indirectly saved his life. Following the "accident," he was really taken to the *revere* to die. Besides Mr. Hoffman, who tended to his leg, nobody paid much attention to him in the *revere* and could not care less whether he lived or died. He had, perhaps, a little more to eat in the *revere* than he would have had in the work detail. Staying in the *revere* also kept him away from the dangerous work in the tunnels, the filthy tunnel air which blackened the lungs of the workers, possible avalanches, exposure to the elements, and unpredictable beatings by the *kapos*. As terrible as it was in the *revere*, it would have been much worse on the outside.

Human lives — especially Jewish ones — were meaningless to

the Nazis. Why, then, did they establish *reveres* in the concentration and death camps? I have no logical answer to this question, except that the "final solution" comes from Heaven's authority.

Mah Nishtanah and Shfoch Chamascha in Ebensee: Passover Seder

"SEDER" MEANS SYSTEM, ORDER. AT HOME, EVERY PART OF THE Passover *seder* is arranged according to a system. In the Ebensee *revere*, the only real system was the cruel one of the captors. Berlin and the SS executed European Jewry with Germanic *"seder."* Nevertheless, a true *seder* inside the electrified barbed wires of one of the most notorious Nazi camps would be a meaningful rebuff to the Germans' *"seder"* of annihilation, and so it was, so it felt, so it happened.

The essence of a Passover *seder* night is telling how an enemy, Pharaoh, wanted to destroy the Jews and how the A-mighty saved us. We sit at our tables with our families, our children and grandchildren, and the youngsters, who have been taught to ask the Four Questions, begin with, *"Mah nishtanah halaylah hazeh?* (Why is this night different from all other nights?)" The parents answer, "We were slaves of Pharaoh, but tonight we are free... ," and go on to recount the story of how Pharaoh wanted to kill the Jews and how the A-mighty protected and rescued us.

It is worthwhile to remember that although we celebrate the Exodus from Egypt, only one-fifth of the Jewish population of the time left Egypt. In comparison, a greater number of Jews — two-thirds of the world's Jewish population — were spared from perishing in the Holocaust.

How can one respond to the questions of the *Mah Nishtanah* when lying in pain on a flat, wooden, filthy pallet in the subhuman conditions of the *revere* in one of the Nazis' most dreaded concentration camps? What can one mean by replying, "We were slaves to Pharaoh in Egypt," when, this night in Ebensee, one is in cruel bondage himself? "This year we are slaves, but next year, we will be free." Could those words from *"Ha Lachma"* be uttered? The answer is yes, because the age-old Jewish qualities of *emunah* and *bitachon*, faith and trust in the A-mighty, lived on even in that cruelest place of bondage.

Miracles can happen — even in the filthy, death-laden Ebensee *revere*. You could say it was something of a miracle that Mr. Hoffman — against whom so many other prisoners were later to bring bitter complaints of torture and mistreatment — took a liking to my husband and helped to save his life.

Yet another near-miracle happened on *erev* Pesach, 1945. The fact that in this inferno my husband even knew when Pesach was approaching was extraordinary in itself, since he didn't have access to a Jewish calendar in Ebensee. Considering the impossibility of preparing for Pesach in this forsaken place, my husband still hoped to create a makeshift *seder* with what little he had.

One night, delirious with fever, my husband envisioned his mother coming from Auschwitz to visit him. Appearing radiant, she sat by his bedside and offered him *chizuk*, urging him not to lose his *bitachon*. The next day my husband still strongly sensed his mother's presence in the room. This gave him the strength to do everything humanly possible to prepare some sort of a Passover *seder* in his tiny corner of the *revere*.

My husband first needed to find a way to obtain the *arba kosos* (four cups) of wine required for the *seder*. He made a deal with a fellow inmate, Dr. Dezso Kramer, from my hometown of Selish. Dr. Kramer, who was ill, shared the same upper bunk as my husband. He agreed to trade his "coffee" for my husband's bread. The "coffee" was neither palatable nor nourishing, but as the only liquid available in the *revere*, it would have to suffice as the drink for the *seder*.

Needing a vessel in which to store the liquid, my husband "organized" one of the bottles that the *kapos* threw away, and hid it underneath his bunk, hoping that it would not be discovered. If it was, cruel punishment would almost certainly follow. Although my husband had to sacrifice the main staple of his diet — his small daily ration of bread — for four days prior to Pesach, he was successful in obtaining the required *arba kosos* for the *seder*.

Deciding what to do with the daily bread rations he would receive over the eight days of Pesach in the *revere* was a monumental dilemma for my husband. According to *halachah*, not only is one not allowed to eat bread, he is also forbidden to have bread in his possession. My husband realized that he would have to continue to trade away his bread portions during the entire eight days of Pesach. This would further weaken him, he knew; he would practically be starving for a substantial amount of time. But he decided to take his chances and not eat his bread ration during the eight days.

Fully aware that in the Ebensee *revere*, the notion of getting any kind of matzah was inconceivable, my husband had resigned himself to not being able to fulfill the *mitzvah* of eating matzah. Then, at what my husband guessed to be approximately a half-hour before sunset on *erev* Pesach, a man hurriedly entered the *revere*, whispering that he was looking for the son of the Rebbe from Szaszregen. My husband could not believe what he had just heard. Weakly he identified himself, hoping that the young man would hear. It was surely *min haShamayim* — decreed in Heaven — that the young man heard, spotted my husband, and came over to him. My husband's heart pounded with eager anticipation as the young man approached. Who was he? How did this young man know his beloved father? How did he even know he was there?

The man leaned over my ailing husband — and in his hand was a small, whole matzah! My husband was astonished. Was this a dream? How could anyone "organize," let alone bake, matzah in a place like this?

The man who performed this incredible *mitzvah* was Mr. Hirsh, one of my father-in-law's *Chassidim*. He came from the town of Targu Mures-Washarhely, which was located in the vicinity of Szaszregen. He had been assigned to work in the camp kitchen, and somehow heard that my husband was in the *revere*. This kind young man handed my husband the small matzah and told him that in the *zechus* of my father-in-law and his family, he managed to make the matzah. Even though he risked his very own life to do so, he was very happy to have fulfilled his mission. "It is not your father's *shemurah* matzah that you had back home,"[8] he explained — but the matzah had been baked on top of the oven, prepared as closely to *halachah* as was possible in a nightmarish place like Ebensee. It would most definitely do.

My husband was speechless after hearing how the young man prepared the matzah. What he must have gone through to bake it was almost beyond comprehension. Imagine the danger into which he had placed himself to perform this great act of *mesiras nefesh*! After presenting my husband with the matzah, Mr. Hirsh disappeared quickly.

One Shabbos, during a visit to *Eretz Yisrael* in 1985, my husband was scheduled to conduct the *shalosh seudos tish* (third Shabbos meal) at the Satmar *shul* in *Yerushalayim*. Just before *Minchah*, a clean-shaven man walked into the *shul* and approached my husband.

"Rabbi Rubin, do you remember me?" he asked eagerly.

My husband replied apologetically that he did not.

The man answered, "I saw the *shul* posters announcing that you were here, and I came to say 'Shalom Aleichem.' I am Mr. Hirsh, the one who gave you the matzah in Ebensee!"

My husband embraced the man. It was a joyous, emotional reunion, and tears flowed from the eyes of both men. "Bless you … and thank you," exclaimed my husband, his voice breaking with emotion.

It was then time to *daven Minchah*. In the Satmar *shul*, there is a custom not to give *aliyos* to anyone without a beard. However, my

---

8. *Shemurah matzah* (literally "watched matzah," from the Hebrew word "*lishmor*," to guard) is a specially protected matzah eaten by scrupulously religious Jews on Pesach. In accord with the Biblical command to "guard the matzos" (*Exodus* 12:17), these matzos are baked from wheat that has been guarded from the time it is cut, to prevent it from accidentally coming into contact with water or moisture. Non-*shemurah matzah*, while baked under rabbinical supervision, is not subject to the same kind of intense scrutiny at every step of the pre-baking process, and hence, most Chassidim do not eat it unless there is absolutely nothing else available, as was the case that year in Ebensee.

husband wanted to call Mr. Hirsh up to the Torah. Quickly, he took the *shul's* rabbi, Rabbi Lipa Schwartz, aside, and R' Schwartz agreed to make an exception in this case. Mr. Hirsh was called to the Torah. My husband cherished this opportunity to express his gratitude to Mr. Hirsh for the great deed he performed in Ebensee.

THE POSSESSION OF THE MATZAH PRESENTED MY HUSBAND WITH A new dilemma. Rabbi David Greenzweig (a friend who survived and

Ve'ahavta Lerei'acha Kamocha
ultimately became the president of the Council of Jewish Organizations [COJO] of Boro Park) who was also in the Ebensee *revere*, heard that my husband had matzah, and asked my husband to share a piece of it with him. This raised an interesting problem for my husband. On the one hand, *halachah* requires one to eat a certain minimum amount of matzah —about one-third to one-half of a whole matzah — to fulfill the requirements of the *seder*. If this amount of the matzah is not eaten, the requirement goes unfilled.

The "Hirsch" matzah provided my husband with the minimum amount required for one person. If my husband were to share the matzah, neither he nor anybody else would eat the minimum amount. On the other hand, if my husband did not share his matzah, he would be denying others the chance to have a portion of this precious matzah on Pesach, small as the piece might be. Being a son of the Szaszregener House, which was built on the foundation of *ve'ahavta lerei'acha kamocha* (caring for others as for oneself), my husband could not have refused others a piece of matzah. He explained his decision by citing an issue raised in the Talmud: "When two people are about to die, and there is one portion of water, must one share it and both die or should one use it all for himself?" According to one opinion in the Talmud, one should share it and not look on as the other dies. My husband knew that he could not bear the silent reproach of his friends were they to see him on the *seder* night eating matzah and not sharing it with them. His choice, then, became simple and obvious. He would make the *berachah* while the matzah was whole, and then share the matzah, thus fulfilling the *Haggadah's* injunction, *"Kol dichfin yaysay v'yaychol, kol ditzrich yaysay veyifsach* (Let anyone who is hungry come in and eat, let anyone who is needy come in and make Pesach)."

My husband created his makeshift *"seder"* that evening with two other men who stole into his bunk. (One of them was his relative, R' David Greenzweig.) These men risked their lives to join the *"seder,"* but they were willing to take that chance — just as the miserable Jewish slaves of yore had been willing to take a chance on the first Pesach by tying up a lamb, an animal worshiped by the pagan Egyptians as one of their sacred gods. The only difference was that in Ebensee, the Jews had not previously been promised by Hashem that they would succeed in their endeavor...

My husband drank the *"arba kosos,"* which was by then moldy ersatz coffee. He broke the matzah into equal pieces and distributed them to those present at his *seder*, saying, "Matzah *zu she'anu ochlin...* (This matzah that we eat ...)." The difference between saying "matzah *zu"* at home and "matzah *zu"* at the Ebensee *seder* was that in Ebensee, my husband and the others felt the meaning of the words "matzah *zu"* more intensely, as if they were really saying "matzah *zu"* in Egypt under the whip of the Egyptian overseer.

They recited the *Haggadah* from memory, each adding his share of remembrance. At the *seder*, we say *"Shefoch Chamascha,"* asking the A-mighty to pour His anger on those who deserve it. Never before, and never since then, did my husband say that prayer as intensely and surely as he and the others said it at that dark *seder* in Ebensee.

There was no pillow on which to recline, no *seder* plate, no wine, no gleaming white tablecloth, no glittering tableware, no fine china, no delicious food — and above all, no family. Muddy ersatz coffee replaced the wine; their actual fear reminded them of *Mitzrayim*; but the little matzah was real, and so was their spiritual belief and strength. Bereft of the fine trappings, surrounded by vicious oppressors who treated them as slaves, my husband and his guests were able to strongly identify with their ancestors and the bitter, tortured lives of bondage they lived in the quarries and mud-pits of Egypt. There was, however, one — and only one — similarity between my husband's makeshift *seder* and the events of *Mitzrayim*: *chipazon* — speed, doing everything in a hurry.

In psalm 23 *of Sefer Tehillim*, it says, *"Taaroch lefanai shulchan neged tzorerai* (Thou [G-d] prepare a table for me in the full presence of my enemies)."* Those words, written by the great David *HaMelech* in thankfulness to the A-mighty for protecting him and sustaining him even as he hid from Saul's army, were as true that night in the accursed Ebensee as they were in King David's day. The A-mighty had indeed prepared a table — their bunk — for my husband and the others in the presence of their enemies. No *kapo* came through the doorway to interrupt them while they prayed and went through our ancient ritual — only the invisible presence of Eliyahu *HaNavi*,[9] with his promise that freedom and redemption were on the way.

For the remainder of Pesach, my husband continued to trade away his pieces of bread for "coffee" and a small portion of margarine. He grew thinner that week, but felt strengthened spiritually. Recently, a young yeshivah *bachur* told me that he met Mr. Jonah Klein from the Belz community of Bnei Brak, who was originally from Selish, the son of our worthy neighbor R' Pesachye, *H"yd*. The *bachur* told me that Mr. Klein was in Ebensee with the Muzsayer Rebbe — my husband — who was the only individual who managed to refrain from eating bread throughout the entire Pesach.

MY HUSBAND SAW THE BEGINNING OF MAY IN THE *REVERE*. SPRING was in the air, and he could hear birds chirping outside the win-

The Final Days Before German Capitulation dows. Those well enough to talk to their neighbors exchanged rumors they had heard about the Allies closing in. Liberation couldn't be far behind! The optimists believed the

---

9. The Prophet Elijah. Scripture teaches that Elijah will herald the imminent arrival of the Messiah. Traditionally, a cup of wine – popularly known as the "Cup of Elijah" – is poured at the *seder*.

SS cowards would run away to avoid capture, and leave the *revere* patients behind. Others were convinced that the SS would murder all of the patients in the *revere* before fleeing, leaving no witnesses behind to testify to the atrocities which had taken place there.

In his weakened condition, my husband chose to stay out of the arguments — although he, too, secretly feared the worst. Instead of voicing this opinion, he closed his eyes and prayed for a miracle.

Liberation at Last!

THE ALLIED ARMIES SMASHED INTO GERMANY FROM TWO SIDES, the Russians from the east and the British and Americans from the west. Ebensee lay in the path of the western attack, and on the afternoon of May 6, 1945, U.S. tanks bulldozed their way through Ebensee's camp gates.

The morning of May 6, 1945, began as another typical day of living hell in the *revere*. The sickroom was unusually quiet, but this extreme stillness spoke volumes, and my husband remembers feeling that something — either favorable or not — was about to happen.

Soon the stillness was replaced by tension. Some of the patients who were well enough to get up stumbled over to the window to look outside. My husband, unable to stand, watched them anxiously, hardly daring to breathe, waiting for them to say something — anything. What did they see? What was going on? Finally, one of the men shouted, "I see tanks on the hills and it might — just might — be the Americans!"

"It is the American Army!" exclaimed another. "See? Their tanks are entering the camp!"

"Are we free? Are we free?" cried an inmate.

"Yes! We're free! We're liberated!" voices screamed in unison.

With tears in their eyes, the men embraced, then ran back to the window to make sure that what they were seeing was really true. No *kapos* (including the notorious Hans) made their usual appearance that morning, nor were any murderous German soldiers seen anywhere alive. The Allied Forces had taken over the camp and the only visible Germans were those who had fallen and now lay lifeless on the ground. Some of the stronger patients — now former inmates — were dancing with delight, while the rest of the patients, including my husband, absorbed this exciting moment lying down.

My husband recited *Modeh Ani* with fervor and a new feeling of thanksgiving to Hashem for granting him a new day of life. Outside, the rumbling of the heavy tanks grew louder while the excitement intensified inside. The Americans arrived at Ebensee's gates around 2:50 P.M. that day.

The following morning, the American soldiers who entered the *revere* were not prepared for what awaited them there; it was simply beyond the comprehension of decent human beings. They could not believe the squalid conditions to which these sick patients, many of whom were suffering from typhus and malnutrition, had been subjected by the Germans. Living human skeletons lined the sickroom wall to wall, examples of the ultimate in human misery, victims of the "noble" Third Reich which wanted to dominate the European nations and destroy the Jews purely for egotistic reasons — to create *lebensraum* (living space) for the Germans. As time passed, the Americans would witness the painful deaths of countless liberated inmates from the effects of starvation, illness and exposure to the harsh elements.

Some of the patients sobbed uncontrollably and embraced the soldiers in desperation and relief. Others, too weak to move, stared blankly at their liberators with enormous eyes bulging from deep eye sockets.

The American doctors weighed and measured the ill men, one by one. My husband's weight was down to approximately 40 kilos — slightly under 90 lbs. In an attempt to quickly put some flesh back on the bony, emaciated men, the U.S. Army served them generous portions of food including heavy, starchy foods such as soup, macaroni and bread. Many of the starved men ate ravenously —

but their shrunken stomachs simply could not digest the food properly. Some became very sick and others died as a result of eating too much, too soon.

The army should have known better. The command did not send in local doctors to examine and care for the infirm, nor were the sick taken to nearby hospitals. Only army-appointed doctors and nurses cared for the sick and wounded.

My husband and other Ebensee survivors, many of them injured or seriously ill, had to spend their first days as free men in cramped barracks. Living conditions were extremely unpleasant and uncomfortable. One might think that after what they had endured — being crammed into concentration camps, losing most or all of their families, and being subjected to barbaric forms of physical and mental torture daily — the survivors would have been treated better after liberation. For instance, the Ebensee survivors were not too far from the empty summer villas and mansions of the wealthy Nazis and supporting Germans. Why couldn't the liberated prisoners be housed there temporarily, to recover in comfort and regain their strength and health? But nobody arranged it.

Tragically, many former concentration-camp prisoners died immediately after their liberation. My husband said that he cried for those who had come this far and died, not at the hands of the cruel SS or the wild Ukrainians, but as free men. He was later to find out that his beloved brother, R' Yosef Mayer Rubin, *ztk"l*, was a victim of such circumstances.

R' Yosef Mayer was liberated in the camp of Theresienstadt, in Czechoslovakia. Many others in the camp were deathly ill with typhus and other diseases. The British divided the camp into two sections: one for the ill patients and the other for the healthier ones who needed a minimum amount of medical care. R' Yosef Mayer had contracted typhus and was placed with the deathly-ill patients. The current Satmar Rebbe, R' Moshe Teitelbaum, *shlita*, was also placed there, but was able to convince the British that he was well enough to be taken out. The wife of R' Baruch Yehuda Lebowitz, *a"h*, was an inmate there as well, and knew that R' Teitelbaum was interned there. She provided him with food and helped him survive. She did not know that R' Yosef Mayer was there, too. R' Yosef Mayer died a few days after liberation.

The Czechs decided that the bodies of the innocent victims, R' Yosef Mayer included, would be cremated instead of buried to prevent the risk of contagion. The ashes of each body were buried individually in Theresienstadt, and each grave was marked with a number and a cross. The numbers were matched with names in a book of records, which was kept inside the camp. In 1966, my husband, R' Rubin, returned to Theresienstadt and looked up the number of R' Yosef Mayer's *kever* in the book of records. The names and dates were still clear. R' Yosef Mayer's remains were removed and flown to *Eretz Yisrael* for burial in a cemetery in Tiberias — the same place where the Baal Shem Tov's disciples were buried. My brother-in-law, the Sulitzer Rebbe, *shlita*, was present when the remains were taken from Theresienstadt to Tiberias.

The first American soldier who approached my husband was a young Jewish man from Boston. He looked well, and appeared neat and clean in his tidy army uniform and polished boots. He introduced himself and assured my husband that he would receive the best medical care for his leg. While conversing, the soldier informed my husband that he had been able to eat kosher food even while fighting on the front. The U.S. Army allowed his mother to send him canned kosher food oversees, and saw to it that the food reached him, regardless of where he was. He showed my husband the kosher canned goods.

The grave of my brother-in-law, R' Yosef Mayer Rubin, in Tiberias, Israel. The cemetery in Tiberias is the resting place for many disciples of the Baal Shem Tov — among them some of R' Yosef Mayer's great-grandfathers.

THE RESCUED RELIGIOUS JEWS DECIDED TO ORGANIZE A PROPER Shabbos in Ebensee. There were a number of *rabbanim* and

Friday Night Tish in Ebensee Chassidic people among them including R' Greenwald, the Chuster Rav, *zt"l*, and my first cousin, R' Teitelbaum, the Kiralyhazer

Rav, *zt"l*, both of whom eventually settled in Boro Park.

Since the American Army was unable and unprepared to provide the men with kosher food, my husband and the others were left to figure out a way of securing kosher food on their own.

R' Yecheskel Wertzberger, *a"h*, attempted to solve the problem. He was able to secure a knife and arranged for someone to bring him some chickens from a German civilian. After slaughtering the chickens according to *halachah*, R' Wertzberger plucked and cleaned them in preparation for *kashering*. When he opened the carcasses of the chickens, however, he discovered a problem inside, resulting in a *she'eilah* about their *kashrus*. Nevertheless, the chickens were cooked, and a Friday night *seudah* was prepared. Everyone assembled in a large room for the *seudah*, where they sang *zemiros* from home.

That Shabbos can be compared to the *"Hamotzi"* of Rosh Hashanah — one side of the *challah* is coated with sweet honey, and the other is covered with salt. It can also be compared to the Pesach *seder* with the matzah — the symbol of liberation — and the bitter *maror* — symbol of slavery — eaten together.

My husband said that he hesitated to eat the chicken that night. The chaplain noticed, and offered my husband some canned kosher food. My husband gratefully accepted the canned food and was able to enjoy a *pareve* (containing neither dairy nor meat products) kosher meal that Shabbos evening.

The other *rabbanim* present at the *tish* were not feeling well enough to deliver a *dvar Torah*. Although my husband was extremely weak himself, he agreed to speak.

In his *dvar Torah*, he stressed that the survivors of *Churban* Europe must rebuild their lives from the ashes, and in the process, they must especially emphasize the rebuilding of their spiritual strength as well. He quoted a *dvar Torah* which was originally delivered by his holy and great ancestor, R' Naftali Tzvi Horowitz, *zt"l*, the founder of the Ropshitzer dynasty. R' Horowitz had said that an important question must be raised from *Bereishis*. Why are we told that the earth was *tohu vavohu* (empty and void)? My husband quoted his *zeide* as answering that it is to teach us that from nothingness can come something.

In that same vein, the survivors of the Nazi camps had, in many cases, lost everything, and were *tohu vavohu* — without families, friends, health or dignity. With *emunah*, however, the survivors could rebuild their world and must, in effect, create something out of nothingness. Like the Jews in the desert who were ordered to build a *Mishkan*, the survivors, although living in a wilderness, were obligated to rebuild their *"Mishkan"* from home.

As he continued speaking, my husband pointed out that Hashem gave the Jews a second set of *Luchos* with the *Aseres HaDibros* (Ten Commandments) after Moshe *Rabbeinu* broke the first set. Then he drew the parallel: even though all those assembled there in Ebensee had lived through a time when the *"Luchos"* were destroyed before their very eyes, they should not give up because there will be, with G-d's help, a second set of *Luchos* which will last forever as the Jews rebuild their lives.

Thinking back to that *dvar Torah* almost half a century later, we see before our eyes the fruits of those words: the rekindling of Torah and *Chassidus*, the rebuilding of families deeply steeped in the teachings of Torah. Out of the ashes of the Holocaust came new roots, and from those roots sprouted new branches of families. These were the offshoots of the few survivors of a generation meant to be completely wiped out by the Hitlerites. We proudly hold the *"Luchos Sheniyos"* — the "Second Set of Tablets" — in our hands, and proclaim to the world that Heaven does make the final decrees

BEFORE DEPARTING FROM EBENSEE, THE SURVIVORS DECIDED to have a special *Yizkor* service — a memorial and a spiritual

Eulogy at the Ebensee Crematorium

farewell at the crematorium for those who had perished there. They wished to depart emotionally from the dead, say prayers, and ask forgiveness from the *kedoshim*. Among those who perished there were my first cousins, Zishe and Yechiel, sons of the famed Sigheter Rav, *zt"l*.

The warm May breezes blew gently into the faces of the mourners as they stood by the crematorium, over the mass grave in which were buried thousands of their murdered Jewish brothers and sisters. The wind carried the stormy cries of the martyrs, their bitter accusations and harsh indictments, up to the peaks of the grand Tyrol Mountains, and higher still ...

The other *rabbanim* there did not want to speak, so my husband, the youngest among them, stood up — his injured leg notwithstanding — to deliver a *hesped* (eulogy). He was overcome with emotion but managed to compose himself and begin.

He started with a question: How could we best avenge ourselves against Nazi Germany? While we, the assembled, had lost families and had been robbed of many happy and productive years, we must start anew by reestablishing families and communities. This, he said, would be the Jews' most effective revenge against the Hitlerites. He quoted from *Vayikra*, which concerns the various sacrifices brought by the ancient Jews first to the *Mishkan*, and later to the *Beis HaMikdash*. He likened them to the sacrifices *Klal Yisrael* had just made: even though a part of our people had been sacrificed during this period, the other part was not, and that part must live on and rebuild a new life.

After my husband finished speaking, everyone said *Kaddish* together and retreated from the site, walking backwards to give honor to the dead.

My husband still has a copy of this *hesped*, which left a lasting impression on the listeners. A member of our *shul*, Mr. Yeshaya Blau, was there and remembers the episode, and Mr. Wertzberger, now living in Boro Park, said to R' Rubin many years later, "I remember your emotional *hesped* in Ebensee," and quoted a few sentences.

During the remainder of his stay in Ebensee, my husband feared the trap of Stalin and warned people not to cross the Russian borders into the occupied Russian territories lest they be trapped there by the Communist authorities. (Actually, it took the Russians a few years until they managed to close the borders.) Later, however, he decided to return to Budapest after he learned that I had been there.

AN ARMY DOCTOR ADVISED MY HUSBAND TO HAVE AN OPERATION performed on his leg in order to save it. The bone would need to be

Out of Ebensee

reset immediately.

The army made arrangements for the sick to stay in a convalescent home in Bad-Ishel, a town near Ebensee. My husband would need to go to the convalescent home first because he was still too weak to undergo surgery. From there he would be sent to a hospital in Salzburg, Austria for the corrective leg surgery. A high officer of the U.S. Army had engaged the famous surgeon-professor, Dr. Dominic, to perform the surgery, and he had also arranged to send the material needed for the operation to the hospital. Everyone there knew who Dr. Dominic was;

his superb reputation spoke for itself and the Jewish chaplain assured my husband that he would be in the most capable hands. The operation would be performed in the best-known and largest medical facility in Salzburg, using supplies from the U.S. Army.

My husband left Ebensee on May 16, 1945. It was finally time to say farewell to a horrific place whose legacy was to prove that people who were considered intelligent and civilized could turn into barbarians practically overnight. For the sake of *"Deutschland uber Alles,"* the Germans created — then jeered at — the most awful human misery. To the rest of the world, Ebensee looked like a beautiful vacation resort — but for the victims interned there, it was sheer hell.

The former prisoners boarded the truck and positioned themselves for the trip. As my husband lay his head back and carefully elevated his broken leg, he could not halt the deluge of memories flooding his mind: the brutal expressions of the German guards and *kapos* as they beat overworked and ill men to death ... the terror in the eyes of the victims ... the harrowing death march in sub-freezing temperatures ... the gasping voice of the *tzaddik,* R' Landau, begging his comrades to let him drop to the snow to die ... the DAW foreman from Budapest (Where was he now?) ... the appalling smells and sights of the tunnels in Ebensee where death lurked around every bend ... the uproarious laughter of the Ukrainians as they looked down on my husband where he lay on the ground, screaming in pain after his contrived accident ... the image of my mother smiling at him as she approached the iron doors of the gas chamber ...

And above all else, he wondered, agonized: where were his loved ones now?

Soon my husband arrived at the town of Bad-Ishel and was taken to the convalescent home. He was assigned a bed in a large, sterile-looking white room filled with many other recuperating survivors. His worldly possessions were so meager that he was able to put everything he owned — a few articles of clothing received from the American Army, and one or two personal items, including a toothbrush and hair comb — into the small wardrobe and tiny drawer of the night table.

After living in filth for so many months, my husband marveled at how sparkling clean the convalescent home was. The floors shone and the walls gleamed. Shafts of sunlight poured through the huge, spotless windows. The smells of disinfectant and rubbing alcohol permeated the room; that plus the fresh air blowing in through the windows made him feel more vibrant and alive.

In this clean and comfortable convalescent facility, my husband managed to get the rest that he so desperately needed and began to feel somewhat stronger. The infection in his leg cleared up and his fever came down. It was at the convalescent home, too, that my husband received a *tallis katan* and a *siddur* from a Jewish army chaplain — the first since his own were taken away in Auschwitz. He still did not have *tefillin*.

The Operation

THE DAY BEFORE HIS SCHEDULED SURGERY, MY HUSBAND MET Dr. Dominic, who explained the procedure he would use to reconstruct the leg. The doctor told my husband that the bone would have to be pieced back together at the sites of the three breaks. He could not guarantee complete success since the bone fragments had been disconnected for a period of time, but said with assurance that he would do everything possible to enable my husband to walk normally once again. Dr. Dominic seemed highly competent and my husband trusted him, even though he was a devoted Austrian. (According to the Americans, he had not belonged to the Nazi party.)

The operation was complicated and took the better part of a day. Even today, such an injury requires many hours to correct. How much more so was the case right after World War II, nearly 50 years ago, when medical techniques and technology were nowhere near what they are now! Although the proceedings were complex, they were uneventful. All went according to plan, and the renowned Dr. Dominic used his considerable skill to reunite the shattered pieces of bone. In fact, Dr. Dominic's technique was so masterful that even decades later, when my husband had occasion to be examined at New York's Memorial Hospital, his doctors were amazed by the perfection of his reconstructed leg.

After the operation, Dr. Dominic checked on him often and told him that the cast would be off in a few weeks.

Once my husband was feeling better, he was more than grateful to receive visitors. Among the visitors was Rebbetzin Pessia Sherashewsky, a former activist in the Bais Yaakov movement in Lithuania, who patiently listened to my husband's account of his harrowing experiences in the camps. Then she and my husband engaged in a conversation comparing the different points of views of leading *rabbanim* in Hungary to those in Lithuania and Poland regarding the establishment of the Bais Yaakov schools for girls in Europe. My husband told her that he once attended a *derashah* given by my uncle, the Satmar Rebbe, in the town of Szamosuyvar, in which my uncle said, "In our communities, forming a Bais Yaakov — a Torah school for girls — means the destruction of *tzenius*." However, years later, when the Satmar Rebbe formed his *kehillah* in Williamsburg, Brooklyn, he founded a girls' school and named it Bais Rochel after his beloved departed daughter. In his monumental book *VaYoel Moshe*, the Rebbe explained that in today's changing, modern world, the establishment of girls' schools is necessary. We must assume that the same was true in Poland before the Second World War.

Others who came to visit my husband included fellow Jews from a nearby displaced persons' camp. Since the hospital did not have a kosher kitchen, his visitors always came well-stocked with kosher food to ensure that he had enough to eat. R' Rubin will always be thankful to them for their *mitzvah* of *bikur cholim*.

A few weeks later, Dr. Dominic removed the cast with a device which resembled an electric saw. The doctor assured my husband that contrary to its appearance his leg was fine, and that the way it looked was not unusual immediately following the removal of a cast. The physical therapy which followed was extremely arduous.

My husband was hospitalized for about nine weeks. Under the care that he received from the doctors and nurses, his health improved substantially, and he gained back some of the weight he had lost during those eleven months in the concentration camps.

R' RUBIN WAS FACED WITH THE DECISION OF WHAT TO DO NEXT. HE knew he could not risk returning to Hungary because, as he had

A New Life warned in his *derashos*, the Russian Army had conquered and occupied most of the countries in which we had once lived. Visiting those countries was dangerous, because once people were in Communist territory, the Communist government would sometimes not let them out again.

Because of this my husband decided that he would remain in Germany for the time being, much as he despised the idea of remaining in the birthplace of Nazism. It also pained him deeply that he would not have the immediate opportunity to search for his family.

Before his release, he was told about a displaced persons' camp set up in Fehrenwald, Germany, located in the vicinity of the city of Munich. Word had it that Fehrenwald was already considered to be a Chassidic camp under the leadership of the camp's head rabbi, the Klausenburger-Sanzer Rebbe, R' Y.Y. Halberstam, *zt"l*. R' Halberstam, who had lost his Rebbetzin and eleven children in Auschwitz, was my first cousin by marriage; his father-in-law, the Sigheter Rav (the *"Atzei Chaim," zt"l*) was my mother's brother.

Comfortable with the idea that he would be among *Chassidim* again, my husband made arrangements to go to Fehrenwald.

He was released from the hospital at the end of August 1945, able to walk with the support of a cane, but limping. Chassidic clothing was not to be found anywhere in Austria, so, like everyone else, he received "modern" clothing. In his brown suit and colored hat, he certainly did not look like a Chassidic rebbe! But the clothing was clean and freshly pressed.

A warm reception awaited my husband in Fehrenwald. Several *Chassidim* eagerly escorted him to meet the Klausenburger Rebbe who was in his study, a large room in one of the camp's buildings. The Rebbe greeted him with a friendly "*Shalom aleichem,*" then looked him over from head to toe and asked, "*Azoi zeht ois ayer taten's a kind?* (So this is how your father's son looks?)" Soon afterward, people in the camp found Chassidic clothing somewhere in Munich. They brought back a *Chassidishe* hat for my husband, and slowly he started to make his way back to looking like his father's son.

After settling in, my husband decided to go for a short walk with some of the other *Chassidim* to see if he could find anyone he knew and to check out the overall conditions of the camp. It did not take long to realize that the camp was overcrowded, its small houses packed with innocent survivors who had suffered so much, both physically and psychologically, at the hands of the SS tormentors.

These were people whose lives had been destroyed at the hands of the SS, who had lost many or all of their family members and no longer had homes to which to return, who continued to suffer the effects of prolonged illness. Weren't these refugees, these battered and broken survivors, entitled to better accommodations?

Fehrenwald was uncomfortable enough, but not too far from it was another D.P. camp called Feldafing. There, dozens of married couples had to share their barracks with other married couples and had absolutely no privacy.

R' Rubin blames the indifference towards the Jewish refugees, and their poor treatment after the war, both on the American Occupation Army and the German authorities, who had a great influence on the Americans. Please do not misunderstand. My husband will be forever grateful to the American army for having liberated the Jews interned in Ebensee, for having done what it could to allow them to have kosher provisions and, on a more personal note, for having made arrangements to treat his injured leg.

Nevertheless, he feels that the American authorities, however helpful they were in many other areas, adopted a hands-off policy vis-a-vis civilians when it came to the matter of providing living quarters for Jewish survivors. Of course, it goes without saying that after 12 years of having brutalized and oppressed us, the local German officials could not reasonably have been expected to show any sort of sympathy for the dignity and sensibilities of the Jewish survivors. However, more was expected from the Americans and the United Nations Relief Agency, and we were disappointed when they didn't come through.

Many German vacation mansions and villas belonging to officials of the German government, the Nazi party, and wealthy private Nazi citizens were left unoccupied during the off-season. The German authorities, under the orders of the American Occupation Army, could have easily made some of them available to the unfortunate Jewish survivors who had suffered so much — but that did not happen. Didn't the Holocaust victims deserve to be housed in these comfortable villas while they convalesced from their illnesses and injuries?

Among the owners of these villas were the Krupp family and other industrialists who were partners in the German war effort. Many of these wealthy industrialists were indirect accessories to war crimes, yet the American Occupational Government and the German authorities ignored this fact. German industrialists who profited from our slave labor were allowed to continue their dilettante lifestyles, even to benefit financially from the Marshall Plan, while the Jewish survivors, many of whom had once been loyal German citizens, were left to rot in the overcrowded conditions of the D.P. Camps. We were classified as "displaced" or "stateless," while the Germans remained the owners or inhabitants of whatever private homes were available. Where were our stolen fortunes? Why were we displaced? Was anybody there responsible for that? There is no valid explanation for this insensitivity and indifference, and for the resulting post-war mistreatment of the Holocaust victims.

At Fehrenwald, R' Rubin and several hundred other *Chassidim* assembled and learned with R' Halberstam in his *beis midrash* on a daily basis. The Friday night *tish* there was extraordinary and inspiring, despite the grim camp surroundings, and R' Halberstam's inspiring *divrei Torah* provided true *oneg Shabbos*.

Nights were not kind to the lonely men. Alone in the still darkness, many were confronted with vivid nightmares which brought the horror of their wartime experiences back to life. My husband recalls being awakened out of his own troubled sleep many times by the screams and wails of others. Sometimes he also awoke with a start, bathed in sweat and weeping. Many times he agonized over how — if he and I were ever to find one another again — he would break the heartrending news to me that he had witnessed my mother entering the gas chamber in Auschwitz.

The Days of Awe of 1945 were soon upon them. As my husband thought back to where he had been just one year ago, he was grateful to the A-mighty for allowing him to see this Rosh Hashanah and Yom Kippur as a free man. The men had all the *siddurim* they needed, didn't have to look over their shoulders when they *davened*, and had fresh, clean and presentable clothing to wear.

Yizkor means remember. The natural way of the world is for a child to eventually say this prayer in memory of his or her parents. But now, unfortunately, many had to say *Yizkor* in memory of children and spouses who were murdered during the 12-year Reign of Terror. Seldom in history were so many names remembered at once as during that painful *Yizkor*. This was the first real opportunity for my husband and others to say *Yizkor* for their dear, departed relatives who, they were certain, were looking down upon them from *Gan Eden* in Heaven.

My husband did not do much dancing that first Simchas Torah after liberation — after all, his leg was still healing from his serious operation. And in his heart, he, like many other survivors that year, was troubled by the fact that he had no way of knowing for sure what had happened to many of his loved ones — his mother, his father, his brothers and sisters and, of course, me. This uncertainty had eaten at him during the weeks following his liberation and subsequent operation, when he lay flat on his back, recuperating from his Ebensee ordeal and from his leg injury. He made inquiries of those who came to see him, of course, but nobody seemed to know anything. This was a widespread problem among Holocaust survivors trying to pick up the pieces in the chaos that was postwar Europe. He reasoned that if his own journey had taken him from Auschwitz to Ebensee and then to Germany, I too had probably been shuttled to more than one camp, which, in fact, proved to be the case. Assuming I was still alive, I might be anywhere in continental Europe, including the vast sector now occupied by the Russians. The same, of course, held true for his other loved ones.

Although his mobility was still limited — he was hobbling about on a cane — my husband resolved to try to find me and his other family members. He continued to make inquiries after the *yamim tovim,* and word got out that the Muzsayer Rebbe was searching for his family. This brought him the news that his sister in Alba Iulia and her family had survived the war, and led to an unexpected encounter with a total stranger that ultimately helped lead to our reunion.

IN THE FALL OF 1945, THINGS FINALLY FELL INTO PLACE. ONE EVENING in Camp Fehrenwald, not too long after the *yamim tovim,* somebody

Our Reunion: My Husband's Story

approached my husband and asked whether he was the Muzsayer Rebbe. When my husband confirmed that he was, the man told him he had heard that I was alive and had been seen in Budapest looking for him.

My husband stared at this man in astonishment. It was highly uncommon in Fehrenwald or any other D.P. Camp for a husband and wife to both have survived. His first thoughts were that his holy father from Szaszregen, *ztk"l*, and my holy uncle from Satmar, who had led us to the *chuppah* just days before Berlin occupied Budapest, must have had a Heavenly intuition that if we were separated during the war, we would find our way back to one another later.

The Klausenburger-Sanzer Rebbe advised my husband not to go to Budapest. Crossing the borders from American-occupied Germany to Russian-occupied Hungary was still dangerous. He urged my husband to remain in Fehrenwald and wait for me to track him down there. However, my husband decided to take the risk, and prepared for the journey.

Instead of heading directly to Budapest, my husband first set out for Alba Iulia. This town, located in southwestern Romania in the vicinity of Sibiu, was considered "off limits" to the SS, who did not occupy Romania. As a result, the lives of my husband's sister Rebbetzin Chana and her family had been spared. Unable to wire in advance, my husband could not notify his brother-in-law, Grand Rabbi Nachman Kahana, the Spinker Rebbe, and Rebbetzin Chana of his impending arrival.

The journey from Fehrenwald to Alba Iulia was difficult. Sleeping among the gentiles, crossing borders without official papers, putting on *tefillin* while standing between moving train cars were but a few of the hardships encountered. Finally, he arrived in Alba Iulia and found the house of the Spinker Rebbe and Rebbetzin. When my husband showed up on his sister's doorstep, the family was stunned by his sudden appearance, but overjoyed to see with their own eyes that he had survived.

My husband's reunion with his brother, R' Mordechai David, was especially emotional. The last time he had seen R' Mordechai David was at our wedding, which seemed like an eternity ago. He noted that his brother had changed; he appeared pale and skinny, and his dark brown eyes, once filled with life and hope, now reflected the suffering and pain that he, too, had endured. R' Mordechai David imparted the welcome news to my husband that R' Shmuel Shmelka was also alive and was traveling with me in search of him. My husband learned that a few weeks after his brothers had arrived, his uncle, R' Moishe Frisherman, the Tomashover Rebbe, had also showed up at Rebbetzin Chana's house. Although he was already aware of the fact that his revered parents, of blessed memory, had been led to the gas chambers with his little sister, Shprintza, he did not know what had happened to the rest of his family. R' Mordechai David had the sad task of informing him that their sister Leah, her husband, and their beautiful children had also been sacrificed *al kiddush Hashem* in the ovens of Birkenau.

During the selection process, my husband's uncle had seen Mengele motion my two other brothers-in-law, Usher Yeshayah and Yosef Mayer, to the right. The family was hopeful that perhaps they too were still alive. As the weeks went by, however, they learned that Usher had collapsed and died while on a forced march in Germany during the final days of the war. The family was later told by the Chuster *tallis* manufacturer that he and some colleagues managed to bury Usher in the vicinity of the town of Kurfirstenstein. They also learned of Yosef Mayer's death in Theresienstadt, again near the end of the war.

My husband's sisters Yocheved and Mirel had passed the initial selection by Mengele, but then vanished. At the time of my husband's arrival in Alba Iulia, the family had not heard from them, or about them.

R' Mordechai David had bittersweet news to tell my husband about me. He recounted to him that while I was alive and relatively well, I did not have any definite information about his whereabouts. As a result, R' Mordechai David continued, I had decided to travel to *Eretz Yisrael* to temporarily stay with the Teitelbaums, with the intention of returning to Europe when conditions were safer, and continuing to search for him.

This news came as a shock to my husband. Why hadn't I stayed at Rebbetzin Channah's house and waited a little longer? Of course, in hindsight, he realized that my decision had been perfectly understandable.

My husband insisted that he would set out for Italy immediately to try to intercept me before I boarded the ship for Palestine. Besides his fear that he would not find me in time, he worried about what could happen should I board the ship to Palestine.

R' Mordechai David decided that he would travel to Italy with my husband. With the help of the Spinker Rebbe and the agents for *Aliyah* (known at that time as *"Brichah"*) to *Eretz Yisrael*, my husband and his brother were ready for travel early the following morning, a Wednesday. Rebbetzin Channah sent them off with packages of food for their long train ride which would take them through Romania, Hungary, Austria, and finally, Italy.

By Friday morning, *erev* Shabbos, they had passed over the border into Austria. Around noontime, my husband and brother-in-law realized that they had to get off the train and find a place to stay for Shabbos, even though they were only slightly past the midpoint of their journey. They got off at Salzburg. As they stood on the train platform in Salzburg, they looked at each other and wondered where they should go next.

Having been raised in a family descended from the Baal Shem Tov, founder of the Chassidic movement, they had heard many stories of how Rebbes found themselves places to stay for Shabbos, even under the most difficult circumstances. They asked people in the street where to find a Jewish community. They were directed to Parsh, a small township just outside of Salzburg.

My husband and brother-in-law boarded a bus to Parsh and arrived at a religious Jewish camp, where they received a warm reception. They made it just in time for Shabbos.

At the Friday night *tish,* my husband noticed two men staring intently at both him and his brother. Finally, one of the men approached him and said that a couple of Polish men had just helped smuggle them and a few other Jews over the border between Italy and Austria. A young Chassidic gentleman — who they said resembled my husband — was in the group, accompanied by a slight young lady who said that she was his sister-in-law. She said that she was on her way to Germany to look for her husband. My husband's heart seemed to stop for a moment — this sounded like a description of his brother and me! After asking more questions, my husband was finally convinced that the man was, indeed, referring to us.

The following evening, as soon as possible after *Havdalah*, my husband and his brother were on the first train back to Germany, to Fehrenwald, where he and I were finally reunited.

CHAPTER 9
The Survival Story of My Brothers-In-Law

ALTHOUGH THE WAR WAS FINALLY OVER AND SOME OF US HAD been reunited, it took some time until we were able to discuss our individual wartime experiences, until we were able to piece together the tragic and heroic details of our lives apart. In time, however, my husband and I learned what had happened to his family, and received first-person accounts from R' Shmuel Shmelka and R' Mordechai David, *shlita*, (known today as the Sulitzer Rebbe and the Szaszregen Rebbe, respectively) regarding their own harrowing experiences.

AFTER MY IN-LAWS RETURNED TO SZASZREGEN FOLLOWING OUR *chasunah* in Nyir-Bator, their lives would never be the same. German

Waiting for the Axe to Fall troops had occupied most of Hungary, including the Transylvanian region, and the Jewish community lived in constant fear of the Germans' next move.

During the days before Pesach, the SS announced that its soldiers would be permitted to move into any civilian homes of their choosing — a nightmare for Jewish families at any time, and even more so during the Pesach season. For my mother-in-law this would be particularly difficult, as she was used to observing the inherited *chumros* (stringencies that go beyond the letter of *halachah*, adopted to ensure that a *mitzvah* was observed fully) of the Premishlaner dynasty, known for the strictness of its Pesach preparations. (For example, it was the practice within Premishlaner circles to put little white linen "socks" on the family cat before allowing it to come into the house from outside, lest the animal inadvertently track in tiny crumbs of *chametz* on its paws!) And now this meticulous lady might have to contend with Nazi soldiers living under her roof during Pesach.

All were under orders to provide quarters for the soldiers, and it was the bad luck of my in-laws that their home was among those commandeered by the SS. A German officer and several soldiers showed up at their house one day, rudely pushed their way in, and made themselves at home.

My mother-in-law carried out her Pesach preparations with her usual precautions, sensing the Germans watching her every move and snickering at her intense efforts to rid her home of *chametz*. R' and Rebbetzin Rubin shuddered as they listened to these coarse ruffians carousing in their quarters — the grating din echoing through rooms which normally reverberated with the sounds of my father-in-law's melodious voice reciting *tefillos*, singing *zemiros* and learning Torah, and the children's sweet chattering and laughter. Now my dear in-laws feared for the virtue of their young daughters and for the safety of all their innocent children.

The soldiers eventually left and returned to the front, but the German officer remained. He took a room for himself and left the family alone, but the Rubins felt that their home had been permanently violated by the presence of the hostile occupying forces.

Pesach finally arrived, and my father-in-law sat at the head of the table, dressed in his sparkling white *kittel*. He led the *sedarim* in a tranquil manner, elevating himself above his own worries and fears and imbuing the *seder* with a true atmosphere of *kedushah*.

By April 15, 1944, Jews in the Maramaros area were being taken from their homes to the ghetto. During the last week of April, the Jews of Szaszregen were unofficially told to prepare provisions for two or three days. No reasons or explanations were given, but everyone feared the unknown.

ON MONDAY, MAY 1ST, VERY LATE IN THE EVENING, THE RUBINS HAD an unexpected visitor. Mr. Shmuel Ganz, an honorable textile busi-

A Message From the Mayor

nessman in the community, asked to speak privately with my father-in-law. The two men conferred briefly behind closed doors, and then went to another room to speak with my mother-in-law. The tension was maddening for the children, who did not know what was being discussed so solemnly by the grownups.

It seemed that Mr. Ganz had come to speak to my father-in-law on behalf of the gentile mayor of Szaszregen, Dr. Smith. Mr. Ganz explained that a new decree against the Jews was scheduled to go into effect at 6 o'clock the following morning, May 2nd. This official directive would order the streets to remain *Judenrein*, effectively placing all Jews under house arrest. Only one member of each family would be allowed to leave the house for a short period in the evening to shop for food.

Mr. Ganz said the mayor, who had a great deal of respect for my father-in-law, wanted to help the Rubins escape before it was too late. They would only have an hour to pack; at midnight, the mayor would arrive in his car to drive them approximately thirty-two kilometers to the town of Sarmas, on the Hungarian-Romanian border, and leave them there. Under cover of darkness, the Rubins would then steal across the border to Romania and find their way to Alba Iulia and a safe haven in the home of their children, their daughter Rebbetzin Chana Kahana and her husband, the Spinker

Rebbe. The plan was risky, but at least it provided the Rubins with a chance for survival.

The children heard my mother-in-law sobbing in the next room. She did not want to leave her married children behind in Hungary. My father-in-law was reluctant to abandon his followers. He was also concerned for the safety of his family. What would happen at the border? What guarantee was there of a safe crossing? My in-laws told Mr. Ganz to thank the mayor for his generous offer, but they decided not to accept it.

There is an ironic twist to the story of Mr. Ganz. My in-laws had turned down the proposition he conveyed on behalf of the mayor, an offer which might have saved the lives of the family. A short time later, however, Mr. Ganz made someone else a proposal which, tragically, was accepted: At the Birkenau ramp, Mr. Ganz pleaded with Mengele not to send him to the right, but to the left with his father-in-law, R' Avraham Leib. Mengele was only too happy to oblige.

A Turn for the Worse

AS MR. GANZ HAD WARNED, THE AXE FELL THE FOLLOWING MORNING. The community was awakened by the thunderous sounds of the town crier pounding his drum, proclaiming the sadistic new edict in a raucous voice. Early that evening, German soldiers and Hungarian gendarmes burst into my father-in-law's *shul* and stormed up the stairs to the Rubins' home. They ordered the Rubins to pack up two days' worth of food, and banished the family to the second-floor terrace on which the *succah* was built each year. The Germans sealed off the apartment so the Rubins could not re-enter it. With broken hearts, the Rubins looked through the glass doors; everything they owned was within sight but out of reach.

Their cherished *beis midrash* was also sealed off. Only silence and emptiness filled the rooms which had witnessed the prayers and echoed to the sounds of beautiful Chassidic songs throughout the generations. In the *beis midrash*, the *sifrei Torah* remained unopened inside the *aron kodesh*. The doors were firmly shut to keep out the many *Chassidim* who had previously filled the *beis midrash* to capacity every day to *daven*, learn and listen to my father-in-law's inspiring words.

The Rubins knew that soon they would be sent away, but they had no idea when — or to where. Did they wonder whether they had made the wrong decision by not heeding the mayor's warning and not accepting his offer? Knowing their thorough belief in *hashgachah pratis* (Divine Providence), I am reasonably sure that they were at peace with their decision to stay.

ON THURSDAY, MAY 4TH, AT APPROXIMATELY 10 O'CLOCK IN THE morning, the Hungarians, supervised by the Germans, staged a surprise

Confined to the Ghetto raid. The Jews of Szaszregen were driven out of their homes and ordered to a ghetto called *Teglagyar* (or, in German, "*Ziegelfabrik*") — an old brick factory on the outskirts of the town. The Jews were told to take all they could carry and to assemble outside their homes. The gendarmes commanded them to hand over gold, silver, diamonds, jewelry and all other valuables. My brother-in-law, R'Mordechai David, trembled as he held out his gold watch.

The Jews were ordered to carry their rucksacks and food to the waiting horse-drawn wagons which had been hired by the government to transport them. At that moment, my father-in-law asked the gendarmes to allow him to say good-bye to his *beis midrash* and to his beloved *sifrei Torah*. The three officials who accompanied R' Rubin to the *aron kodesh* were so moved by his actions and words that they granted him a few precious moments alone in peace before ordering him to leave the premises. With dignity, R' Rubin gently kissed the *sifrei Torah*. As he passed through the doorway of the *shul*, he touched his fingers to his lips and lovingly transferred a kiss to the *mezuzah* with his hand. Would he ever return? When R' Rubin stepped outside, his sons noticed tears streaming down his face like a string of pearls.

By a Heavenly final solution, those tears watered my father-in-law's branch of the Ropshitzer family tree, which continues to bloom with a new generation of *Chassidim*. Today this generation, a link which lengthens the golden chain of inheritance from the Baal Shem Tov, his children and *talmidim*, continues to learn and pass on his teachings. About one hundred children and grandchildren, along with many followers, are learning my revered father-in-law's writings which can be found in the following books: *Zera Kodesh*, reprinted by our son, the Ropshitzer Rebbe of Boro Park with permission from his great-uncle, the late Satmar Rebbe, R' Yoel Teitelbaum, *zt"l*, and *Or Yesha*, published by my brother-in-law, the Sulitzer Rebbe of Far Rockaway, New York.

Slowly, the procession to the ghetto began. Parents and other adults walked behind the wagons which carried the children. Machine-gun-toting gendarmes, supervised by German soldiers, brought up the rear.

After walking approximately three kilometers down the dusty road, the procession arrived at the ghetto. One extra street had been walled off beyond the brick factory. This space was to house the entire Jewish population of the town, as well as that of the immediate vicinity. As the scorching rays of the midday sun beat down on the sore and frightened people, all they could think of was obtaining a drink of fresh well water, but on this march, no water was to be had.

The Jews were greeted by a so-called civilian committee seated behind long tables, and given another chance to surrender their jewelry and other precious items. As the SS watched, members of the committee searched all bags for valuables. Then living quarters were assigned. Space was at a premium, and all houses were filled beyond capacity.

One of the ghetto overseers was Schiller, the erstwhile secret Nazi who lived next door to my in-laws. As he noticed my brother-in-law, who was carrying a *siddur* and *tefillin* under his arm, his eyes hardened. He viciously grabbed the *siddur* away, then walked over to the authorities and whispered something. The authorities turned towards the Rubins, staring at my brother-in-law in particular, and smirked.

Moments later, several SS soldiers ordered the Rubins to begin marching. Approximately half a mile into the ghetto, they reached a shabby brick building. The Rubins were pushed inside, into a dark room with a floor of packed earth. Mold covered the clammy walls. The Rubins were warned not to leave the premises, nor to allow anyone to enter.

Once the family was left alone, my terrified sisters-in-law broke into sobs. Rebbetzin Rubin held them gently in her arms and tried to soothe them. The Rebbe and his sons stepped aside to *daven Minchah*. The powerful words of *Ashrei*, "Fortunate are those who dwell in your house," provided a bit of comfort to the Rubins on that dreary afternoon.

My mother-in-law brought out food, but no one was hungry. Recounting the experiences of our forefathers, she encouraged the children not to lose *bitachon*, and urged them to say *Tehillim*. All the children, from the oldest to the youngest, heeded their mother's words.

Just as the Rubins were about to drop off to sleep, the door to their shabby room was suddenly flung open. A number of hostile Hungarian and German soldiers burst in and ordered the Rubins to surrender their rucksacks. Frozen with terror, the Rubins watched the soldiers ransack their belongings and toss them on the floor. Little Shprintza began to cry in her mother's arms. In a mocking tone, the soldiers told the Rubins that they would be back later. Then they left, slamming the door behind them.

When evening came, the Rubins slept on the hard earth, shivering with cold and terror.

THE RUBINS PREPARED FOR SHABBOS IN THEIR DISMAL SURROUNDINGS.
Although the atmosphere was hardly conducive to the spirit of

Shabbos in the Ghetto

Shabbos, the Rubins beckoned in the Shabbos Queen just as they had always done before.

Throughout that Shabbos, as the frightened children looked to their father for guidance, the Rebbe gently assured them that they had nothing to fear because they put their lives into the hands of the A-mighty every day. The boys accompanied him as he sang *zemiros,* and the haunting melodies brought a measure of *menuchah* and eased the tension somewhat.

The Rubins spent most of that Shabbos *davening.* Their intense cries soared beyond the four mildewy walls, the ramshackle roof and the entire ghetto itself, straight to *Shamayim.* According to the Talmud, the voices of our forefathers split the Heavens when they recited the psalms of *Hallel* in Jerusalem on Pesach (Tractate *Pesachim*). The Rubins' prayers on that particular Shabbos must have reached and split the Heavens with the same magnitude.

APPROXIMATELY TWO WEEKS AFTER THE RUBINS' ARRIVAL, A NEW decree was issued: all boys and men between the ages of 16 and 60

The Labor Brigade

would be taken away to *arbeitslagers* (work camps) where they would be consigned to hard labor under the supervision of the Hungarian army and the SS. My brothers-in-law were no exception, and one day the gendarmes stormed into their dark room and ordered them to pack. They had only 10 minutes to get their meager belongings together and say goodbye to the most important people in their lives, their beloved family. Their heads spun. The teenagers looked at the crestfallen faces surrounding them, not knowing what to say. What could they say?

My father-in-law handed his sons *siddurim* and *tefillin,* and gave each son a *gartel* to wear around his waist. My tearful mother-in-law and her daughters quickly assembled most of what little food they had left and packed the items into rucksacks. The anguished parents were overwhelmed with worry about what would happen to their sons. Little did they realize how much worse things could have been: by working in the labor brigade, R'Shmuel Shmelka and R'Mordechai David would be spared the fate of being sent to the extermination camps.

Within moments the gendarmes returned. I can only imagine how helpless my husband's parents and sisters felt as they watched the two youths being led away at gunpoint.

The gendarmes took away approximately two hundred forty men and teenage boys from the ghetto that day and marched them to a waiting train. By nightfall, the train arrived at a labor camp and the new labor brigade was met by SS soldiers who directed the exhausted group of men and youths to an empty wooden barrack and shoved them in. There was no place to sleep except on the floor.

The following day, the group was taken to the town of Toplitza but was not put to work. Instead, the SS marched everyone to the Marosh River and locked them inside a building for the night. From there, they were dragged off to another *arbeitslager* in Toplitza where the SS ordered them to march back and forth on the premises for several hours. The soldiers then forced the group to stand at attention for a seemingly endless period of time before dismissing them for the night.

Nighttime provided little, if any, relief for the exhausted laborers. Often the SS did not allow the men to sleep in peace.

One night, while my brothers-in-law and the other workers were still in Toplitza, a ruthless SS man woke the men with shouts of *"Abresto! Abresto!* (Get up! Get up!)" Startled and groggy, the men were rushed out of the barrack into the chill night air and led to the river. The SS man ordered everyone to march into the river. Barely able to see in the dark, the frightened victims soon found themselves chin-deep in icy water. The SS man ordered them to halt. As he stared at the terrified, shivering young men and boys, some of whom were already weeping and crying out the *Viduy*, the sadistic SS man burst out laughing. Moments later, the

German ordered everyone out of the river and back to the unheated barrack. With no clothes to change into, the men trembled and shivered in their soggy garments all night long. By morning, many of them were ill.

As the days and weeks passed, the laborers' stomachs shrank from lack of food. In the morning they were given weak, foul-tasting "coffee"; at noontime they ate watered-down soup with a few pieces of barley, beans or rotten potatoes; and at dusk, they received another cup of "coffee."

Once a week, the laborers were given small portions of bread. Each group of two men received a slice of coarse black bread called *"kumis,"* measuring approximately four to five inches by two inches. The bread happened to be distributed on Friday mornings. My brothers-in-law waited the few hours for sundown in order to welcome Shabbos and say a proper *Kiddush* over the whole piece of bread.

Toward the end of May, my brothers-in-law and the others were assigned to lay tracks in a railroad yard. From there, they were taken to an airplane landing field to assemble airplane parts. Their next stop was the town of Manos-Falva, where they were once again assigned to work on the train rails.

On Friday morning, June 2nd, my brothers-in-law were lining up with the others at the Manos-Falva station for early morning "coffee." A short distance away, they saw a long string of cattle cars pulling into the station. Suddenly, my brothers-in-law and the others heard people calling their names. The cries were coming from the direction of the cattle cars. Forgetting for a moment that they were under heavy guard, the laborers rushed toward the train. Their hearts pounded as they got closer: the people in the cattle cars were their families and friends from home!

My father-in-law saw his sons in the distance and called out to them through a small, barbed-wire-enclosed slit at the side of the cattle car. My sister-in-law Mirel, (today the Sawasher Rebbitzin), then standing at her father's side in the stuffed cattle car, still remembers his words: "Mother is here! Your sisters are here! Don't be *machmir* (strict) on *she'eilos* (questions) of *issur d'rabbanan* (rabbinical prohibitions). Do what you can to stay alive!"

Those were to be his last words to his sons.

As R' Shmuel Shmelka and R' Mordechai David tried to catch more of what their father was saying, the gendarmes and SS dashed toward them and chased them away from the train. Other SS men hurried toward the train and spoke to the conductor. The train sped away from the station. As it turned out, that was the train which would carry my beloved, esteemed parents-in-law and their three sweet, innocent young daughters, Yocheved, Mirel and Shprintza, to Auschwitz.

During the sweltering months of July and August, the men and teenage boys were transported to the town of Ilva, Hungary, where they were forced to build a railroad roundhouse. This excessive physical labor beneath the scorching sun was excruciating for the workers, whose badly sunburned skin became inflamed and covered with blisters. Many also suffered from work-related injuries caused by handling sharp pieces of metal track and tools. The SS stood in the shade, sipping ice water and cold beer while snickering at the sweaty, dehydrated laborers struggling to get through another excruciating day of work.

By the end of the summer, my brothers-in-law and the others had been reduced to walking skeletons. Their soiled clothing hung on their bony frames.

One warm September day while the workmen were still toiling over the railroad tracks in Ilva, the SS ordered the entire brigade to line up. The SS pushed them into cattle cars. Inside the train, the men tried to figure out where they were headed. There had been rumors around camp that the Russian army was quickly advancing and the Germans were retreating just as quickly to remain one step ahead of their adversaries. Some men speculated about where they were going; perhaps to Solnika, Hungary? In their weakened state, however, many no longer cared.

Since the SS were constantly looking out for advancing Russians, they were cautious about traveling. Train schedules were disrupted; sometimes the train stopped at a station for a long period of time, sometimes the train changed course and went in the opposite direction. As a result, it took approximately three weeks for the transport to reach its destination, which was indeed Solnika. It was a brisk October day in 1944 when the train finally pulled into the station.

For the entire course of the three-week journey, the men of the brigade were forced to remain inside the stuffy cattle cars. The Germans fed the laborers diluted "soup" which was eaten inside the cars, and occasionally allowed someone to empty the waste bucket and to fetch a pail of fresh water. When the SS finally allowed the half-dead laborers to alight, the emaciated men gulped in the crisp clean country air. Even though they were in vast fields and could easily have lost themselves in the tall wild grass, no one dared think about escaping. They were too weak to outrun the scores of SS men surrounding them.

As with many other Holocaust survivors, fate took a strange twist for my brothers-in-law and the other religious men in their group. They did not have to work on Rosh Hashanah and Yom Kippur because they were still confined in the cattle cars. Some of the men had calendars, so they knew the exact dates of the *yamim tovim*. The *bitachon* and *ahavas Hashem* of my brothers-in-law remained steadfast, even in their hopeless situation. They and others tearfully *davened*, asking that the A-mighty inscribe and seal their names into the *Book of Life*. On Yom Kippur, my brothers-in-law gave their "soup" portions to those who were unable to fast.

In Solnika, the Germans continued to mock the fragile, half-dead slave laborers and to make their lives miserable. Working conditions remained difficult and hazardous and the abrupt change of weather was a further shock to their already weakened bodies. The brisk fall winds whipped straight through to their bones, no longer insulated by fatty tissue. Mornings were especially difficult; at roll call, their teeth chattered and they shivered in their thin clothing, which was threadbare and caked with dirt. Some men had lost their will to live. However, my brothers-in-law managed to keep their hopes up; they still had each other. Fond memories of their family in happier times and hopes of seeing them again gave them the will to try to survive.

One Shabbos in mid-October, their brigade was not assigned any work. Instead, an SS man took the group to a steep hill covered with sharp, jagged stones. Using his machine-gun to point, the German indicated a side road and ordered the laborers to climb the hill. When the workers reached the top, panting with exertion, the German ordered the men to tumble down the hill! The men gaped at one another in disbelief. Their skin would be torn and lacerated if they were to obey this insane order!

The machine-gun pointing in their direction left them no choice, and the men began rolling down the hill. Miraculously, everyone made it down to the bottom, banged up and bruised but still alive. This infuriated the SS man, who ordered the men back up the hill and forced them to tumble down once again. And again. Although in agonizing pain, my brothers-in-law and the others managed to survive this ordeal nine times within 2 hours. The German finally tired of this unique form of torture and allowed the battered men to stop.

A Narrow Escape

DAYS LATER, THE WORKERS WERE TRANSPORTED TO AN AREA IN Solnika that overlooked the Danube River. One bitterly cold night, the Germans discovered that the Red Army was practically on their heels. The only way to stall the Russians was to blow up the massive bridge that towered over the river. The labor brigade was instantly ordered to set mines on the bridge, then blow it up. The panicked Germans ordered the men to do the job quickly — or else.

The men had to walk to a warehouse about a mile away, and carry back metal boxes filled with dynamite. Since the boxes were heavy, two men were assigned to each box. Once the men had retrieved all the metal boxes, the Germans handed them pieces of wire and ordered them to start mining the bridge.

The men were exposed as they worked, easy targets from any angle. As usual, the possibility existed that the Germans would begin spraying them with machine-gun fire. But now they were in danger as well of being shot by the Russians. If bullets were to start flying, and if any would hit the dynamite, the workmen could be blown to smithereens within seconds. My brothers-in-law were convinced that the pounding of their hearts could be heard a mile away.

The men had not yet finished mining the bridge when they heard frantic shouts from the Germans to get back inside the transport train, at the far end of the bridge. The German cowards ran right behind them, jumping on board without looking back or locking the doors of the cattle cars. The train took off like a shot. Bewildered men toppled over one another as the train hurtled down the track at full throttle, then made a sharp turn. It seemed that they were all about to fall through the open doors and plunge into the icy river below.

Suddenly, a violent tremor shook the entire train. Everyone looked backward and watched in horror as the entire bridge blew up behind them. In a matter of seconds, the huge, solid structure came apart and pieces of wood and metal debris were flung into the air. Sections of the bridge crashed into the water. Even though they were some distance away inside the cattle car, everyone had to shield himself from the flying fragments.

The noise of the explosion continued for a few more seconds, then, in the eerie silence which followed, the workmen began to shake violently. Some wept quietly, while others remained in a state of shock. My brothers-in-law whispered their thanks to the A-mighty for their narrow escape.

Later the men found out what had happened. The Russian Army was approximately three kilometers away from the bridge when, from a distance, they saw the Germans surrounding it. The Russians started shooting, causing the Germans to panic and order everyone back onto the train.

THE BRIGADE WAS TRANSPORTED ONCE MORE. AT THE TOWN OF Felso Galla, they were assigned more rail work. On Friday,

Early Signs of Freedom
December 22, 1944, the group awoke to the sounds of explosions and felt the ground shake beneath them. Hope and optimism prevailed. Were the Russians advancing? Would their cruel captors finally be defeated? Or would the Germans force them to move to another undisclosed location?

Soon they had an answer. The Germans stormed into the barrack and ordered everyone outside for work detail. While the laborers worked on the tracks, British airplanes flew overhead and bombed the station house. The train and platform were blown up along with the small building. My brothers-in-law and the other men ran for cover. The terrified Germans also sought shelter. As soon as the planes disappeared into the clouds, the Germans ordered the men back to work.

Later in the day, stranger than usual events began to occur. First the Germans ordered the men back to the barrack, with no explanation at all. A couple of hours later, they ordered the workers out of the barrack and marched them to an aluminum factory one kilometer away.

The Germans abandoned the aluminum factory for a few hours, leaving the laborers on their own. Shabbos had arrived. Morale was up. Had the Germans run away? In spite of their hopes, nobody attempted to step outside. Much to their disappointment, however, the Germans returned on *motza'ei* Shabbos, barking orders at the men to load aluminum pieces on trains bound for Germany.

For 72 hours straight, the brigade carried the heavy stacks of aluminum to the trains. Tasting freedom close by, they poured their last reserves of strength into the task they fervently hoped would be their final work assignment.

On one trip back to the train, R' Mordechai David dropped a heavy piece of aluminum on his foot. He cried out in pain and fell. R' Shmuel Shmelka began to run toward his brother, but the Germans stopped him. They forced R' Mordechai David to pull himself off the ground and pick up the heavy load himself. Clenching his teeth in pain, R' Mordechai David struggled to comply as his brother stood by helplessly and watched.

ON MONDAY EVENING, DECEMBER 25TH, THE GERMANS MARCHED the men back to the aluminum factory building, which was by then

A Plea and a Decision
completely empty. Exhausted, most of the men fell asleep on the bare floor. R' Shmuel Shmelka was finally able to examine his brother's foot. It had become swollen and infected, and R' Mordechai David moaned in pain. R' Shmuel Shmelka tore off a piece of clothing and used it to bandage his brother's wounded foot. Soon R' Mordechai David fell asleep next to his brother on the floor.

Sometime during the night, the men awoke to the thunder of explosions. The ground trembled beneath them. Several Germans raced into the factory, shouting, *"Alle raus! Alle raus!"* Unable to pull himself to his feet, R'Mordechai David begged his brother to leave without him. Much against his will, R'Shmuel Shmelka was forced outside with the others, while R'Mordechai David remained behind with the other weak and injured men.

The men lined up just yards away from the aluminum factory. This was the first time that my two brothers-in-law had been separated since being conscripted into the forced labor detail, and R'

Shmuel Shmelka was sick with worry, with the knowledge that he could not protect his brother from the Germans.

Suddenly, as if in a dream, R' Shmuel Shmelka saw R' Mordechai David limping toward him! How had he managed to pass the Germans without getting shot? This was nothing short of a miracle! R' Mordechai David finally reached his brother, crying that he could not bear to be separated from him, and pleading with R' Shmuel Shmelka to return with him to the factory.

Even though R' Shmuel Shmelka wanted to comply with his brother's request, he realized that it would be impossible for him to leave his place, as the Germans had already counted him. But finally, unable to continue denying his brother's pleas, R' Shmuel Shmelka stepped out of line and followed his brother into the factory. The two of them managed to slip past the guards at the door to the factory, and quickly found places on the floor.

A short while later, a panicked German dashed into the factory with news: they were surrounded by Russians and would have to move out quickly! He ordered the men to follow him outside, but they remained on the floor, too exhausted to obey. The room grew still.

The frantic German pointed his revolver at the man closest to the door, which happened to be R' Shmuel Shmelka. Pressing the cold gun barrel against his forehead, he bellowed, "Come with me!"

"I am sick. I cannot move," R' Shmuel Shmelka responded quietly.

The German held his position for a few more seconds, the gun still pressed against R' Shmuel Shmelka's head. R' Shmuel Shmelka tried to maintain outward calm, but inside he was trembling. Finally, as if in slow motion, he felt the pressure ease and the gun was removed. The German moved on to the next man, then the next, repeating his words and actions with each until he reached the last one. The men continued to lie face down on the floor, many with their eyes closed, trembling.

The exasperated German moved to the back of the room. Suddenly the silence was shattered by a loud blast of gunfire;

the German had fired a shot into the ceiling. "Fools!" he screamed. "Don't you realize the Russians will kill you when they find you?" Nobody responded. Finally the German walked out of the factory, alone.

Right there on the ground, R' Shmuel Shmelka and R' Mordechai David fell asleep, too exhausted at the time to fully appreciate the miracle that had just occurred. (Later they learned that only a handful of those men who had marched off with the Germans survived. They were taken to Austria, where many perished in the notorious Mauthausen death camp.)

Sometime later, loud bombs and powerful ground vibrations jolted everyone in the factory building awake. The men opened their eyes to bolts of blinding white lightning, as shrapnel and fragments of shattered glass flew all over. Instinctively shielding their heads with their hands, everyone ran for cover, but when the roof above their heads blew off, there was no place left to hide. Some of the men began to panic.

A few veterans of the First World War can be credited with saving their comrades. With measured calm they explained the necessity of finding an underground bunker in which to hide. Assuring the others that they would recognize a safe hiding place when they found one, the former veterans led the others out of the factory. R' Mordechai David leaned on his brother for support.

Bombs were exploding everywhere, but the weak and sickly victims quickly adjusted to the grave danger. Drawing on unknown and unsuspected reserves of energy, they managed to run to save their lives. In spite of his wounded foot, R' Mordechai David kept up with the others.

They ran into a field of wild sugar beets. Some of the men, including R' Shmuel Shmelka, managed to yank a few beets out of the frozen ground and shove them into their pockets. When one of the veterans discovered an underground bunker, the others hastily followed him through the narrow entrance.

Before entering the bunker, a few men had noticed that the sky was getting lighter: the sun was rising! A new day was dawning.

Would these be their last moments as prisoners? Would they finally be free men again? It was Tuesday, December 26, 1944.

The bunker was dark and airless, but it protected the men from the bombs, flying shrapnel and whizzing bullets. Those who had sugar beets in their pockets took them out and shared them with the others, devouring the dirt-coated vegetables in two or three bites.

As the men tensely sat in the bunker, they were aware of the earth rumbling over their heads. Little did they know they were sitting beneath advancing Russian tanks! Ultimately the bunker stopped shaking and silence prevailed in their tiny hiding place.

The younger men turned to the veterans. What should they do now? A few people wanted to go outside immediately, but the older men felt it would be safer to first make sure that the bombing would not resume. After a few hours of stillness, everyone agreed to exit the bunker.

Liberation

ONCE OUTSIDE, MY BROTHERS-IN-LAW AND THEIR COMPANIONS SAW a red flag flapping in the wind, not too far from where they were standing. The Russian army had arrived, and the area was liberated! A handful of Russian soldiers approached the laborers, shocked to see this group of bloody, dirty, skeletal men.

The stillness was broken when a Russian soldier noticed R' Shmuel Shmelka concealing something in his pants pocket. Fearing it might be a hand grenade, the soldier motioned to my brother-in-law to surrender whatever he was hiding. The Russian's face grew visibly more tense as he watched my brother-in-law reach into his pocket ... and take out a beet. An expression of relief crossed the soldier's visage when he realized it was not an explosive, while nervous laughter skittered among the soldiers and newly liberated men.

"You are now free, comrades," said the Russians. "Throw your dirty beets away. We have bread and soup for everyone."

HAD MY BROTHERS-IN-LAW AND THE OTHER FORMER PRISONERS not been so weak, they would have cheered and danced. But all

Freedom and Hardship

they could do now was manage weak smiles as they collapsed onto the cold ground.

The soldiers told the group, "You are free to go now. *Dwey domo.* (Go home.)"

After being held captive for so long, my brothers-in-law and the others could barely absorb the import of these words. Were they dreaming or were they actually free to go wherever they wanted without anyone standing over them? My brothers-in-law and most of their companions were weak, but not ill. With a little sleep and some light food, they would be able to get on their feet and slowly move on. Many other survivors required hospital care after liberation. Had my husband or I been there, we would not have been able to leave on our own.

Now it was time for my brothers-in-law to go home, as the soldiers had said, or at least find out if "home" still existed. Who in the family was still alive?

R' Shmuel Shmelka and R' Mordechai David hoped they would find most of their relatives, including their parents. They decided to begin their search in the town of Alba Iulia, Romania, and prepared to set out on the long journey to the home of their sister, Rebbetzin Channah Kahana.

My brothers-in-law traveled light. The only possessions they were left with after the war were their *siddurim* and *tefillin*, which they had managed to hide and hold on to during their captivity in the labor camps. Being able to fulfill the *mitzvah* of putting on *tefillin* every day raised their morale during those dark days.

The Russians did not send them off with food rations, and since they had no money, they would have no means to purchase food. They also had no means of transportation, and would have to travel by foot. By then, walking had become an excruciating ordeal.

Their own shoes had fallen apart ages ago and their feet were encased in makeshift footgear consisting of pieces of wood held together by strands of wire.

The brothers began their journey. On their first night of freedom, my brothers-in-law approached a farm alongside the road and told the farmer they were Hungarians who had been imprisoned by the Germans. Now liberated by the Russians, they added, they were on their way home.

These words apparently frightened the farmer. Russian soldiers had been going from one village to another and looting houses. Afraid that my brothers-in-law had some connection with the Russians and might attempt to rob him, he tried to placate them. He invited them in and served them a light meal of bread and milk, which my brothers-in-law consumed ravenously.

After the meal, the farmer led my brothers-in-law to a bedroom. For the first time in many months, the youths slept in comfort on a real bed and enjoyed the luxury of quilted blankets. The following morning, R' Mordechai David and R' Shmuel Shmelka bade their host farewell and thanked him for his hospitality. They would not enjoy such a luxurious night again until they reached Alba Iulia. Subsequent farmers would only provide them with shelter in their barns.

Over the next couple of days, they begged farmers for fruit from their orchards or a small cup of milk from their cows. Many of the peasants took pity on my brothers-in-law, especially on R' Mordechai David, and allowed them to pick apples or pears from their trees. Other farmers sent them to the cows' barn for milk. On some occasions, my brothers-in-law even milked the cows themselves.

By Friday afternoon, R' Shmuel Shmelka and R' Mordechai David realized they had to stop for Shabbos. They found an abandoned barn and rested there from sundown Friday until early Sunday morning. R' Mordechai David was especially grateful to have this time to rest. Without medical help, he knew he would have to rely solely upon the Doctor in Heaven to heal his injured foot.

Early Sunday morning they left the barn and continued on their journey. A few days later they reached the Danube River. They needed to get across the Danube to reach their destination, but the river was too deep for them to wade through, and too wide for them to swim across. There were no bridges to walk over, nor were there any available boats to ferry them to the other side.

As they sat by the water's edge trying to figure out a solution to this problem, some other Hungarian survivors, who were also trying to find their way home by foot, stopped to speak with my brothers-in-law. They informed them of a riverfront town about ten or twelve kilometers away where they might find a way to cross the Danube.

The strain of the long walk took its toll on R' Shmuel Shmelka and R' Mordechai David, but their determination and strong will enabled them to persevere. Hours later they finally reached the town and met some other survivors also desiring to cross the river. They proceeded together to the riverbank, where they found a small raft tied to a tree. They helped one another onto the unsteady craft which bobbed up and down in the choppy waters. The current seemed to pull them in the opposite direction from where they wanted to go, and the men tried desperately to push the raft forward with branches, which served as oars. The raft was pushed back several times by the current, but they did not give up.

When they finally reached the other side of the river, the passengers all toppled off the raft and dropped to the ground. My brothers-in-law bid farewell to the others and decided to rest before continuing their journey.

R' Shmuel Shmelka and R' Mordechai David awoke from their short nap and looked up to see guns pointed at their faces by Russian soldiers. They froze in disbelief. Was this a nightmare, or was it really happening? They had just been liberated by Russian soldiers, only to be held at gunpoint by others!

The soldiers ordered R' Shmuel Shmelka and R' Mordechai David to get up and follow them, threatening to send the two to Siberia if they dared make any escape attempts.

My brothers-in-law slowly rose and allowed the Russians to take them away. They soon found themselves at another rail yard, repairing damaged rail lines for the Russians. Other wandering survivors who had been captured by these Russian soldiers were also working on the rails. By nightfall, the Russian soldiers marched my brothers-in-law and the others to a barrack.

The Russians left without closing the door. My brothers-in-law weighed their options. Should they try to escape? Was the open door a sign from Heaven?

Among the prisoners was a man by the name of Mr. Mendel Stein who overheard their conversation and advised them against escaping. My brothers-in-law decided to take the risk, and invited Mr. Stein and the other workers to join them. Tragically, Mr. Stein and the other workers who stayed behind were taken to Siberia. We heard that they spent the next 10 to 15 years of their lives there.

My brothers-in-law tiptoed unnoticed out of the barrack and continued walking until they were some distance away from their new Russian captors. They resumed their routine of journeying along the roads by day and sleeping in barns at night. Sometimes the local farmers gave them a piece of bread, a cup of milk, or some fruit.

To their shock, my brothers-in-law were once again stopped on the road — this time, by a Russian officer. The officer claimed he had heard my brothers-in-law speaking Yiddish, and asked them if they were Jews. Yes, they answered truthfully. The officer motioned that they should follow him.

Their hearts pounding wildly, the two young men dutifully followed the officer. Much to their surprise, the officer led them into the army kitchen and motioned them to a long counter. He handed them extra rations of bread, followed by cups of steaming hot coffee. Puzzled over the unexpected kindness of this Russian, my brothers-in-law stared at one another in amazement. Was he being sincere or did he want something? What could they possibly offer a Russian officer? They waited to see what would happen next.

The officer assured them that everything was all right. Looking over his shoulder to make sure that nobody else was watching, he reached into his pocket, slipped them a hundred-pengo coin, and advised them to clear out as soon as possible. As they left, the officer gave them several loaves of bread. He insisted on escorting them to the tracks, where he helped them get places on a train heading east. "I am also a Jew," the officer whispered by way of explanation as they parted.

Once they were safely aboard the train, my brothers-in-law wondered who this helpful and kind man was. Where did he come from? Indeed, his appearing to them out of the blue was like the appearing of an angel sent by the A-mighty to help them out of their difficult situation.

The train was jammed with Russian soldiers and other survivors wandering through Europe, trying to find their way home. Wedged in among hordes of people, it was not a terribly comfortable ride; however, compared to the trips in cattle cars, sitting on ordinary train seats was practically a luxury.

Since this train's run ended far from their destination, my brothers-in-law spent the next few days getting on and off other eastbound trains. They were able to survive on small amounts of food, purchased with the money they had received from the Russian officer.

Before dawn on a Friday morning they arrived in Arad, Romania, a town on the border between Romania and Hungary. They wandered into the empty train station and found places to sleep for a couple of hours. When it was light enough outside, my brothers-in-law walked into town. Much to their happiness, they discovered a *shul*. There was actually a Jewish community remaining in Arad!

My brothers-in-law were welcomed warmly by the Romanian Jews as they entered the *beis midrash*. The men in *shul* immediately realized that my brothers-in-law were camp survivors and were shocked over how emaciated and ragged they looked. After *davening Shacharis,* the men in the shul invited R' Shmuel Shmelka and R' Mordechai David to join them for a light breakfast. My brothers-in-law learned that the Jewish community of Arad was one of the few which had not been destroyed by the Germans.

One of the men approached them and asked if they were the sons of Szaszregen Rebbe, R' Yaakov Yisrael V'Yeshurin Rubin. This man was R' Walvesh Motzen, the *shochet* of Arad, a very pious man who was well-regarded in the community. R' Motzen said he had once known their father and had the utmost respect for him.

My brothers-in-law eagerly asked R' Motzen whether he might have heard anything about the whereabouts of their father or anyone else in their family. R' Motzen sadly answered that he had not, and asked my brothers-in-law when they had last seen their parents, and where they had gone after that. R' Shmuel Shmelka and R' Mordechai David told him the story of what had happened at Manos-Falva when they spotted their family on the train, and about their own experiences in the labor camps. They then informed R' Motzen that they were heading toward Alba Iulia, Romania, to look for their family.

R' Motzen decided that my brothers-in-law, who looked so tired and thin, needed a rest. He invited them back to his home, a short distance away, and insisted that they not leave until they had put on some weight.

In their weakened condition, the two youths were only too happy to accept his warm invitation. Upon arriving at the Motzen household, they were introduced to Rebbetzin Motzen and the rest of the family. Tears filled the Rebbetzin's eyes when she saw how wan and emaciated my brothers-in-law looked.

During the next couple of weeks, the brothers took hot baths with strong soap, received freshly laundered clothing, and enjoyed the luxury of sleeping in real beds again. R' Mordechai David's foot was properly cleaned and bandaged.

They also ate delicious food prepared by the Rebbetzin. Since R' Motzen was a *shochet,* he continually brought home meat for the family. The Rebbetzin prepared mouth-watering *fleishig* meals; she and her husband urged their houseguests to eat the *fleishig* meals twice a day, if possible. As with the rest of us who survived the camps, my brothers-in-law's stomachs had shrunken to the point where they were unable to consume too much food — especially at the heavier *fleishig* meals — at one sitting.

About two weeks later my brothers-in-law had filled out a bit and some color had returned to their faces. It was time to continue their journey to Alba Iulia. Along with their *siddurim* and *tefillin* from home, the Rebbetzin sent them off with clean clothing and food.

Once again they traveled on trains full of Russian soldiers. The trip from Arad to Alba Iulia was treacherous at times. At one point, the train heading east was overcrowded, so my brothers-in-law hoisted themselves on top of one of the train cars. As the train roared over the tracks, they were terrified of falling off, either as a result of the force of the winds whipping through and around them, or as a result of the sharp turns.

At one point, the train approached a tunnel. R' Shmuel Shmelka and R' Mordechai David closed their eyes and prayed. Even though the train (along with its two extra passengers riding on top) fit easily under the top of the tunnel, my brothers-in-law had visions of being crushed to death. When they finally opened their eyes they were relieved to see that they were back in the open air again.

After two days of travel balanced on that precarious perch, the two of them found room inside the train. R' Shmuel Shmelka and R' Mordechai David were astonished to discover that windburn had reddened their cheeks.

This was the last leg of their journey. Approximately four weeks after liberation, my two brothers-in-law arrived at Alba Iulia eagerly anticipating a reunion with their family. This expectation was only partly fulfilled, and over time they learned who had survived the war and who had perished.

CHAPTER 10
Adjusting After the Churban-Shoah

OUR DAYS IN FEHRENWALD PASSED SLOWLY AND QUIETLY. My husband, R' Rubin, continued with his learning. As for me, my bout with typhus had left me in a weakened state, and sitting outside in the warm autumn sunshine helped speed my recovery. Some color returned to my pallid face, and I began to regain my health.

The Yeshivah

The nights were bad. Terrible dreams held us in their grip night after night, and sometimes I cried out in my sleep for my beloved father and mother. My husband and I tried as best we could to comfort one another.

The Klausenburger-Sanzer Rebbe, R' Halberstam, *zt"l*, taking what was considered an innovative step for a Chassidic Rebbe, established a *mussar shiur* for women. My husband considered these lessons part of the order of the day, which was to strengthen the *emunah* of the people, weakened so terribly during the Holocaust.

The Klausenburger Rebbe z"tl

Actually, what happened during the Holocaust was definitely above nature, unexplainable. However, only *"mevinim"* realized that.

R' Halberstam established a yeshivah in the D.P. camp, in the same building as the *beis midrash.* Although the school was not large, it was adequate. The boys grew to respect and love their *Rosh HaYeshivah,* and began to feel hopeful about life again.

One day, R' Halberstam unexpectedly sent for my husband and informed him that he was preparing to travel to America on a fundraising mission for his yeshivah and community in Fehrenwald. He asked my husband to assume the temporary position of acting *Rosh HaYeshivah* in his absence.

My husband, R' Rubin's short tenure as acting *Rosh HaYeshivah* was an enjoyable and unforgettable experience, filled with new challenges and rewards. In accordance with the European yeshivah style, the *Rosh HaYeshivah* gave a daily *shiur* in *Gemara* (Talmud) and *Tosafos.* There was nothing more rewarding than to share the enthusiasm of the *bachurim* as they completed a section of *Gemara* and *Tosafos.*

My husband also shared in the pain and tears of his *talmidim.* Sometimes the loss of their parents, siblings, and other family members was too much for the youngsters to bear. It was, however, a source of comfort for them to have my husband nearby, knowing he cared and worried about them as if they were his own. One of the leading *talmidei chachamim* in the yeshivah, R' Judah Rosenberg, *z"l,* was a tremendous support to the yeshivah and to my husband during that time. They continued to converse about halachic matters for many years to come.

Three months later, R' Halberstam returned, reassuming his position as Rebbe and *Rosh HaYeshivah*, and continuing to be an inspiration to the Chassidic community.

Helping Others to Start Over

OTHERS IN THE CAMP REGARDED US WITH AT LEAST A LITTLE BIT OF amazement and awe. We were the very exceptional couple, as both of us had survived the war and then managed to overcome the innumerable obstacles that might have prevented us from finding each other. Sometimes we assumed the role of surrogate parents to many young men and women who were lost, alone and broken-hearted. Some of these individuals had been married, or were about to be married, when the 12-year Reign of Terror burst into their lives like a murderous tornado. In order to help these forlorn individuals create new lives out of the ashes, people were trying to arrange *shidduchim*.

Although the order of the day was to rebuild Jewish family life, a huge problem existed. Tangible or documented proof that one's spouse had actually died in the Holocaust did not always exist (the records from Auschwitz and Theresienstadt were not yet available), and therefore many surviving spouses found themselves in the untenable position of technically still being married (even though their spouses were in all probability no longer alive), and needed to be permitted to remarry and begin new families. This halachic problem, the *"agunah"* issue, affected Jewish survivors throughout Europe. Eventually the rabbi from Niamz, Romania, was accepted as the authority regarding these *halachos*. He worked out guidelines to solve the problem and put his full authority behind his *psak*, thus allowing the bereaved survivors to remarry.

BY THE WINTER OF 1946-47, WE FELT AS IF WE HAD BEGUN TO RECOVER .
It was time to move on — but where should we go?

D.P. Leipheim   We doubt that we would have stayed in Germany had it not been for R' Baruch Yehuda Leibowitz, *z"l*, the Rabbi-*shochet* of Hallash, Hungary. A very strong-minded and energetic individual, he was intensely Chassidic and deeply committed to the furtherment of *Yiddishkeit*. While we were in Fehrenwald, R' Leibowitz served as both rabbi and *shochet* in the D.P. camp of Leipheim, Bavaria, one of the largest Displaced Persons camps. In early 1947, he came to us with an unexpected proposition: would my husband become the Chief Rabbi of the D.P. camp in Leipheim?

He explained that the large camp, consisting of approximately 3,000 desolate Jewish survivors, did not have a full-time rabbi. The schools were controlled by non-religious organizations; the camp lacked proper *kashrus* supervision; it had no *mikveh* (ritual bath), and no one to properly advise the survivors regarding matters of marriage and family purity.

R' Leibowitz painted a poignant picture of people in distress, noting that not only had many of the people in the camp lost all their loved ones, their homes, and their possessions — but they were now in great danger of losing their *Yiddishkeit* as well. This was particularly true of the youth. A school teaching secular subjects had been established by the Department of Culture of the *Sochnut HaYehudit* (Jewish Agency), the Palestine-based organization set up by various non-religious Zionist groups, which acted as the Jewish "government" in Palestine during the British Mandate. The *Sochnut* had an office in Munich from which it provided certain educational, cultural and social services to the people in the D.P. camps. Among the camp's inhabitants were families from Budapest and Romania who had survived the deportations. The children would need a *cheder*, R' Leibowitz stressed, to keep them on the path of Torah.

But not only the youngsters were in need of spiritual guidance. Some of the older people, once religious, had become depressed as

R' Rubin in Leipheim DP camp — Left: Performing his duties as Chief Rabbi.
Right: Walking through the camp with the secretaries of the rabbinical office.

a result of what had been done to European Jewry by yesterday's "friends" and "civilized" people. These poor Jews, young and old, would need a competent, compassionate, kindhearted rebbe to guide them and help them find their way back to *Yiddishkeit*. Could we move into the Leipheim camp?

My husband had serious doubts about accepting this position; he was not sure he would be up to the task of serving as rabbi to so large a group of people. After all, he was still young, and his only experience consisted of observing his father at home and in the *beis midrash*.

The large community of Leipheim would be looking to its rabbi for hope and answers. Would my husband be able to bear such an awesome burden on his shoulders? We were not even sure we wanted to remain in Europe. My husband, always appreciative toward my uncle, the Satmar Rebbe, for his devotion to me, knew how much I wanted to be reunited with the Teitelbaums. As a result, we were seriously considering the option of traveling to Palestine to stay with them despite the difficulties. Another option was to travel to the United States and start a new life there, although the doors of the United States were not open for us at that time.

Nevertheless, R' Leibowitz pleaded with my husband to consider his request seriously. The community was in desperate need of a good, *heimishe* rabbi, and the position would be temporary. He assured my husband that we would be free to leave as soon as we made final plans regarding our future. As a further incentive, R' Leibowitz said that the camp administration would provide us with a comfortable apartment with all the conveniences we needed.

My husband told R' Leibowitz that he would need more time to decide, and wanted to discuss the offer with me. R' Leibowitz agreed to return in a few days for an answer.

We all needed help to heal our hearts, broken into a million pieces. We had to deal with suffering, with deep emotional wounds that began to open and bleed as the weeks and months passed. The initial shock was beginning to wear off, and we were only now beginning to fully comprehend the reality of what had been done to us, to our families, and to European Jewry. Even now, half a century later, it is still not fully comprehended. This seemingly impossible, unbelievable tragedy had truly occurred; the eyewitnesses could not be denied. We had to strengthen one another and rebuild the ruins. Even as I write this book today — half a century later — the memories remain incredibly difficult and painful to deal with.

My husband was keenly aware of his relative youth and inexperience as a rabbi and, courageous though he was, it was entirely natural and proper for him to entertain some doubts about accepting this position. I watched him sit quietly, trying to weigh the pros and cons. Even though we had plans of our own to make, I knew that his good heart ached for those Jewish refugees who needed his help. We talked long into the night about this truly daunting challenge. Where could he begin? How could he make these people feel whole again? Would he have the good fortune to arrange marriages and help young people rise from the ashes and reestablish families? Would he be able to advise them on whether they should remain in Europe, or start new lives abroad?

A major factor that influenced my husband's decision was the fact that R' H. Lichtenstein, zt"l, the venerable rabbi of Krasna and a close friend and admirer of my husband's late father, was the Chief Rabbi of another nearby camp, in Landsburg. My husband contacted R' Lichtenstein, who encouraged him to accept the position and promised to make himself available day and night for any questions my husband might have.

Thus it was that after considering all the pertinent factors, my husband and I agreed that he should accept this position. With the help of the A-mighty, my husband hoped he would successfully fulfill his obligations as Chief Rabbi of Leipheim.

R' Leibowitz, z"l, was enthusiastic and excited to learn of our decision. A handshake between the two *rabbanim*, R' Rubin and R' Leibowitz, made the appointment official. Within a few days our bags were packed and we bid farewell to the Klasuenburger Rebbe, to our friends, *talmidim* and acquaintances at Fehrenwald. We were off to Leipheim. My brothers-in-law, R' Shmuel Shmelka and R' Mordechai David decided not to leave Fehrenwald, since it had an environment of Torah and *Chassidus*. However, they did come to Leipheim sometimes for Shabbos, to visit with us.

THE CAMP DIRECTOR AND OFFICIAL REPRESENTATIVE OF U.N.R.A., the United Nations Relief Agency, at the Leipheim D.P. camp was

Respect for the Rabbinate Mrs. Robertson, a member of the cabinet from Ireland, who had volunteered to serve the survivors of the German-Nazi war machine. As soon as my husband and I arrived, she greeted us warmly and invited us to her office, where she outlined the background of the camp and explained the hopes she had for its future. Mrs. Robertson struck us immediately as a good-hearted, truly democratic lady. She sincerely seemed concerned about the many Jewish refugees wandering through the camp. As we were soon to find out, the same thing, ironically, could not be said for everyone involved in

Slowly the survivors began to rebuild their lives. Here, a young man (center) is about to be married. My husband is sitting immediately to the chassan's right.

Rabbi Rubin (holding a Kiddush cup) officiates at a wedding at Leipheim DP camp

Just before the chuppah. (L to R) Rabbi Rubin, the young chassan and a relative of the chassan's.

Rabbi Rubin at a seudas mitzvah with members of the congregation from the Leipheim DP camp. Seated to my husband's right is the Terzel Rav.

the camp community, especially the atheistic, left-wing *Sochnut* man who tried strenuously to turn the Jewish population against Torah and traditional Jewish values and customs. He and my husband were to have a few conflicts during my husband's tenure as Chief Rabbi there.

Mrs. Robertson showed us my husband's new office, which even included a telephone. We were amazed because telephones were a

relative rarity 50 years ago, particularly in the chaos that charac-
terized Europe immediately after the war. Certainly the use of a
telephone in Leipheim would make my husband's job much easier,
since he could more efficiently reach R' Lichtenstein and other *rabbanim* to consult with them about halachic issues. This was quite a
different situation than that which my martyred father-in-law, the
elder R' Rubin, *ztk"l*, had to contend with when he was Rabbi at an
internment camp during the First World War. He was completely
on his own, and had to answer *she'eilos* armed only with his own
considerable knowledge of Torah.

The fact that my husband had been assigned an office, particularly one with a phone, was a sign that the camp administration
apparently recognized the importance of having someone meet the
spiritual needs of the Jewish refugees there — even if the bureau-
crats at some of the ostensibly Jewish organizations (as we were
later to find out), did not.

Mrs. Robertson then escorted us to our new apartment. It was
newly furnished and filled with modern conveniences. For the first
time since our days in the ghetto, we had privacy.

After my husband and I had settled in, Mrs. Robertson gave us
a complete tour of the camp. It was a former *Luftwaffe* camp. We
saw blocks of similar-looking buildings, sectioned off by roads.
Many people were milling about; some staring into space. Word
was already out that a new rabbi had been appointed for the
community, and some of the people looked in our direction,
pointing and smiling. Perhaps he was just the person they were
waiting for, the one who would restore hope into their despondent
hearts.

Just as in Fehrenwald and other D.P. camps, the refugees in
Leipheim were trying to piece their lives back together. The Torah
tells us that when Lot's wife disobeyed the commands of the
A-mighty's angels and looked backwards after the destruction of

the wicked cities of Sodom and Gomorrah, she became a pillar of salt. The same could be said for the situation after the Holocaust. For those who had lost their *emunah* during the Holocaust years, or who did not have *emunah* in the first place, it was not difficult to look back at what had happened and become as cold emotionally as a pillar of salt. Such people became broken, empty, devastated, cynical, unfeeling and bitter. It would now be up to my husband to provide them with spiritual elevation.

In many ways Leipheim — a much larger camp — was physically different from the D.P. camp at Fehrenwald, although here, too, the Jewish survivors were housed in overcrowded, cramped quarters. It tore at my heart to see the victims of the worst tragedy ever known to humanity dwelling in such appalling conditions.

Unlike my husband, I had no official role in the camp, so I resolved to do what I could to aid him in his efforts.

Time passed quickly, and my husband soon gathered a group of single boys and formed a yeshivah. I prepared the meals for them — and remember frying over three hundred *latkes* for the *seder*. With the energetic assistance of R' Leibowitz and the help of the Joint Distribution Committee, my husband managed to bring in a *melamed* and establish a *cheder* for the youngest *talmidim* as well, in an attempt to counter the influence of the non-religious *Sochnut* school.

It was my husband's task to give daily *shiurim* in *halachah* and *parashas hashavua*, and talks about the importance of maintaining faith in the aftermath of the *Shoah* (Holocaust). On Fridays nights and Shabbos afternoon *shalosh seudos*, a *tish* took place, presided over by my husband. Over time, many young men and women came to us for advice.

ACCORDING TO *CHAZAL*,[1] A JEWISH COMMUNITY'S ABSOLUTE FIRST obligation is to build a *mikveh*, or ritual bath. The monthly visit to

The Mikveh   the *mikveh* is necessary for women to fulfill the halachic obligation of *taharas hamishpachah* — Jewish family purity. Customarily, it is also used daily by men for immersion. (Before accepting the Torah at Mount Sinai, all men purified themselves in water.) Finally, new dishes — both cooking and eating utensils — are required to be dipped in the *mikveh* (*tevilas keilim*) before they can be used. Unlike a *shul* or yeshivah, which can be established almost anywhere and with a minimum of architectural requirements in *halachah*, a *mikveh* needs to be built according to certain rigorous halachic specifications in order for it to be kosher.

My husband's biggest accomplishment in Leipheim was establishing a kosher *mikveh*. From start to finish, building the *mikveh* was a challenging but necessary struggle.

Before the actual *mikveh* was built, several obstacles needed to be overcome, beginning with a lack of funds. The American Army chaplain, R' Cohen, was one source of assistance. Immediately after receiving a phone call from my husband, R' Cohen was on his way to Leipheim to meet with him and to offer his services.

The visit was very pleasant. As it turned out, R' Rubin and R' Cohen even discovered that they were distantly related. R' Cohen was the son-in-law of the Chernobyl Rebbe of Boro Park. My husband is a descendant of the original Chernobyl Rebbe, *zt"l*.

Mrs. Robertson also helped to raise funds for the *mikveh*. She acquired a sizable amount of cigarettes from the U.S. Army for this purpose. (Scarcity of both cigarettes and of hard currency made a carton of "Old Golds" almost as good as real gold as a medium of exchange in postwar Europe.) When we obtained cigarettes, we were able to barter them for badly needed commodities such as building materials and labor for our *mikveh*.

---

1. An abbreviation for *Chachameinu zichronom livrachah* (Our Sages, may their memories be blessed).

Once the funds were raised for the *mikveh*, my husband's next step was to supervise its actual planning and construction. It was built according to the specifications of the Chasam Sofer, the famous Rav of Pressburg, Czechoslovakia. R' Rubin was grateful to receive help and advice from R' Lichtenstein in Landsburg, and also consulted *rabbanim* in Munich and Fehrenwald.

When it was time to begin the actual construction, my husband worked closely with the local architects and assisted them with their blueprints and the building of the structure.

One great obstacle remained to be overcome. How would water be supplied for the *mikveh*? *Halachah* specifies that a *mikveh* must contain well-water or natural rainwater in order for the immersion to be considered kosher. There weren't any natural springs in the Camp Leipheim area, and it hardly rained while we were there. Since time was of great essence, as a *mikveh* was needed every day, it was decided that natural ice would be used. In fact, it was my uncle, the venerable Sigheter Rav, *zt"l*, who had once ruled that natural ice was allowable when in dire need, and it was this ruling which provided the precedent in the case of the Leipheim *mikveh*.

Many blocks of ice would be needed. These ice blocks, formed from natural rainwater, were delivered to the site on planks and thrown in the pit according to halachic specifications. That this immense undertaking succeeded was due in no small part to the understanding and cooperation of the officers of the American Occupation Army, who arranged for the transportation of the ice blocks.

Much to the credit of my husband's perseverance and determination and the unified efforts of the community and the American Army, a dream was brought to fruition. Before long, the *kehillah* rejoiced upon the completion of their new *mikveh*. Going to *mikveh* once again restored feelings of hope to the hearts of many survivors, and helped many others find the road to *Yiddishkeit*. A debt of gratitude is due to Mr. Alter Lebowitz, secretary of the rabbinate in Leipheim (who now resides in Boro Park, Brooklyn), for his energetic help.

Unfortunately, not everybody shared the community's enthusiasm over this major accomplishment. One day, a U.S. Army general came to Leipheim to inspect the conditions of the camp. My husband accompanied the general on his tour of the religious sections of the camp. The inspection remained uneventful until they reached the building which housed the *mikveh*. The general seemed perplexed over the purpose of this building. He knew that my husband had coordinated the project from start to finish, so he began to ask questions. He demanded to know the significance of this "community bath" which had cost thousands of cigarettes to build. Calmly, my husband explained our belief in the existence of *tumah* — defilement and spiritual impurity — and quoted the Torah source (*Leviticus* 11:36) teaching that by plunging into well-water, or pure rainwater, the impurity disappears.

The hard-faced general did not quite know what to make of this information. He took a good, long look at my husband, almost as if he were questioning his sanity! My husband waited for the general to reply. Instead, the general turned away without saying a word, and walked off in a huff. Later, the interpreter confided to my husband that he was under the impression that the general did not believe his explanation. Nevertheless, the facility had already been built, and our community at last had a working, kosher *mikveh*.

A SHAMEFUL TRAGEDY WAS NARROWLY AVERTED DURING MY husband's tenure as rabbi in Leipheim.

"Who Here Believes in G-d?" It all began early one morning while my husband was walking toward the *cheder* and noticed that everyone in the street seemed jubilant and excited about something. Glad to see such joy in their faces, my husband asked what the excitement was about.

He was told that a soldier from Palestine had just arrived and had promised to take care of the people's needs in camp. Sure enough, down the street strode a tall, young, powerful-looking *sabra*, dressed in a clean khaki uniform. On his shirt bore the Hebrew inscription, *HaSochnut HaYehudit* (the Jewish Agency). As it turned out, the young man was not actually a soldier but rather a representative of the *Sochnut*.

It cannot be overstated what an uplifting effect it had on these broken, dispirited people, who had just lived through the era of the German "solution," to see what appeared to be a Jewish soldier with Hebrew words on his uniform. Here was a living, breathing symbol of Jewish pride and strength, so unlike the powerlessness, humiliation and degradation the survivors had so recently experienced.

This charismatic young man had been sent to the camp from *Eretz Yisrael* to encourage the Jewish survivors to make *aliyah*, to serve as a source of inspiration and hope to the children, and to supervise the teaching of cultural affairs. Many of the impressionable young boys looked up to him with unrestrained admiration and more than a twinge of envy. But the visitor soon revealed a more sinister agenda.

One day, a messenger came to my husband's office with an urgent communication from one of the teachers in the secular school. The teacher complained that the newcomer had come into her class and asked the children, "Who here believes in G-d in Heaven?" When most of the children raised their hands, the young man stared disapprovingly at them and proceeded to tell them that such beliefs are *"buba meises,"* superstitious old wives' tales. As it turned out, this young man continued doing this in class after class. Was this his true mission, even more important than merely encouraging *aliyah*?

Needless to say, my husband was shocked and appalled. Of course, he certainly knew that not all Jews were religious — unfortunately, many were quite irreligious. Still, he found it inconceivable that such an *apikoros*, a militant non-believer, had officially been dispatched to our camp all the way from Palestine and was apparently trying to brainwash the innocent minds of Jewish children and fill their sweet young heads with his noxious, atheistic propaganda. Surely, thought my husband, a mistake must have been made in dispatching such a man to the camp. He resolved to put an end to the matter before the atheist was able to inflict any more damage on the children's pure souls.

My husband's initial shock over this man's activities, however, was nothing compared to the nasty surprise he received when he tried to remedy the problem. He telephoned the leader of the camp community and described the young *sabra's* arrogant behavior and actions. There was a long pause at the other end of the line. Finally, my husband received a matter-of-fact response. The man had been instructed by the people in Munich who had set up the *Sochnut* school that the *sabra's* lessons on "Jewish culture" were not to be interfered with. With that, he hung up on my husband.

This conversation left my husband greatly perturbed. In the very country which had instigated the murder of millions of Jews by people who later said they "were only following orders" and could not interfere, a Jewish bureaucrat was telling my husband that he could not interfere in what amounted to the spiritual murder of young Jews because he "had his orders." Incredible!

R' Rubin then called the Culture Department in Munich where those "orders" had supposedly originated, and tried to explain the situation to the director. He was coldly rebuffed and told to mind his own business. "Your assignment is to deal with the needs of the religious population in the camp," the Director of Culture informed my husband. Anything else was outside his jurisdiction — including the *Sochnut* school for the non-religious children. The Director of Culture stressed that my husband was to focus his attention on running the *cheder* for the religious children only — and to let the young man from Palestine do his job. R' Rubin told him he would not tolerate this.

The bureaucrat was unmoved, and continued to insist that my husband had no jurisdiction over what the *Sochnut* school taught its pupils.

R' Rubin decided to go over the head of the Director of Culture to resolve the situation, and requested a meeting with Mrs. Robertson, the camp director. She represented the people who actually ran the camp — the United Nations Relief Administration — and so was not beholden to the *Sochnut*. He had no doubt that Mrs. Robertson would help him; from the time we first met her, she was friendly, sympathetic and decent. My husband was saddened that he had to appeal to a non-Jew for help because Jewish officials — such as the head of the camp community and the *Sochnut* man in Munich — acted in opposition to their own religion and Torah.

From the moment my husband walked into her office, Mrs. Robertson knew that something was seriously wrong. He explained the situation to her, how this was a desecration, a blatant *chillul Hashem*, and she listened sympathetically, expressing shock and concern throughout his recital. As soon as he was finished, she wordlessly pushed her chair back from the desk and picked up the phone.

When she got through to Munich, the bureaucrat in the *Sochnut* office repeated the instructions previously given my husband and bluntly told her to mind her own business. Bristling with anger, Mrs. Robertson said that such behavior was unacceptable under her jurisdiction. She then placed another call — at the time my husband didn't know to whom — and explained the situation to the person at the other end of the line. At one point, Mrs. Robertson even threatened to resign if the situation were not corrected. "It's either him or me," she fumed, and hung up the phone.

"Rabbi, please wait a few minutes," she requested, turning to my husband.

We later found out that her second call had been to the commanding general of the area's American occupation forces. The general must have been impressed with Mrs. Robertson's determination because he called back a few moments later and advised her that effective immediately, the visitor from Palestine would be replaced. The new teacher would be a religious person from the *Mizrachi* (religious Zionist) movement. Oddly enough, his name was also Rubin. It is, indeed, a small world.

MY HUSBAND CONTINUED AS CHIEF RABBI OF LEIPHEIM UNTIL the spring of 1947. His feelings of unease persisted regarding the

Krumbach great responsibility he had assumed in undertaking to care for such a large community in such complicated circumstances. He decided to leave the position, but first he had to find a suitable rabbi as a replacement.

Whereas the camp provided a *cheder* for the younger children, it did not have an established yeshivah for the older boys and men.

While my husband was trying to solve the problem of establishing a yeshivah, he learned about a small Jewish *kehillah* that had once existed in a nearby community named Krumbach. All that remained were a few buildings from the former *kehillah*. The Gestapo had wiped out the entire town, making it virtually *Judenrein*. My husband saw the potential of using the buildings, and arranged a time for us to visit the town. Upon arriving in Krumbach, we were greeted by a single, elderly Jewish man named Dr. Milhauser. The only survivor from the original community, he was happy to take part in transferring the former Jewish property. Legally, only with his signature could any plans be carried through.

My husband was surprised to find a well-water *mikveh*. True, both the *mikveh* and the structure, neglected for 10 years, needed to be refurbished, but at least the Germans had not destroyed the structure, and the *mikveh* itself was untouched.

As we continued our search for property formerly owned by Jews, my husband asked his guide about various buildings. Dr. Milhauser remembered that only a few short years ago, two buildings had been occupied by the Jewish community as communal buildings. He showed us the site of the destroyed old *shul*, the place where he and his family had once lived, and pointed out the dwellings of other Jews, including those of some relatives and friends. Tragically, those homes had been taken over by local gentiles, who helped themselves to whatever remained after the Nazis had liquidated and looted the Jewish community. We could not help but notice the marks on the right side of the doorpost indicating the spots from where *mezuzos* had been torn off. The day was gusty, and it seemed to us that the wind carried to our ears the cries of the town's innocent victims, so brutally murdered despite being such devoted German citizens.

After spending a few hours there, my husband decided to pay tribute

Among the most famous founders of European Ashkenaz Jewry was the Torah commentator Rashi. The Nazis destroyed part of Rashi's synagogue in Worms but did not harm his nearby beis midrash, the interior of which is shown here with his famous chair. After R' Rubin founded the kollel in Krumbach in 1947, he and the members of the kollel managed to visit Rashi's beis midrash in Worms.

to this small Jewish town by rebuilding it. The *mikveh* could be restored, a *yeshivah* built for the *bachurim* and a *kollel* established for newly married young men. Newlyweds could begin their wedded lives there, and start new families.

We felt that the restoration of this Jewish community would serve as a memorial to those who were lost, a fitting way to deny the Nazis their victory. Although Dr. Milhauser was not an Orthodox Jew, he was sympathetic toward my husband's dreams and goals.

A joyous moment at the Krumbach Yeshivah as kollel members celebrate the upsherin (ritual first haircut) of the little boy to the left near the lamp.

The dormitory of the Krumbach Yeshivah

R' Rubin officiates at a funeral in Leipheim DP camp. Several American army officers were also there to pay their respects to the deceased.

A letter of thanks to R' Rubin for his help, from those who carried on the "Rabbinats Hochschule" in Krumbach. Among the kollel members mentioned in the letter are R' Shulem Weiss, the Uheler Rav zt"l, and R' Yosef Klein, the Tober Rav zt"l.

This would be a monumental undertaking, but the conviction in my husband's eyes announced his determination to succeed. We were both confident that once word got out that he was reestablishing this small township, displaced Torah families like those we had seen in both Fehrenwald and Leipheim would settle there, and a new Torah community would emerge from the ashes.

Once the decision had been made, several major obstacles needed to be overcome. For starters, since non-Jewish families were living in the space stolen from its rightful Jewish owners, how could my husband reclaim those buildings for the Jewish community? How would he be able to evict the gentile families from the apartments? Then, once the buildings were vacated, how could they be renovated to include a newly rebuilt kosher *mikveh*, kosher kitchen, *shul*, *beis midrash*, and living quarters for the *Kollel* students and their families?

Filled with eager anticipation, we discussed nothing but this new

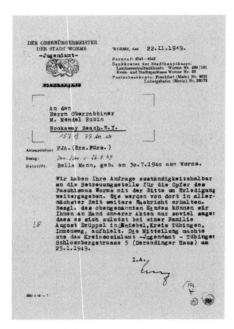

DER OBERBÜRGERMEISTER
DER STADT WORMS   WORMS, den   22.11.1949.
-Jugendamt-

Fernruf: 4041—4042
Bankkonten der Stadthauptkasse:
Landeszentralbankkonto Worms Nr. 480/181
Kreis- und Stadtsparkasse Worms Nr. 29
Postscheckkonto: Frankfurt (Main) Nr. 9810
Ludwigshafen (Rhein) Nr. 29072

An den
Herrn Oberrabbiner
M. Mendel Rubin

Rockaway Beach. N.Y.
157 β 77 th st

Aktenzeichen: FJA. (Frm. Fürs.)
Bezug: Ihr. Schr. v. 26. 9. 49
Betrifft: Bella Mann, geb. am 30.7.1940 aus Worms.

Wir haben Ihre Anfrage zuständigkeitshalber
an die Betreuungsstelle für die Opfer des
Faschismus Worms mit der Bitte um Erledigung
weitergegeben. Sie werden von dort in aller-
nächster Zeit weitere Nachricht erhalten.
Bezgl. des obengenannten Kindes können wir
Ihnen an Hand unserer Akten nur soviel sagen
dass es sich zuletzt bei einer Familie
August Drüppel in Kniebel, Kreis Tübingen,
Immenweg, aufhielt. Die Mitteilung machte
uns das Kreissozialamt -Jogendamt - Tübinger
Schlossbergstrasse 5 (Derendinger Haus) am
25.1.1949.

I.A.

When R' Rubin took the kollel members to Worms, he found that one Jewish child out of the entire community had survived the war. He began a long correspondence with authorities in an attempt to rescue this child. He continued his efforts even after we relocated to America. Shown here is one of the letters received in reply. Sadly, the child was not handed over to a Jewish family or group.

project as we traveled back to Leipheim. Upon his return home, my husband first turned to the occupying American Army for assistance. My husband also went to the U.S. Joint Distribution Committee and then to the Refugee Office in Munich. Additional assistance for this project came from the *Vaad Hatzalah*, headed by R' Baruch.

Since my husband was working without a staff or proper facilities, plans to restore this Jewish community were easier made than carried out. Nevertheless, he was young, enthusiastic and resourceful. Strengthened by his belief that the A-mighty would help him achieve his noble goal, and spurred on by his strong drive to rebuild the ruins left by the Nazi destroyers, my husband was determined to see his dreams become a reality, and make the Jewish community of Krumbach come to life again.

Once the plans to rebuild the community had been set in motion, my husband submitted his resignation as Chief Rabbi of Leipheim, and chose the Terzaler Rav, R' Rosner, *zt"l*, to succeed him, confident that he would be a more than adequate replacement. In April 1947, my husband and I once again packed our bags. The Leipheim community arranged a very moving farewell for us. A tearful R' Leibowitz acknowledged his gratitude for my husband's efforts. Mrs. Robertson and other members of the U.N.R.A. camp

In Krumbach, reading a letter from my uncle the Satmar Rebbe, zt"l.
From left: the Mishkolzer Rebbe, z"tl, R' Rubin, the Nasoder Rebbe, shlita.

administration were also there to say good-bye to us.

Upon our arrival in Krumbach, one of the first people we met was the town's mayor, who introduced himself as an anti-Nazi and impressed us with his fine manners. He was helpful and found living quarters for us.

Once we were settled, we began the long, arduous task of bringing my husband's dream to fruition. With the help and cooperation of the American occupation forces, the dilapidated buildings that once belonged to the Jews were cleared of German squatters and were refurbished. Then the Yeshivah and Kollel She'eiris HaPleitah (literally,

קלג.

מענין הצלתו מהרהרי האכזרים וממחלתו באה"ק*)

ב"ה.

שלו' וכט"ס אל כבוד ידידי ש"ב חי"א האברך היקר הרב
המאוה"ג חריף החסיד המפואר המפאר כנשיק סאליים ותרשישים כש"ת
מורה מנחם מענדיל **ראבין** שליט"א והאברהק"ק מאושי צי"ו
עם כבוד זוג' היקרה ב"א החביבה החכמת תחי' לי"ט...

הנה לא אוכל לספר לכם את גודל השמחה שהיי לי מטו שראיתי את
מכתבכם שהח"ל נודעתם יחד אחר שעזר לכם השי"ת להשאירכם בחיים אחרי
רוב התלאות והצרות ר"ל אשר עברו בכל משך הזמן לא פם זכרינו, והיויתי סקוה
בכליון עינים לשמוע ממם בשורה מובה, ואקוה שגם להלאה החב"ה ברוב
רחמיו וחסדיו לא יעזוב ויא ימוש אתכם, ותובו עוד לחיי נחת במקום מנוחה
הרהבת חלב לבנות בית גאון לתורה ועבודה עדי ניבה בסהרה לראות
בישועת כל ישראל ושמחתו.

והנה לא אוכל לספר ולתאר על הגליון רוב הנסים והפרי השיית'ה שנעשה
גם עמדי בכל משך הזמן תחת הרשעים האכזרים היודעים ימ"ש, ובאשר
זכיתי לבא לכאן עיהק הי' חש כחי מאד בתכלית החולשה מנוחל התלאות
והצרות ר"ל, גם עבר עלי בחתולה ב"איתי לכאן מחלה כבידה ר"ל של ליקת
הסרה ונפיחת הכבד בצירוף דליקת הריאיה ר"ל, ומל אלה חוברו יחדי
שהייתי מוטל בזה קרוב לשני חרשים על ערש דוי בימורין וחולשה ר"ל, אבל
השי"ת ברוב רחמיו הי' בעזרי גם בזה, והסיר ממני המחלה ותרפאותי,
ובעחה"ית הוטב לי חרבה במצב הבריאות ומה אשיב לה' כל תגמולוהי עלי.

ובענין המצב פה גם בענין מצבי קצר היריעח מהכיל לבאר על הגליון
וכומה כמה מנסים וסיבות שנתחבכו מסיבות כל הסיבות וכל להיות שאסע
על איזה ירחים למדינת אמעריקא, ועדיין אין הדבר ברור, אבל יהי' איך
שיהי' את אם אשים הדרך מעני להסיעה זו דעתי לחזור אי"ה בקרוב לאה"ק
בעדר איזה ירחים. ורוב המעמים והסיבות שהביאוני שהביאני לזה א"א לבאר בכתב
והרבה מעמים וסיבות נתחבכו בזה וחבל הוא בחשבונה.

והנה עשיתי השתרלות לחשינ גם עבורכם רשיון כניסה (צערטפיקאטם)
לאה"ק, וסה מאד היתיר משחוקק להתרצות התרצאות אתכם ולדבר עמכם פא"פ אבל
לע"ע קשה להשיג הרשיון הנ"ל, כי הצערטפיקאטין הם ביד"י האינגעלאצים
אשר אינם מצירינו ואינם פרים לשמעתעירנטו°. בפרט כעת שהממשלה אינה
נותנת אלא מספר כם שאין לחם כו כדי הלוקת, גם כמה עיכובים בדבר.
ולע"ע בעניה העול גליות כבד מאד ר"ל על בני ישראל וכשרים בכל אחר
ואחר, והשי"ת ירחם וישמח את לבנות בני ישראל וימנה הנראמות וינתנו
במקנ'ר צדק למען שמו יני אר"ינו הוש מהר גאולת עולם בישועת אמירית
בב"א.

והנני ידידכם דודכם הד"ש באה"ר עומד וסאפה לשמוע מכם בשורה
ולהתראות אתכם בקרוב בישועת כל ישראל ושמחתן.

הק' **יואל מיטעלבוים**

The letter from my uncle, the Satmar Rebbe zt"l, "I cannot express my great joy at your having been rejoined, thank G-d, after, with His help, you survived..."

Yeshivah of the Survivors) of Krumbach was founded, and some of the young *bachurim* we had known in Leipheim moved to our new community. My husband selected noted newlywed scholars, who moved in with their wives, and before long the *talmidim* were learning and thriving. We were privileged to witness the amazing metamorphosis of these young men from weak, lost souls into individuals filled with new hopes and dreams for the future.

Within a short time, approximately fifty people had established themselves in Krumbach. Among them was R' Yosef David Klein, *zt"l*, the Rabbi of Tob, Hungary, who later became a rabbi in Montreal, Canada. Others who joined our Krumbach *kollel* included R' S. B. Berkowitz (Secretary of the Central Rabbinical Congress), R' J.W. Safern of Bobov, *z"l*, R' J.E. Berkowitz (Williamsburg), R' Yeshayah Sprung Raver of Belz, R' Lazar Hierfeues (Kiryas Yoel), and R' David Singer of Pupa.

My husband devoted himself to giving *shiurim* and also providing all material and spiritual needs for the new members of the Jewish community. Often he had to travel to Munich to fight for — and to obtain — provisions for the Krumbach community.

MY TWO SURVIVING BROTHERS-IN-LAW, R' SHMUEL SHMELKA and R' Mordechai David, were still learning in Fehrenwald. Finally

The Surviving Family Is Reunited

they joined us in Krumbach, and once again we were together as a family.

We had heard rumors that my sister-in-law Mirel was alive in Sweden, but we did not know where in Sweden she was — assuming, of course, that the rumors were true in the first place. We wrote letters and sent them to every Displaced Persons camp and school in Sweden, hoping one would reach her. Finally our letters reached Mirel, and we arranged for her to come to Krumbach.

The day of Mirel's arrival was an emotional one for us. Even though more than 2 years had passed since liberation, Mirel still did not look like her former self. She was pale and thin — and this, after receiving humane, excellent care in Sweden. She told us the bitter news of the untimely death in Bergen-Belsen of my dear, gentle sister-in-law Yocheved, who passed away on *erev* Pesach — on the *yahrtzeit* of the head of our dynasty, R' Usher of Ropshitz, *zt"l*. Finding out about the death of loved ones was tragically common after liberation, but for those of us who had survived, each new account was heartbreaking.

Mirel lived with us for approximately a year after we arrived in Krumbach. During this time we became close as sisters, and this relationship has endured until today.

The story of her fight for physical survival in the death camps and for spiritual survival after her liberation is truly amazing.

CHAPTER 11

"Remember Who You Are!"

The Survival Story of Rebbetzin Mirel Meisels the Sarvasher Rebbetzin

"Die Kinder Stube Geht Mit"
(The Childhood Home Accompanies You)

AFTER MY BROTHERS-IN-LAW WERE TAKEN AWAY TO THE LABOR camps from *Teglagyar* (the brick-factory ghetto to which the Rubin family and the other Jews of Szaszregen had been taken), my three sisters-in-law, Yocheved (age 15), Mirel (age 13) and Sprintza (age 7), were the only children remaining with my husband's parents. From *Teglagyar*, the Rubin (Eichenstein) family was transported to Auschwitz.

They arrived at Auschwitz-Birkenau very early on Sunday morning, June 7, 1944/14 Sivan, 5704 — the same date that we arrived! Never did we meet, however. Long trains full of Jews were arriving daily, creating a backlog of new victims. The selection, numbering and shaving — and the gas chambers and the ovens — could not accommodate so many people at once. As a result, many unfortunate victims had to wait inside the cattle cars. My in-laws' transport was among those chosen to remain locked until nightfall.

It happened once that my uncle, the Satmar Rebbe, came late to a *chuppah*. Citing the phrase used to describe the proper time that an event should occur — "*besha'ah tovah* (in a good hour)" — he observed, "Maybe *now* is the good hour" (even though it was later than originally planned). A similar explanation can be offered as to why the soon-to-be-martyrs were forced to suffer the additional torture of waiting in the sealed trains before being sent to die: even to die *al kiddush Hashem*, the victims had to await the predestined hour.

My father-in-law turned to his family and, in his gentle, firm manner, gave his loved ones some final advice. Rebbetzin Mirel vividly remembers his words:

"Since I am not a prophet — none of us are — I don't know what is going to happen when these doors open. Should we become separated, make sure that you eat what you can to stay alive. Do what the Germans tell you so they won't beat you up. And when you get out of here, *im yirtzeh Hashem*, remember who you are!"

The family agreed that if they were to be separated, they would search for one another in Budapest after the war. Then the Rebbetzin and her daughters, along with R' Rubin, descended into a deep silence; there was no need to say more.

According to Mirel, her revered father's last piece of advice, "Remember who you are ..." saved her life many times during the following desperate years.

By nightfall, the Germans came for them and pulled them from the boxcars. In the chaos, my father-in-law realized he had left his *tallis* and *tefillin* behind. He quickly approached one of the *kapos* and asked him to retrieve the items from the boxcar. The *kapo* — a Jewish man himself — coldly denied his request. When my mother-in-law made a desperate plea for the *kapo* to go into the boxcar and hand her the *tallis* and *tefillin,* the *kapo's* face hardened. His reply was, "Where you are going, your husband won't need them!" He then hurried away. (Actually, under normal circumstances, a *tallis* is supposed to be buried with its wearer's remains.)

Within seconds, R' Rubin was gone, having been ordered to line up with the men. Rebbetzin Rubin and her daughters held on to each other and fearfully awaited the next development.

Cries and screams were heard from the front of the women's line. The line moved up quickly and, almost before they knew it, Rebbetzin Rubin and her three daughters were being subjected to Mengele's cruel gaze. He immediately motioned my mother-in-law and Shprinza to the left. When Mirel stood in front of him, he asked her how old she was.

"Thirteen," answered Mirel truthfully.

For some reason, Mengele motioned her to the right.

Next, Yocheved stood in front of Mengele and she was also motioned to the right.

The girls unwillingly separated from their mother and little sister. They did not know that they would never see their dear parents or sweet sister again.

THREE DAYS AFTER THEIR ARRIVAL AT BIRKENAU, YOCHEVED AND Mirel were assigned to an outgoing transport. Once again they

Camp Plaszow

found themselves in a boxcar, this time with one change of clothing and a small bag of food containing a piece of stale bread and a smidgen of jam. Crammed against the walls of the crowded boxcar, the girls had no idea where they were headed.

Finally the train jerked to a stop. Everyone was ordered out and chased onto trucks which then transported them to a camp called Plaszow. The camp was built on land which was part of an old Jewish cemetery in the vicinity of Cracow. The commander of the camp, a ruthless German Nazi named Amon Goeth, rode a white horse and carried a whip which he used freely on anyone not moving quickly enough for him. Goeth, who often personally shot prisoners on a mere whim, was hanged as a war criminal after Plaszow was liberated. Arrogant to the end, his final words were, "Heil Hitler!"

The girls' first job in Plaszow was to break up cement with a heavy steel pick, a task which left them exhausted and bruised by the end of the day. One day, the chief of the camp decided that he wanted a garden on the hill in front of his *lager*, so he ordered Yocheved, Mirel and the other girls to dig up the earth with axes to cultivate the soil. This was backbreaking work, as the earth could only be tilled in small portions with axes, and the work had to be done in a hurry.

But the worst work detail of all was when the girls were forced to dig up corpses behind the camp, carry them in their bare hands and throw them into a fire. Often pieces of skin would peel off the corpses and stick to their own bodies.

Only the fact that they were together afforded Yocheved and Mirel any comfort in Plaszow. When one sister felt as if she could not go on, the other offered words of encouragement. Their *bitachon* and *emunah* were unwavering — even in those horrid surroundings.

Months later, the Russians began closing in. The SS liquidated the camp and placed everyone on outgoing transports. To Yocheved's and Mirel's horror, they found themselves back on the Birkenau ramp where they had last seen their venerable parents and younger sister, and had to submit to the selection process yet again.

From Auschwitz, the girls were transported to an ammunition factory in Guben, a town near Berlin. By midwinter, the fleeing German cowards ordered the Guben workers on a death march. The girls had to walk at a fast pace in the sub-freezing temperature, wearing nothing more than their thin prison dresses. Their legs were bare and their feet bled from frostbite. Starvation and exposure to the cruel elements weakened them even further.

FINALLY YOCHEVED, MIREL AND THE OTHERS FOUND THEMSELVES IN Bergen-Belsen, a death camp near Hanover, Germany. The camp was

The Tragedy at Bergen-Belsen named after the German village of Bergen, which was located approximately four kilometers from the camp. During the war, the village of Bergen served as a stopover for the weary German soldiers, a place where they found housing and entertainment.

Bergen-Belsen played an unimportant role during the peak of the war. At the end of the war, however, when the Germans were facing imminent defeat, Bergen-Belsen became a convenient dumping ground for the remaining European transports. Many innocents died from typhus and other diseases which resulted from unsanitary conditions. Huge mountains of corpses lay around camp, many of which had begun to deteriorate in the muddy earth. The stench from the decaying bodies intensified daily. The latrines, grossly inadequate for the thousands of prisoners, were usually overflowing. Among those who perished there was the famous Dutch teenage diarist, Anne Frank.

The day on which my dear, gentle, sweet sister-in-law Yocheved tragically passed away in Bergen-Belsen — *erev* Pesach — was just one week before the liberation of the camp. On that day, Yocheved was unable to pick herself up from the floor of the barrack. Mirel gently placed Yocheved's burning head into her lap and held her, trying to offer her dying sister the fortitude to hold on. Yocheved heard Mirel's words, but, crying softly, insisted she didn't have the strength to take another breath. Her eyes slowly closed for the last time, and her head slumped on Mirel's lap. Mirel held her dear sister tightly, sobbing, and slowly said *Shema. H"yd*

Mirel and the other concentration-camp prisoners were liberated

on April 15, 1945, by the British Army. The soldiers were aghast over what they found when they liberated the camp. The inhumane cruelty of man against man was evident everywhere, and many soldiers were sickened by what they witnessed. But today, 50 years later, one may ask: What did we, or anyone else, learn from that?

AT THE TIME OF LIBERATION MIREL WAS DEATHLY ILL. DELIRIOUS WITH high fever at the time, she later could not remember her liberators

Mirel's Long Journey Back to Life taking her to the hospital set up outside the camp where, along with approximately 1,500 other sick and wounded women, she was placed in a huge ward.

One day, a man from the Red Cross in Sweden came to the hospital. Declaring that the Swedish King wished to help rehabilitate the concentration-camp victims, he announced that the patients would be moved to Sweden, where they could be better cared for. Ambulances showed up a couple of days later, and the patients, too sick to weigh their options or make their own decisions, were transported across the Baltic Sea to Sweden.

In Sweden, the liberated prisoners found a truly humane nation and society — the very opposite of that which had attempted to destroy them. They were first taken to a clean, bright, makeshift hospital that had been set up in a local school building. One day, the King came to visit the ailing patients and spoke to each one personally. Mirel remembers him as a friendly, benevolent man who sympathized with their plight.

From the nurses in the Swedish hospital, Mirel learned that she weighed only 40 kilograms (approximately 85 pounds). Her swollen legs were covered with raw, painful sores. When she felt strong enough, the nurses escorted her into the garden for a healthy dose of fresh air and sunshine. A bit of color returned to Mirel's sallow cheeks and she began to regain some of her lost strength.

From the hospital, the patients were taken to a convalescent home situated in a sprawling country house on a hill. The picturesque gardens surrounding the house, combined with the peace and quiet of its isolated location, provided the atmosphere of serenity so sorely needed by the survivors in the recovery process.

In the home, patients received printed sheets from the Red Cross containing the names of survivors. Mirel was overjoyed to find the name of her brother — my husband — on the list, but saddened when she did not see the names of her other family members. She remembered that her grandmother — my father-in-law's mother, Rebbetzin Sara Shlomtza, z"l — lived in *Eretz Yisrael* at the time, and she decided to attempt to contact her. Even though Mirel didn't know her grandmother's address, she remembered that she lived in *Yerushalayim* and was hopeful that the letter would reach her. In those immediate postwar days, the community in *Yerushalayim* was not large, but Rebbetzin Rubin (Eichenstein), already a well-known personality, would be relatively easy to trace.

One sunny morning, approximately six weeks after sending her letter to *Eretz Yisrael*, Mirel told her friend that she dreamed that she was about to receive a letter from her grandmother, in which she would learn that three of her brothers were alive. The woman looked at Mirel as if she were losing her sanity — a not-uncommon phenomenon among the survivors — and quickly summoned a nurse.

By the time the nurse arrived, Mirel was getting ready to walk down the hill to wait for the mailman. The nurse suggested that Mirel relax instead. But Mirel was firmly convinced that her dream would come true. After all, such things had happened before in her family. Wasn't that how her own father had received his name "Yeshurin," based on a message that Rebbetzin Sara Shlomtza, his mother, received in a dream while still pregnant? Mirel left the room and waited outside for the mailman who finally arrived and presented her with a letter from *Yerushalayim*, just as she had expected!

With trembling hands, Mirel showed the letter to all the people in the parlor, some of whom gasped from the shock of Mirel's prediction coming true. However, her grandmother had not written the letter; it was written by a cousin and it stated that two, not three, of her brothers (R' Shmuel Shmelka and my husband, R' Mendel) were alive and temporarily settled in a D.P. camp in Germany. (The cousin was not aware that R' Mordechai David had also survived, so indeed, although she did not know it at the time, Mirel's prediction regarding surviving family members turned out to be accurate.)

Since Mirel was still unable to travel to us, she sent a letter informing us of her whereabouts and her general state of health. In the weeks that followed, we corresponded with her and anxiously awaited the day when we would all be reunited. It would take time for us to make arrangements for her to join us.

WHILE MIREL WAS AWAITING OUR REUNION, THE SWEDISH GOVERN-ment set up schools for the displaced children. When their health

Battles for Yiddishkeit

had improved, Mirel (who was now 14) and approximately one hundred eighty other children were taken to an orphanage which had been transformed into a school.

Mirel's experiences in the school turned into a nightmare, although of a different sort than those at Auschwitz, Plaszow and Bergen-Belsen. While her physical safety had been endangered in each of those places, now, in the seemingly safe environment of free, affluent Sweden, she faced a battle for her spiritual and moral well-being (just as our students in Leipheim did with the *Sochnut* agent sent from *Eretz Yisrael* to "teach" them Jewish culture). The *madrich* (leader) sent to fill the role of head counselor to the children was, as usual, a left-wing atheist from *HaShomer HaTza'ir* (a Marxist-oriented Zionist *kibbutz* group from *Eretz Yisrael*). This group was totally hostile to traditional religious ideals and practices, scorning them as an "opiate of the people."

Much to Mirel's shock and dismay, the young man came to the classrooms and tried to convert as many children as possible to his way of thinking. He made every attempt to turn them away from *Yiddishkeit*. Many of the children, young and impressionable — without the guidance of their parents and former teachers and rebbes — listened intently to his words and believed him. The *madrich's* goal was to bring some of the children back with him to *Eretz Yisrael* someday to start a new life, and he wanted them to follow his kind of socialist lifestyle. This situation created a deep inner struggle for some girls, who ultimately lost their way and blundered off their original paths of a Torah-true life. *Baruch Hashem*, the *rebbishe* house in which Mirel had been brought up, along with the strong-willed nature with which she was blessed, prevented her from being swayed by the counselor's words. In the course of her stay in Sweden, she would be challenged more than once — and would triumph in her fight for *Yiddishkeit*.

When Mirel first came to the orphanage, she was dismayed to discover that kosher meals were not being served to the children. She and five other girls who were *shomrei mitzvos* tried to get this situation remedied, but were thwarted in their efforts by their group leader, Joseph, who took a strong stand on keeping the kitchen the way it was. Joseph told Mirel that she and the others should be grateful just for being well fed! Mirel stared at him in horrified disbelief.

She and her five partners decided to stage a hunger strike in protest against the *treif* kitchen, and word of this soon spread throughout the school. Knowing that Torah was on her side, and feeling her father's eyes upon her from *Gan Eden*, Mirel maintained her position. She asserted that while eating *treif* food would harm the *neshamos* of those who ate it, eating kosher food would not harm anyone — religious or not.

The director was surprised by the girls' strong stand and impressed by the depth of Mirel's convictions. She listened intently to what she had to say and was swayed by her fervor. After considering the pleas of the six girls, she arranged for the kitchen to be *kashered* (made kosher).

Mirel's hardships did not end with her battle for *kashrus*. One evening, the school organized a coed social. Mirel refused to go. When the director noticed that Mirel was not at the social, she sought her out and asked her why she did not attend the function. Mirel answered with an explanation about her Chassidic upbringing and values.

The director, in turn, confided that she herself had been raised in a traditional Jewish home, but as she grew older, she moved away from that kind of life. With a melancholy, faraway look in her eyes, the director thanked Mirel for bringing back memories of a simpler, happier time for her. After a while, the director had to return to the social. Mirel remained alone in her room that night, feeling as if she had won yet another victory. Yet how many thousands of boys and girls from Torah homes were unable to withstand pressure and temptation and were torn away from *Yiddishkeit*?

A Talmid From Szaszregen in Sweden!

THE SWEDISH GOVERNMENT SENT REPRESENTATIVES TO VISIT THE schools and then report back to certain philanthropists who wanted to donate money to various schools of their choice.

One day, a representative from the Swedish rabbinate in Stockholm came to Mirel's classroom. He was clean-shaven and wore a modern suit. He walked around the room and conversed with the children. After staring intently at Mirel, he asked her for her name and that of her hometown. As it turned out, he had been a student of R' Rubin (Eichenstein) until his family left Szaszregen in 1939. Mirel was surprised to see her father's student dressed in non-Chassidic clothing. At her request, he had her transferred her to a religious school, and she was grateful to him for his help. However, she wasn't happy in her new school, either.

Through word of mouth, she heard of a Bais Yaakov school operated by R' and Mrs. Jacobson in Lidingo. She asked the Swedish government to transfer her there and, in time, they agreed. The Swedish government provided tuition for all the displaced students.

Mirel was happy in the Lidingo Bais Yaakov and enjoyed many hours of learning there while waiting to hear from us about our impending reunion. Finally she received a postcard from R' Hager who said we had asked him to inform her that we were trying to arrange her trip to Germany. Mirel anxiously prepared for her trip, and sure enough, a couple of weeks later she was in Germany. R' Shmuel Shmelka was waiting for her at the train platform.

Of all the daughters born to my revered mother-in-law, Mirel was the only one to survive the Holocaust. Her personality, courage and faith were recognizably strong in both the concentration camps and after liberation. With the help of the A-mighty, she is now the matriarch of the Sarvasher *rebbishe* family in Boro Park, a family which brings credit to the Rebbetzin's venerable father's last words: "Remember who you are!"

CHAPTER 12
Leaving Germany
for America

MY UNCLE, THE SATMAR REBBE, WROTE TO TELL US THAT HE had visas for us to go to *Eretz Yisrael*. But by early 1947 we received word that the Teitelbaums had gone to America. They settled in Williamsburg, Brooklyn, where the

To America
Satmar Rebbe ultimately established a huge Chassidic following. His supporters at the time consisted of a limited number of *Chassidim*, notably including Mr. Feish Moskowitz, *zt"l*, and his worthy family. The Rebbe's followers were mostly new European immigrants, Holocaust survivors who wanted to revive their Chassidic lifestyle in a new land. This resurgence of Chassidic life was largely due to the strong will and leadership of the Rebbe. We decided to follow my uncle and aunt and emigrate to the United States.

Although my husband and I felt that we had accomplished a great deal in Krumbach, we knew it was time to leave. I wanted to be with my uncle and aunt once more. Having missed the opportunity to join them in *Eretz Yisrael*, I very much looked forward to finally seeing them in America.

One of our major concerns about emigrating to America was our very limited ability to read or converse in English. While still in Germany, my husband found a Yiddish-speaking soldier who gave him private English lessons and provided him with dictionaries. This enabled him to confer with the Americans in English while they worked together to establish the *kollel* buildings in Krumbach. Nevertheless, my husband's knowledge of the language was at best limited, and mine even more so.

Entry to America right after the war was by no means automatic. Those with relatives already living there were given priority, as were people with sponsors who guaranteed that the new immigrants would have jobs and not become a public burden. In order to meet this second requirement, we needed a rabbinical contract to show the American authorities, proof that my husband would indeed be productively employed. The Bostoner Rebbe, *zt"l*, whose Rebbetzin is our close relative, intervened for us with the well-known Yeshiva Torah Vodaath in Brooklyn, and the *menahel* (principal), R' Dovid Bender, *zt"l*, sent us such a contract. Days before that contract arrived, however, we received another contract from the Melitzer congregation, initiated by our beloved uncle, R' Avraham Simcha Horowitz, the Melitzer-Dzikover Rebbe, *zt"l*. Those were the papers that we sent to the American Consul. We are grateful for the assistance of the venerable Bostoner Rebbe and everyone else who helped us come to America.

I would like to add a note about the Melitzer-Dzikover Rebbe, *zt"l*, my father's brother. R' Avraham Simcha Horowitz was in the United States quite by accident. He had come here temporarily from Melitz, Galicia, but then war broke out. His wife and children perished in the Holocaust, and he lived in America shattered and alone. His followers cared for him, but the loss of his family, the destruction of his hometown, and the annihilation of most of European Jewry left him broken-hearted. Nonetheless, his *bitachon* and *ahavas Hashem* remained intact. He finally emigrated to *Eretz Yisrael*, picked out a *kever* in *Yerushalayim*, prayed there every *erev Rosh Chodesh*, and is buried there.

As we began to make arrangements to leave for America, we were devastated to learn that the quota for young immigrants under the age of 18 had already been filled. My sister-in-law Mirel would therefore be denied a visa and would not be able to come with us. The thought of being separated from her once again was disheartening, but we realized that giving up our own visas would benefit nobody, and besides, this separation would only be temporary.

We searched for another way to send Mirel to America, and discovered that youngsters 18 and under could go to Canada. From Canada, Mirel would ultimately be able to emigrate to the neighboring United States.

In the meantime, the Joint Distribution Committee paid for our passage on the steamship *Marine Flasher*, which was to leave from the German port city of Bremerhaven before Pesach. The ship was scheduled to arrive in America just in time for us to be at the Teitelbaums' *seder* table. Much to our disappointment, however, our plans were thwarted when we learned that the ship was running behind schedule. As a result, my husband, the Rebbe, would have to conduct our two *sedarim* aboard ship.

We packed a few bags with our meager possessions and prepared for the long sea voyage. On the day of departure we were tearful — my brothers-in-law had to remain in Europe for the time being, and so did Mirel. But we smiled through the tears, hoping that soon we would all be together in America.

Our farewell *seudah* in Krumbach took place on a well-known day in Chassidic circles, 21 Adar, the *yahrtzeit* of the Rebbe of

Lizensk. (My husband is a descendant of the Lizensker Rebbe, known by the title of his *sefer, Noam Elimelech*.) In his outstanding speech, my husband articulated his heartfelt yearning to go to *Eretz Yisrael*, and declared that he was not so much going to America as leaving Germany. To this day he still wishes to live in *Eretz Yisrael*. My husband told his *kollel* members that as soon as he had an address in the United States he would forward it to them, and they would always be welcome to contact him.

With mixed feelings we left the Krumbach Torah community. Before setting out for Bremerhaven, we visited the D.P. camp in Bergen-Belsen to pay tribute to the memory of my sister-in-law Yocheved, who had passed away there. My husband wept bitterly for his sweet and gentle sister who, after fighting so hard to survive all those months in German captivity, succumbed to death just one week before liberation.

In Bergen-Belsen we met with R' David Mordechai Meisels, now a resident of Monroe and Williamsburg, whose parents were admirers of my father-in-law. He arranged for my husband to bake *shemurah matzos* for our journey and provided us with wine and some other food. This was one less worry, knowing that we would have *shemurah matzos* for our *sedarim* aboard ship.

We reached the Bremerhaven harbor and boarded the ship. For a while we were unable to eat anything. Once the seas calmed down a bit and our appetites returned, we were limited, for reasons of strict *kashrus*, to eating only the food we had brought along with us. Vegetables were plentiful, and we had eggs; I recall cooking eggs for breakfast one morning over a burning candle.

Pesach on the High Seas

NOWADAYS, CELEBRATING PESACH ON THE HIGH SEAS — AND conducting shipboard *sedarim* — is considered a luxurious vacation for a Jewish family. For us, however, on board the *Marine Flasher* back in 1948, it was quite a different experience. Conducting a *seder* in the middle of the choppy Atlantic Ocean, where all one saw for miles was the hazy blue horizon above meeting the deep blue water below, made us feel totally cut off from the world — in a watery *galus*. Moreover, we were confronted with a major dilemma: how would my husband be able to lead our two *sedarim* aboard ship in strict adherence to *halachah*? He sought out the captain to solicit his assistance in this matter.

My husband returned from his meeting with the captain looking relieved. *Seder* arrangements had already been made. A lovely room on the ship would be set aside on both nights for our use, and the captain had ordered brand-new dishes for our *sedarim*. A huge supply of Pesach wine, matzos and canned goods had also been ordered. When it became known aboard ship that my husband, a Chassidic *Admor*, would be conducting the *sedarim*, approximately two hundred people asked to participate.

We were pleasantly surprised and pleased to see how helpful the ship's crew had been in setting up an elegantly appointed room, with festive tables set for all. I managed to prepare a *seder* plate, which was carefully arranged and placed at the head of the table where my husband, R' Rubin, would be sitting and conducting the *seder*. The wine and covered matzos were placed alongside the *seder* plate; I made sure that the wine had been handled only by *shomer Shabbos Yidden*.

More than two hundred people participated in our *sedarim*, conducted by my husband according to the Zidichoiver customs he had learned at home. The songs and lyrics were the same ones that my husband had sung during his childhood, those taught to him by his holy and revered father. When my husband conducted his first *seder* in Selish the first year we were married, this *nusach* was strange to both my mother and myself. We had only been accustomed to *sedarim* conducted in the Sigheter or Dzikover manner. Now too, many of the people in attendance were unfamiliar with my husband's customs from home, but were moved by the way he led the *sedarim*. They could sense his deep *kavanah* (pious intentions) and his great knowledge in every step of the *seder*, and they participated joyously.

For my husband and me, these *sedarim* were quite an emotional experience. We had personally experienced what amounted to a modern-day version of the suffering of the Israelites and the redemption from Egypt through our experiences in Auschwitz, Stutthof, and Ebensee, and our survival and liberation therefrom.

We still meet people who were present at our *sedarim* aboard the *Marine Flasher* and who fondly remember how very special they were. Our *sedarim* were, as many said, an "experience of a lifetime."

Arrival in America

MANY YEARS AGO, EUROPEANS EMIGRATING TO AMERICA CALLED their destination the *"Goldene Medinah* (the Golden State)." For us freedom-starved refugees, America was the "Land of Freedom."

As our ship steamed into New York Harbor, we gazed around in awe. The sun was shining brightly; the great Statue of Liberty glistened in all her dazzling glory from afar, and the salty sea breezes gently blew on our faces. We had learned already what this statue represented, and we hoped that the welcome it extended would be sincere, that the promises it implied would come true, for the sake of all of us who had witnessed first-hand in Europe the exact opposite of the ideals that "Miss Liberty" epitomized.

We passed through customs and found ourselves on a dock filled with hundreds of people greeting family members. There we were met by a delegation representing the Satmar Rebbe and Rebbetzin, headed by R' Lipa Friedman, *z"l,* a prominent Selisher who had been an important guest at our wedding. The reunion with R' Lipa brought back memories of our recent past, and the pain was still very raw.

R' Lipa sensed how we felt, and used his good humor to help lighten the situation. As we surveyed the thousands of people milling about, he commented jokingly to my husband, "You see, all of these people know that you are an important survivor of *Churban* Europe, and have come to welcome you to America!"

Together with the group of people who actually were sent over to meet us at the dock, we set out by car from lower Manhattan to the Satmar Rebbe's house in Williamsburg.

As we drove through lower Manhattan, my husband and I were awed by the sights of New York City. Countless automobiles thronged the streets, and we saw huge skyscrapers for the first time. Elegant storefronts dazzled us as we passed one block after another. Even

R' Rubin, around the time of our arrival in America

though we were tired from our long trip, we stayed awake just trying to absorb our new surroundings. Everything looked so different — so strange compared with what we were used to in Selish or Szaszregen — even when compared with the large European cities we had seen, such as Munich and Budapest. Driving through Chinatown as we headed toward the Williamsburg Bridge was perhaps the most fascinating part of the trip. We saw row after row of Oriental shops, restaurants, signs and faces.

We passed from Chinatown to the Lower East Side — along East Broadway, up Essex Street, then onto Delancey Street where we saw a myriad of signs in Hebrew and Yiddish. We were told that this was *"Yiddishe America."* Then we crossed the impressive Williamsburg Bridge. Once on the Brooklyn side, our hearts beat with excitement at the sight of the many people in traditional Chassidic clothing walking down the streets where, again, stores displayed signs in Yiddish. Even in Europe that was rare!

ALTHOUGH WE HAD CORRESPONDED WITH THE TEITELBAUMS WHILE we were still in Europe, thousands of miles had separated us. Our letters were mostly factual and pragmatic, and did not express the kinds of thoughts and feelings that surface only in

The Emotional Reunion With the Satmar Rebbe

personal encounters. Our first meeting with the Satmar Rebbe and Rebbetzin — the very first following our terrible wartime experiences — was so moving and emotional that initially none of us knew what to say. Words were simply too shallow to convey the deep feelings which spilled from our hearts. Instead, we read one another's facial expressions — in particular, the eyes. Excitement and joy suffused the Satmar Rebbe's face upon seeing us in front of him, alive and well. We understood that his happiness was especially intense as it was due to him that we had been married merely weeks before the destruction of the Hungarian *kehillah*. Seeing the Rebbe and Rebbetzin in front of us after many long years of separation gave us equal joy.

After briefly exchanging pleasantries, the conversation veered toward my esteemed late father-in-law, Grand Rabbi Yaakov Yisrael V'Yeshurin Rubin of Szaszregen-Sulitza, whom R' Teitelbaum had always held in high esteem. "Your father was such a wise man," the Rebbe stated. "Why didn't he cross the Romanian border when he had the chance?" There is no good answer to this important question other than to assume that the Jews of Budapest had not been informed about the true danger they were in.

We had prepared ourselves emotionally to discuss our personal experiences in the camps and my revered mother's tragic death in the Birkenau gas chamber, but the Satmar Rebbe seemed deep in thought. We decided to leave these topics for another occasion.

R' Yosef Askinazy, a relative and the Rebbe's *gabbai* from back home, and his wife were at the Teitelbaums' home during our first meeting. They joined the Satmar Rebbe and Rebbetzin in showing their joy and gratitude to the A-mighty upon seeing us again. In honor of our homecoming, the Rebbetzin prepared a lavish table, as only she could. A pleasant time was had by all there, and I shall always remember that afternoon in Williamsburg with warm feelings.

CHAPTER 13
The Miraculous Survival of the Satmar Rebbe & Rebbetzin

N O ACCOUNT OF THE EXPERIENCES OF OUR FAMILIES WOULD BE complete without the truly astounding story of how the Satmar Rebbe and Rebbetzin — my uncle and aunt — were able to survive after falling into the hands of the SS. The SS, after all, took a special delight in the humiliation and destruction of religious Jewry, and surely the Gestapo knew from their informers that the Rebbe was one of the great leaders of Hungarian religious Jewry.

After Eichmann took control of Budapest and the German Army proceeded to occupy all of Hungary in March of 1944, the Nazis herded the Jews into ghettos. Their goal was to eventually transport the Jews to Auschwitz and other concentration camps, where they would be liquidated *en masse*. Unlike the rest of Hungarian Jewry, the Jews of Budapest were not included in the initial Nazi plans for transport to Auschwitz. But Eichmann had every intention of deporting the Budapest Jews. He simply deceived them into believing they were safe.

Clüj-Klausenburg and Oradea-Grosswardein were two noted towns in Transylvania. Two of the largest Jewish congregations emerged from that region. The towns had been handed over by Romania to Hungary in 1940 and occupied by the Germans in March, 1944.

Clüj had the largest ghetto, and Oradea the second largest. Both towns were near the border of that part of Romania which had not been occupied by Germany as of 1944. King Carol of Romania, who had been a German ally, was by then already leaning toward supporting the incoming Russians, so that part of Romania became a safe haven for some Jews. (Included in this "safe zone" was the town of Alba Iulia which, as already mentioned, was the home of my sister-in-law, Rebbetzin Channah, and her husband, Grand Rabbi Nachman Kahana, *shlita*. It was to this town that my husband, I, and other members of his family headed after the war.)

There were dozens of families who succeeded in bribing their way over the border into Romania, thereby escaping Eichmann's claws. Among them were our cousins, the famous Hager-Vizhnitzer family. The family of the president of our Brooklyn congregation, Mr. Mordechai Friedman, can recount how such a border crossing took place in Oradea, as his father was actively involved in the escape transports, and our *gabbai*, Mr. Judah Bittman, remembers a similar clandestine border crossing from Clüj. The venerable Zidichoiver Rebbe, *zt"l*, father of my sister-in-law, the Szaszregen Rebbetzin, was very effective in encouraging and advising individual families to make that move in Oradea, and thereby helped save the lives of a number of families.

The Satmar Rebbe's son-in-law, R' Lipa Teitelbaum, *zt"l*, was able to smuggle himself out of the town of Satu-Mare, Hungary to

Romania via Oradea two weeks before the ghetto in Hungary was established. The Hungarian soldiers he bribed instructed him to don a Hungarian soldier's uniform. In order to look the part, he also had to cut his beard and *payos*, which he reluctantly did. (In order to save one's own life, one is allowed to violate most statutes of *halachah*, including those related to the prohibitions regarding shaving and dressing like a gentile.) The Hungarian soldiers then told him to enter their jeep and he sat there, inconspicuous among the other soldiers. Since arrangements had been made for that particular jeep to cross the border, the soldiers arrived safely on the Romanian side. Most assume that his Rebbetzin, Roisele, *z"l*, disguised herself to escape on that jeep as well.

Meanwhile, Mr. Nota Gluck, whose sons now reside in the United States, made arrangements with the driver of a Hungarian Army Red Cross ambulance to take the Satmar Rebbe, his saintly Rebbetzin Feige, and his devoted *gabbai*, R' Yosef Askinazy, over the Romanian border to the town of Turda, via Clüj. Arrangements were also made for the Biksader Rebbe, R' Eliezer Fish, *z"tl*, to accompany them on the journey.

On the designated date — approximately three days before the opening of the ghetto — the ambulance was to leave Satu-Mare. The Teitelbaums and the others were instructed to go to the house of Mr. Yeremiah Tessler in Satu-Mare where the ambulance would pick them up. Mr. Gluck made special arrangements with selected acquaintances in Clüj for somebody to take them over the Romanian border.

But despite these carefully made preparations, backed, one assumes, by considerable sums of money paid to the driver and others in the local Hungarian Army command, the journey did not proceed as planned. The ambulance arrived at the Tesslers' house several hours late, in the middle of the night. It seems that the driver somehow misunderstood the exact location of the meeting place.

During the delay, word about this "secret" transport had somehow gotten out, and when the ambulance finally left under cover of darkness, a number of neighbors in Satu-Mare pushed themselves into the vehicle with the Rebbe and Rebbetzin and their party in an effort to escape to Romania. The soldier-driver, in a panic, closed the van and sped off, leaving Mr. Gluck behind.

When the ambulance carrying the Satmar Rebbe and the others reached the town of Clüj, the driver became frightened. At gunpoint, he ordered all of the passengers, including the Teitelbaums, out into the dark street. Then he sped off, leaving them to fend for themselves. The refugees wandered around aimlessly, wondering what to do next. Around dawn, the Hungarian police in Clüj spotted the group and imprisoned them in the local jail with common criminals. The Satmar Rebbe and Rebbetzin were also subjected to this indignity.

The members of the group — now prisoners — wanted to contact the local Jewish community to alert the people as to what had transpired and to stress the plight of the imprisoned Rebbe and Rebbetzin. However, confined as they were, they had no way to make contact with the community. Finally, Rabbi Askinazy devised a solution to the dilemma and managed to position the Satmar Rebbe near a small window in the jail building, with the hope that someone passing by might recognize him. R' Teitelbaum, with his full beard, was instantly recognized by a Jewish man across the street. The Rebbe said the man looked at him and began to weep. Immediately, the same man went off to alarm the *kehillah*, telling them the revered Satmar Rebbe was among those imprisoned. At that time, however, short of sending the prisoners kosher food, the *kehillah* was powerless to take action to save them. By then, the government in Budapest was totally dominated by Berlin, and Jews had no say in their situation.

Soon a ghetto was opened in Clüj. Every Jew in the *kehillah* was interned there, including the Satmar Rebbe and Rebbetzin after their release from the Clüj jail. At its peak, there were over 28,000 people within the Clüj ghetto, 12,000 of whom were from the city itself, with the others brought in from neighboring towns.

The Germans ordered six transports for deportation out of Clüj. The Jews on those trains would ultimately reach Auschwitz.

The fifth transport was scheduled to leave on a Monday. However, on the previous Friday, the Russians bombed the railroad station. As the fifth and sixth transports could not be loaded at the ruined train station, the Germans took the unfortunate Jews from Clüj over to a leather factory named Dermada, where the rails ran right onto the factory grounds. On June 7th, 1944, the last transport from Dermada left. Many of the people from the fifth and sixth transports could have run away to safety, but had been falsely led to believe that they would be working in a labor camp in Hungary called Könyörmezö. (My husband, mother and I had also been told that we would be transported to this fictitious "Könyörmezö.")

Not everyone in Clüj had been deported. According to a number of rabbis and laymen at the time, Eichmann had arranged a deal with Rudolf Kastner, a lawyer and noted personality among Hungary's Zionist leaders, to allow one train with six hundred Jews to escape to Switzerland via Austria. In return for letting the train go, Eichmann and his SS were to receive several suitcases stuffed with diamonds, gold, and foreign currency. This booty was only the tip of the iceberg, the "down payment," as it were.

Years later, when Kastner brought suit in an Israeli court against a journalist who had labeled him a Nazi collaborator, it was revealed that the main price demanded by Eichmann of Kastner and his followers — and his whole reason for allowing the escape train at all — was to lull the Hungarian Jewish community into complacency so there would not be a repeat of the revolts which had broken out in Warsaw and in other ghettos of Poland. Since Clüj was the largest ghetto, and was right near the Romanian border, the German-Nazis were concerned about the possibility of an outbreak there. But they proved to be the masters of making use of human weakness, setting brother against brother in each and every nation, like Petain in France or Quisling in Norway. Even in Germany itself, brother attacked brother and son denounced father to the Nazis. In Hungary, the SS used its criminal intelligence to make an individual such as Kastner lie to his fellow Jews and keep them quiet in the ghetto. It is for this reason that out of the quota of six hundred passengers, three hundred eighteen came from Clüj, including many of Kastner's associates and their relatives.

Even though Hungarian Jews were generally prohibited from train travel, Kastner had the freedom to ride the trains more or less as he pleased. He traveled to Clüj to visit the ghetto and to gather together his family, including his father-in-law, Dr. Joseph Fisher, an attorney, who was among those imprisoned in the Clüj ghetto. According to a former inhabitant, Kastner's visit left behind a false optimism among the Jews of Clüj, an inaccurate view that nothing really terrible was going to happen.

Kastner gathered together those who would make the trip from Clüj to Budapest, where they would board the special train that would take them to Switzerland. Most of those who were selected to be saved were Kastner's associates and family members. Representatives of a fair amount of the local Orthodox and Chassidic communities had been omitted from Kastner's list. (It is known that Kastner refused to include even one of the Klausenburger Rebbe's eleven children from the Clüj ghetto.) Even so, according to the terms of this "devil's deal," some leading personalities from all sectors of the community — even the religious element — had to be on the list of train passengers, presumably to adhere to Eichmann's plan to keep the overall ghetto population tranquil. So it was that the names of the Satmar Rebbe and Rebbetzin, and of R' Askinazy, were included among the three hundred eighteen Jews whom Kastner selected from the Clüj ghetto, along with that of the head rabbi of the Orthodox community, R' Akiva Glazner, and his family.

Kastner secretly transported all of those selected to Budapest, where the special train arrived late one Friday afternoon in June. The Satmar Rebbe walked to the train without taking along his *tefillin*, it being near sunset on *erev* Shabbos. (Budapest had no *eruv* [a boundary around a community which enables its Jews to carry items outside their domain on Shabbos], and besides, *tefillin* are considered in the category of *muktzeh* [items not permitted to be used on the Sabbath which therefore may not be moved on that day].) Later, a man found the Rebbe's *tefillin* and returned them to him in Budapest, to the Rebbe's immense joy. The return of his precious *tefillin* was a tremendous spiritual experience for the Rebbe. (Years later, the Rebbe told my husband that he would one day have those *tefillin*. After the Rebbe passed away, the Rebbetzin sent the *tefillin* to us via messenger, to fulfill this verbal statement.)

In Budapest, others who were scheduled to board the special train to Switzerland did so. For example, R' Jungreis, the *Rav* of Szeged, Hungary, was interned in the Szeged ghetto. He and his family were jammed with hundreds of other Szeged Jews onto one of the death trains bound for Auschwitz. However, one of R' Jungreis' relatives worked in Kastner's office. She arranged it so that when the Nazi transport from Szeged passed through Budapest, the cattle car was opened and the entire Jungreis family was rescued. (His son, R' Yaakov Jungreis, claims that the accusations of collaboration which have been lodged against Kastner in the years since these events took place are wrong, and wrote to my husband to tell him so.)

Ultimately, more individuals than were anticipated had crowded onto the train in Budapest by the time it finally left to go to Switzerland. Rather than the original number of 600, the Swiss counted 1,686 Jews when the train finally crossed the border many months later.

After the train left Budapest, it headed for Switzerland by way of Austria, but was detained in the city of Linz, Hitler's one-time hometown and the hometown of Eichmann. There, what my husband considers to be one of the truly amazing miracles of the Holocaust occurred.

All the passengers — men, women and children — were removed from the train for disinfection. They were forced to have the hair on their bodies cut and were ordered to take a bath. The pale victims were lined up and a doctor inspected everyone's head (and the men's beards) before sending them off to the barber. When the doctor checked the Satmar Rebbe's hair and beard, he said he found both the head and beard clean. He passed the Rebbe through without requiring him to go to the barber.

R' Teitelbaum, to my husband's knowledge, was the only Jewish prisoner who did not have his beard shorn. Furthermore, he was the only individual of all the European Jewish men who fell into the hands of Eichmann and survived, who never once had his beard and *payos* forcibly removed. A number of explanations have been suggested, but one must ask why so many other rabbis (for example, the saintly and venerable R' Yonasan Steif of Budapest, the famous R' Michoel Dov Ber Weissmandl, or the *Rav* of Debrecen) were forced to have their beard and *payos* removed. The fact that the Satmar Rebbe was spared this ordeal is all the more remarkable when one remembers that it was, after all, the common practice of the German-Nazis and their collaborators to humiliate Orthodox Jewish men by publicly shaving their beards and cutting their *payos*. The beard has always been a special symbol to religious Jews, especially among the *Chassidim*, and having it forcibly cut off or shaved caused unbelievable mental anguish and spiritual trauma to those men who endured this indignity. I therefore marvel at the Heavenly providence which spared Grand Rabbi Teitelbaum, the *tzaddik*, from having to endure this supreme humiliation during his time under Eichmann's rule.

From the stopover in Linz, the train proceeded through Austria — but not westward to Switzerland. Rather, it turned north into Germany itself, ultimately stopping at the dreaded Bergen-Belsen murder camp. Perhaps in the *zechus* of the Rebbe's presence among them, those aboard were lodged in a special section of the camp with no hard work or killings. The Satmar Rebbe arrived there on the fast day of 17 Tammuz 5704.

The months in Bergen-Belsen passed slowly, but no harm came to the Rebbe and Rebbetzin, or to the others from the train.

After six months of negotiation, Eichmann's notorious assistant, Kurt Becher, made another "devil's deal" with Kastner: the train would be allowed over the Swiss border in exchange for saving Becher's life after the war by vouching for him with the Allied authorities. Permitting the train to leave was strictly in contravention to Hitler's directives that the liquidation of all Jews every-where under Nazi dominion be speeded up. However, by December 1944, the war was all but lost; Nazi murderers were starting to desert the Fuhrer's sinking ship in droves. They cut whatever deals they could to save their own necks. And so it was done. Becher released the train, and Kastner later kept his part of the bargain by saving him from the hangman's noose. (This action by Kastner caused much chagrin and consternation to many who believed that the notorious Becher truly deserved to die, and that Kastner was being overly fastidious in keeping a promise made so obviously under duress.)

In the Satmar books, the dates of both the arrival at Bergen-Belsen and the border crossing to Switzerland are given. In a letter to the British customs officials in Haifa, dated April 21, 1946, and signed by the Rebbe himself, R' Yoel Teitelbaum wrote, "My wife and I survived miraculously [in] the German camp in Bergen-Belsen where we stayed for seven months." Actually, according to the dates, it was only five months and four days, but it seems that he counted from the date when he was first interned in the Clüj ghetto.

R' TEITELBAUM DEPARTED FROM BERGEN-BELSEN FOR SWITZERLAND on December 6, 1944/21 Kislev 5705, five days before Chanukah.

Chanukah in Bergen-Belsen After the departure of the Satmar Rebbe, R' Rafael Gross (now rabbi of the Keresterer *shul* in Miami Beach, Florida) arrived in Bergen-Belsen and was assigned to sleep in the bed which had been occupied by R' Teitelbaum. R' Gross and his family had been on a transport from the Debrecen ghetto when the railway to Auschwitz was closed. The train altered course and took its imprisoned passengers through the outskirts of Vienna, then through Czechoslovakia, where they passed Theresienstadt. Finally, R' Gross' transport arrived in Bergen-Belsen.

R' Gross told my husband how one day he found eight potatoes hidden by his bunk bed. When he showed the potatoes to the others in his barrack, they related the story of those potatoes.

Beginning a few days before Chanukah, the Satmar Rebbe refrained from eating his potatoes and hid them with the hope of finding oil to make a Chanukah *menorah*. The Rebbetzin took the potatoes and made them into Chanukah oil holders, cutting them into nine pieces and gouging a hole in each piece, eight for the oil or candles, and the ninth for the *shammes*.

Various firsthand witnesses told me that right before Chanukah, a bundle of candles fell down from a shelf in the barrack. They were obtained by the Rebbe, and hidden for use on Chanukah. It seems that the Rebbe had "organized" the candles just in case he could not find oil to fill the potatoes.

There are Chassidic *rebbeim* who have silver *menorahs*, sometimes so large that the rebbe has to walk up several steps to reach the wicks and oil cups to light them. This portrays the great honor given to the *mitzvah* of observing the holiday and the expression of the miracle of the oil. But it is easy to understand that on the scale of the *Beis Din* (Rabbinical Court) in Heaven, which measures our *mitzvos*, those few potato candle-holders made by the Satmar Rebbetzin in Bergen-Belsen, where there was constant hunger and danger, might very well outweigh all of the grandiose ten-kilogram silver *menorahs*.

Since from childhood on R' Yoel Teitelbaum had always taken great care to *daven* with a thoroughly clean body (as required by strict Torah law), even under duress he made sure to exchange food for bathroom paper. However, the Rebbe did not exchange his Shabbos food (as told by R' Shalom Krausz, the Udvarier Rav, *shlita*, who was also in Bergen-Belsen as part of the Kastner group).

In Bergen-Belsen, the Satmar Rebbe's *mesiras nefesh* enabled him to maintain his high standards of *kashrus*. He was extraordinarily particular about what he ate, even when the food was kosher. Usually, his diet consisted of potatoes, eggs or fresh vegetables. Rebbetzin Feige went to great lengths to prepare the food specially for him. I am told that the first time she cooked the food for him in the camp oven, the Rebbe refused to eat it; she had to heat the food with candles instead.

THE SATMAR REBBE AND REBBETZIN AND THE ENTIRE GROUP FROM the Kastner train eventually crossed the border into Switzerland.

Switzerland Once in Switzerland, the Rebbe and others with him were placed in the refugee camp of Caux Kavah. At the time, some of those originally in the group still remained in Bergen-Belsen.

A short while later, Mr. George Mantello, the Secretary of the El Salvadorian Embassy in Switzerland, obtained a visa for R' Teitelbaum. Later, in recognition, Mr. Mantello received a silver cup with a profound personal blessing from the Rebbe.

How Mr. Mantello came to be in a position to help the Rebbe is a story in and of itself (and, again, proof that Hashem works in strange and great ways).

In the vicinity of Szaszregen was a town named Bistritz. The rabbi of that town, R' Moshe Spitz, survived the war years and resides now in Boro Park. A non-observant Jew from Bistritz had previously emigrated to El Salvador, where he changed his name to George Mantello. He went into the service of the El Salvadorian government, and by the time of the war, had become the First Secretary of the El Salvadorian Embassy in Switzerland. In this position, he learned about the murderous activities of the cruel Nazi government and resolved to do something about it. Mantello issued many passports to safety, thereby saving countless Jewish lives. The German Foreign Office — even the world-notorious Eichmann in Budapest — had to respect this embassy's papers, as was the case with the papers issued by the famed diplomat Raoul Wallenberg of Sweden, may he rest in peace.

Mantello performed another important act. Through the Swiss press and ambassadorial channels, he broadcast to the world that Jews and others were being murdered by the Germans. He revealed that in Auschwitz 12,000 innocent men, women and children were being murdered and gassed daily. His alarm opened the eyes of the public to the existence of the gas chambers, a fact that the Germans had kept secret.

Mr. Mantello is still alive and is over 90 years old, may G-d bless him. I wish we could bear a similar debt of gratitude towards certain other Jewish individuals who were in a position to help save Jewish lives in Budapest, in the United States, in Israel, and elsewhere at that time.

Pesach 1945 fell while the Rebbe was in Switzerland. He had a problem obtaining proper matzos for the festival observance. Chassidic *rabbanim* eat only handmade, hand-ground, hand-baked matzos. Baking *shemurah matzos* in that fashion was strange to the Swiss Jewish population at the time. However, certain individuals stood by the Satmar Rebbe, including our worthy friend, R' Moshe Gross, the father of the Boro Park Belzer Dayan, R' Shamai Gross. The Rebbe managed to prepare an oven in a nearby township in which to bake his matzos for Pesach. He was able to get the wheat and material he needed to prepare the matzos. A Swiss inhabitant told my husband how difficult it was to obtain the oven and the matzos. He said that this was the first private matzah oven in Swiss Jewish history. We have a photo print of a *shtar mechirah*, the sales contract selling the *chametz* to a non-Jew, written in hand by the Rebbe himself. In his sales contract, the Rebbe sells his dishes, which was the custom of most rabbis in Galicia, but not of many others.

WHILE IN SWITZERLAND, THE SATMAR REBBE WAS INVITED TO THE United States by his cousin, R' Teitelbaum, z"l, the Laposher Rav **Eretz** from New York City. The Satmar Rebbe wrote to him to **Yisrael** obtain U.S. papers, but as soon as he received the certificate to enter *Eretz Yisrael*, he sent another letter to the Laposher Rav, telling him that he would be going to *Eretz Yisrael* after all. Apologizing, he explained that he had only requested U.S. papers because he had been very doubtful of obtaining a certificate to enter *Eretz Yisrael* at the time, a difficult feat without political connections.

From Switzerland, the Satmar Rebbe and his Rebbetzin went to *Eretz Yisrael*. They arrived in Palestine in 1945. His son-in-law, R' Lipa Teitelbaum, and daughter, Rebbetzin Roisele, were living in *Eretz Yisrael* at the time, having escaped via Romania. I was told that Rebbetzin Roisele, *zt"l*, turned to the Chief Rabbi, R' Isaac HaLevi Herzog, *z"l*, who intervened on behalf of the Teitelbaum family and obtained three certificates to enable the Rebbe, his Rebbetzin, and one other person of their choice to come to *Eretz Yisrael*. The other passenger was his devoted *gabbai*, R' Askinazy, who now resides in Monroe, New York, in the Chassidic neighborhood founded and built through the great efforts of the Satmar Rebbe and Rebbetzin, with the help of R' Askinazy. That section of town bears the Rebbe's name, *Kiryas Yoel*.

My husband, R' Rubin, would like to take this opportunity to publicly recognize the actions of R' Herzog, who obtained certificates for his parents and family in Szaszregen. In 1943, a postcard arrived in the mail from Rav Dr. Jacob Griffel of Istanbul, Turkey, who wrote, "I have obtained certificates for you and your children to go to *Eretz Yisrael*."

My in-laws were undecided and, as already mentioned, the Jews in Hungary were uninformed as to what was truly going on. It would have been a difficult decision for them to make, to leave their married children behind and go by ship overseas. Therefore, my in-laws did not act swiftly.

Dr. Griffel later told my brother-in-law, the Sulitzer Rebbe, *shlita*, that it was my father-in-law's mother, Rebbetzin Shlomtza, *zt"l*, the famous Zidichoiver-Premishlaner Rebbetzin in Jerusalem, who had contacted Rabbi Herzog on my in-laws' behalf. R' Herzog ultimately obtained the certificates and transmitted them to Dr. Griffel. Since Dr. Griffel did not get a fast response from my in-laws, he sent the certificates to another family. Had they known what torments awaited them at the hands of Eichmann, perhaps my husband's family would have taken immediate action and gone to *Eretz Yisrael*. It seems it was Heaven's decree for a different family to be saved by those certificates. We therefore justify Rav Dr. Griffel's decision to give away the certificates to someone else.

When he arrived in *Eretz Yisrael*, the Satmar Rebbe found about one hundred of his followers already there, including the leaders of the Satmar community, the Freund family, and many others. The Rebbe settled in the Meah Shearim section of Jerusalem and did a tremendous amount of *tzedakah* for the religious community.

After my husband founded the *kollel* in Krumbach, Germany, and it was time to decide where we wanted to emigrate — either to the United States or to *Eretz Yisrael* — we wrote to our uncle, the Satmar Rebbe, and asked his advice. He mailed back a long handwritten letter, informing us that he had obtained two certificates to enable my husband and me to emigrate to *Eretz Yisrael*.

In 1947, the Satmar Rebbe and Rebbetzin went to the United States on what was intended to be a very temporary basis. The Rebbe told my husband that he was hesitant about coming to America. He was determined to remain only a short time and then return to *Eretz Yisrael*. "Only when the ship left port in Haifa was I sure that I was leaving," said the Rebbe. He did not take along any of his *sefarim*, and the first year he lived in the United States (1948/5707), he and the Rebbetzin did not have a place of their own. Instead, they stayed with Mr. Mordechai Fleischman, *a"h*, on Rodney Street in Williamsburg, and did not unpack their bags for quite a while. The Rebbe observed Succos for only one day, as is done by a person who lives permanently in *Eretz Yisrael* but is in *galus* during Succos. These actions all point to the probable intentions of the Rebbe to live out his days in *Eretz Yisrael* and await Mashiach there. In his letter to the Laposher Rav, the Rebbe explained that the only reason he inquired about a visa to the United States in the first place was because while he and the others on the transport were in Switzerland, there were rumors that Switzerland was going to transfer them all to Algiers, and he greatly preferred to go to America. But when seven hundred certificates of admission to *Eretz Yisrael* arrived in Switzerland for the Jews of the Bergen-Belsen

Left to Right: The present Satmar Rebbe, shlita, my uncle, z"tl, my husband, R' Yosef Askinazi, and Mr. Mordechai Ekstein

transport, the Satmar Rebbe decided that he would go to *Eretz Yisrael* because, "[his] whole desire [was] to live in the *Eretz HaChaim* (synonym for *Eretz Yisrael*), and wait for the redemption of Jewry which we hope for in the near future" (*Michtavei R' Yoel*, Letter 137, p. 194).

It should be remembered that all of this took place before the official establishment of the State of Israel. The Satmar Rebbe's opinion about establishing the political state of Israel is included in his books.

CHAPTER 14

Our New Life
in a Free Country

AFTER MY HUSBAND AND I ARRIVED IN AMERICA IN 1948, we maintained a very close relationship with our uncle and aunt. R' Rubin spent many hours with the Satmar Rebbe, and had the privilege of engaging in many intimate discussions with him for many hours. He made it a custom to be there every Monday when the Rebbe returned from *Shacharis*, usually after midday. Very few individuals could say they shared so many hours with the Rebbe, and my husband considers himself fortunate to have had that special time with him, mostly discussing serious themes of Torah law and the conduct of Chassidic courts.

DOWN THROUGH THE AGES, JEWS HAVE ALWAYS ASKED THEMSELVES the painful questions: "Where do I go now?" and "Who wants **Rockaway** me?" Once we were in America, we found our-**Beach** selves facing this dilemma, along with so many other European Jewish refugees. In addition, finding an apartment right after the war was a problem.

Adjusting to life in America took some time and was difficult. The transition was made easier by the Teitelbaums' unlimited assistance, for which we were very grateful. They made us feel welcome the entire time we were with them; the affection and encouragement they lavished on us went above and beyond the calls of duty and kinship.

However, the weeks were racing by and we had to make plans for our own future. We could not remain in Williamsburg indefinitely. As the Satmar community was beginning to take root, my uncle, the Rebbe, was under a great deal of pressure, busy day and night meeting with people in the religious community, and fulfilling his many duties. It would have been equally wrong for us to impose upon my other uncle, the Melitzer Rebbe, who lived alone on the Lower East Side and was trying to cope with the tragic loss of his family in Europe.

One day, the Satmar Rebbe received a visitor in the person of R' Berel Moskowitz, *a"h*, who lived with his family in Rockaway Beach, a seaside community on the Rockaway Peninsula in the borough of Queens. Although not a rabbi himself, Mr. Moskowitz, a *Chassid* from Sighet, Hungary — my hometown — owned a *shtiebel* in the Rockaway community. He informed my uncle that a small Chassidic community had been established in his vicinity, and that he was willing to hand over the *shtiebel* to whomever my uncle deemed acceptable to assume the position of rabbi. Later that day, my uncle met with my husband and me, and informed us of Mr. Moskowitz's proposition. He recommended that my husband should assume leadership of the Rockaway *shtiebel* and use it as a base for rebuilding his *rebbishe* dynasty. We decided to try it out, and my husband accepted the offer. Would we wish to settle there permanently? Only time would tell. My uncle made the final arrangements and we prepared for our new life in the Rockaway Beach religious community.

R' Lipa Friedman drove us to Rockaway Beach. We stepped out

of the car and drew the fresh, clean ocean air into our lungs. The peaceful sounds of seagulls calling filled the silence. We stood near the Atlantic Ocean, watching the waves ebb and flow, supremely conscious that our former homeland — now soiled with the blood of our martyred Jewish brethren — stood on the opposite shore. The vast, open sky met the ocean far out on the horizon, stretching back, back, back to where we came from.

Mr. Moskowitz was waiting outside for us. He greeted us in a friendly manner and showed us around, focusing, of course, on the *beis midrash*. The *shtiebel* was a relatively old structure, but we were impressed with the cozy, *heimishe* atmosphere inside. Then Mr. Moskowitz introduced us to his wife, who welcomed us warmly and showed us to our apartment. We had not yet discussed monetary arrangements.

My husband was happy to once again be starting out as the rabbi of a *shtiebel*. The new situation brought back memories of "home" in Szaszregen as well as Selish, Leipheim and Krumbach, where he had been privileged to serve the needs of the religious community and provide help and inspiration. He enjoyed the challenge of responding to *she'eilos* on *kashrus* and other matters, and looked forward to the hours he would spend with members of his new *kehillah*, engrossed in Torah study.

Halachic Problems in Rockaway Beach

WE STAYED IN ROCKAWAY BEACH FOR ABOUT A YEAR, AND WERE treated well by the Moskowitz family and by many in the local religious community, most notably R' Mendel Hausman, *z"l*, and his worthy family. However, although we were grateful for the consideration and friendship of these people, and despite the breathtaking beauty of the natural landscape, we decided against settling there permanently.

This decision was based on our discovery of what Rockaway Beach was like during the summer months. It was a resort community, and the behavior we witnessed on the streets of this

American beach resort was scandalous in our eyes. Brought up, as we both were, to respect the concept of *tzenius* (modesty), it pained us to realize that there were many Jews among the scantily dressed seaside revelers, participating in mixed swimming and other immodest pursuits. We felt decidedly uncomfortable in such an environment, and regretfully informed the Moskowitzs that it was time for us to move on.

We later heard about the generally accepted educational theory that by mixing the sexes, lust is supposedly eased. We know that is wrong. Today, the moral decadence which pervades secular society from the street right up to the upper echelons of leadership is testimony to the bankruptcy of that theory. One can only wonder if the day might not come when separation of the sexes will be adopted in the high schools and other vulnerable areas of society at large.

WHILE WE WERE DEALING WITH THE QUESTION OF WHETHER OR NOT to remain in the Rockaways, the Berbester-Keresterer Rebbe, R'

Flatbush Naftali Gross, *zt"l*, and his Rebbetzin (now in Miami Beach, Florida) happened to visit us. R' Gross told us that relatives in Flatbush, Brooklyn, were urging him to relocate there. He told us that Flatbush was a very clean, quiet, well-kept neighborhood and more importantly, it was a place where Orthodoxy definitely had a future. To be sure, the majority of the approximately 250,000 Jewish residents in the Flatbush-Midwood area were not particularly observant. However, the great Mirrer Yeshivah, once one of the brightest lights of the lost Eastern European yeshivah world, had recently relocated there, coming from Shanghai, China, after the end of the war. The yeshivah, with its *kollel* of several hundred families, was in turn attracting other Orthodox people to live in the area, and they formed growing enclaves within the general population.

The Keresterer Rebbe was tempted by the possibilities that existed in relocating to Flatbush, but decided instead to move to the more established Chassidic community in Crown Heights.

He advised us to go to Flatbush and establish a Chassidic community there.

We went to discuss this matter with our uncle, the Satmar Rebbe. He asked us why we wished to leave Rockaway Beach, and we explained the impropriety of our remaining in a resort community. He gave the issue some thought and then said, "In Rockaway Beach, the street may be *treif*, but the inside of the *beis midrash* is kosher. In Flatbush, the street is kosher but the *beis midrash* may be *treif*." Nevertheless, we could not bear to remain near the beach and decided to settle in Flatbush. (When our *shtiebel* was established, my dear uncle participated personally in every *simchah*. He paid us a visit every year, and said *divrei Torah* at the *shul's* annual *melaveh malkah*.)[1]

The first major problem we faced was organizing a *shtiebel*-type *kehillah*. At the time, establishing a *shtiebel* with a *mechitzah* to separate the men and women and having a congregation that would be willing to stretch the Sabbath or Yom Kippur for 72 minutes after sunset was very difficult. But, please the A-mighty, it was achieved, especially after we had our first congregants from Zeirei-Agudah in Flatbush. The next problem was finding and purchasing a house large enough to fit a comfortably-sized *beis midrash* for the community and an apartment for ourselves. We also had renovation and zoning laws to contend with. Finally, there was the question of money — for without money, there were great limits on what we could hope to accomplish.

The Keresterer Rebbe, *zt"l*, introduced us to a man named Mr. Aba Frankel, a distant cousin of mine from my hometown of Sighet, who now lived in Flatbush. My cousin was happy to learn of our interest in moving to Flatbush, and involved himself in assisting us. He spent many hours searching for a suitable place for us to live and to establish my husband's congregation. He ultimately found a sizable two-story house facing Ocean Parkway, and

---

1. Once, my uncle tried to settle us in the Satmar congregation of Crown Heights or Boro Park, but for reasons unknown to me, it did not happen.

after inspecting the building, we decided to settle there.

We were extremely fortunate to have many people in the community help us towards the goal of raising funds for a down payment. One such individual was Mr. Naftali Wexler, *a"h*. A Ropshitzer follower from the township of Maiden, Galicia, he was instrumental in helping to build our *beis midrash*. A blue-collar worker, he saved his earnings and used most of his savings to help us obtain what we needed. May the A-mighty remember his many good deeds.

The *shul* was finally opened and named "Congregation Yeshurin" in memory of my martyred holy and revered father-in-law, may Hashem avenge his blood. We still live in the same house today and have many rewarding

Congregation and Yeshiva Yeshurin on Ocean Parkway in Flatbush

Russian immigrants attend a shiur (lecture) at Congregation Yeshurin

memories dating back to the early days when we struggled to build a strong Chassidic *kehillah*.

This is the Aron Kodesh (Holy Ark) at the shul in Brooklyn. It was built in 1947 and used in the Kollel in Krumbach.

R' Rubin with the leading Roshei Yeshiva in Flatbush

MY HUSBAND WAS FRIENDLY WITH THE Boyaner Rebbe, zt"l, from the Lower East Side of New York City. When my husband told him

A Berachah From the Boyaner Rebbe

about our plans for Flatbush, the Rebbe gave my husband a special *berachah*. "May there always be at least ten *shomrei mitzvos* [to form a *minyan*] in your *beis midrash*," he said. This was, unfortunately, the kind of reputation that Flatbush had among the very pious at the time — a community in which forming a *minyan* was not always possible. But the reality was somewhat different. The number of Orthodox Jews anxious to live a Torah life and create a strong religious community in Flatbush was on the rise.

MR. MEYER UKELES WAS A POLISH IMMIGRANT WHO WOULD GO ON to become the first president of our congregation. His devotion and

Mr. Meyer Ukeles

strong *emunah* impressed everyone around him, my husband and myself included.

Mr. Ukeles shared a driveway with his next-door neighbor, and when this man insisted on driving his car on Shabbos, R' Meyer lay down on the concrete and cried out, "Over my dead body!" The neighbor was impressed by Mr. Ukeles' strong stand, and eventually ceased his public desecration of the Sabbath.

Mr. Ukeles told us that he once attended a meeting of *Hatzalah-Rescue*, where the issue of rescuing Europe's shattered *klal* was discussed. When the *Rosh Yeshivah* of Lakewood, R' Aaron Kotler, *zt"l*, described the sufferings of European Jewry and appealed for funds with which to aid them, Mr. Ukeles became very emotional, took out his checkbook and wrote a check for $35,000 — a tremendous fortune in those days. His generous donation helped to rescue the Mir Yeshivah community and other Jews who had fled Europe and ended up temporarily in Shanghai.

Mr. Ukeles always credited his wife for her support when he told her about the $35,000 donation. Mr. Ukeles should be remembered for his tremendous *mesiras nefesh*.

Mr. Ukeles was just one of the many fine, devoted people we found when we got to Flatbush, people who would prove instrumental in establishing Congregation Yeshurin.

Mr. Eliyahu "Ira" Rosenzweig

ANOTHER PERSON WHO MUST BE ESPECIALLY REMEMBERED FOR HIS great deeds to further Torah and to help us was a man by the name of Mr. Yisrael Eliyahu Rosenzweig, *a"h*. Many people in the community knew him by his American name of "Ira." When it came to promoting *Yiddishkeit*, he was a powerhouse. He was a founder and supporter of a large local Orthodox synagogue and a founder and major patron of Yeshivah Rambam, a yeshivah in the neighborhood, and a co-founder of the Hebrew Academy headed by Rabbi Gross in Miami Beach, Florida. He *davened* every day in his *shul* on East 3rd Street, and each day people would line up and approach him to solicit funds for all sorts of charities — and they would not be disappointed. When we came to Flatbush, Mr.

Rosenzweig took a great interest in establishing our Chassidic *kehillah* in the neighborhood.

As part of a fundraising campaign that Mr. Rosenzweig organized for our *beis midrash,* he wanted to print a public relations statement in the *Jewish Morning Journal,* accompanied by his picture. Coming from the *rebbishe* House of Szaszregen, my husband hesitated to print the picture. At about this time we were visiting my uncle, the Satmar Rebbe, at his home on Bedford Avenue in Williamsburg. My husband explained his dilemma about allowing a man's picture to be published in the newspaper in order to help raise funds for the congregation. Mr. Mordechai Eckstein, a"h, a well-known public figure and Sigheter *Chassid,* heard the conversation. As he joined in the discussion between the Satmar Rebbe and my husband, he surprised them both with an unexpected observation, "The biggest institutions are after Ira Rosenzweig to get his picture in the paper, and you are hesitating?" For years afterward, Mr. Ira Rosenzweig organized a yearly *melaveh malkah* for our *shtiebel,* complete with obtaining the guest of honor and invariably attracting a sizable crowd.

MY HUSBAND WAS ACTIVE AND ENERGETIC IN STRENGTHENING *Yiddishkeit* in the neighborhood. While there were fine Orthodox

Birth of a New Chassidic Community
shuls such as the Talmud Torah of Flatbush, Young Israel of Flatbush, and others, there were no established *shtieblach* in the community. There were no local glatt kosher butcher shops, nor stores which sold *chalav Yisrael* products, nor was there a school to which a strictly Orthodox family could send its children. The rabbi of the Young Israel of Flatbush, R' Sharfman, and Mr. Nat Kevelson were active in erecting a *mikveh* in Flatbush. My husband took an active part in determining the halachic standards for the *mikveh*. When the *mikveh* plans from R' Telushkin, zt"l, a member of the Agudas HaRabbanim and an authority on *hilchos mikveh,* were presented, my husband and the Shomkuter Rebbe, R'

J. Rutner, *zt"l*, requested stricter standards. Mr. Morty Rosenberg, *a"h*, was instrumental in having the *Mikveh* Committee approve an extra $15,000 for that purpose.

My husband was instrumental in helping to establish the first glatt kosher butcher shop on King's Highway. He also engaged a peddler who sold *chalav Yisrael* products. A Chassidic nursery school was opened for preschoolers, and a *cheder* was started for boys. The first Bais Yaakov was established in our building by the Kaliver Rebbe, R' M.Taub, *shlita* (now an *Admor* in *Eretz Yisrael*). A few years later, the well-known Yeshiva of Brooklyn (Y.O.B.) girls' school moved into the neighborhood, and my husband was helpful in obtaining a building for them on our block on Ocean Parkway. Today it is thriving, and a new state-of-the-art building has been erected to accommodate the large influx of girls attending.

Mr. Rausman opened a new *shomer Shabbos* grocery store on Avenue M, not too far from our block. To celebrate the opening of the first *shomer Shabbos* store in the area, Mr. Ch. A. Fried, the devoted *askan*, hosted a festive *kiddush* in our *beis midrash*. In my husband's *derashah*, he said, "I can now explain the words of the wise Shlomo *HaMelech* in *Koheles*: "It is better to go to a house of mourning than to a house of celebration." Why is this so?

"My great father, *zt"l*, once called together his *kehillah* in Sulitza, Romania, to inform them that the local grocer was secretly selling his products on the holy Sabbath through a back door. The members of the congregation burst into tears upon hearing of this

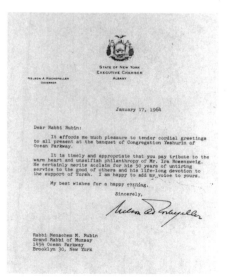

A tribute to Mr. Ira Rosenzweig from then-Govorner Rockefeller

Our shul logo, designed at the initiative of Mr. Rosenzweig

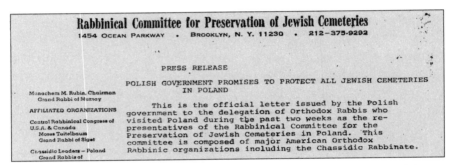

Rabbinical Committee for Preservation of Jewish Cemeteries
1454 OCEAN PARKWAY • BROOKLYN, N. Y. 11230 • 212-375-9292

Menachem M. Rubin, Chairman
Grand Rabbi of Muzsay

AFFILIATED ORGANIZATIONS

Central Rabbinical Congress of
U.S.A. & Canada
Moses Teitelbaum
Grand Rabbi of Sigat

Chassidic Leaders – Poland
Grand Rabbis of

PRESS RELEASE

POLISH GOVERNMENT PROMISES TO PROTECT ALL JEWISH CEMETERIES
IN POLAND

This is the official letter issued by the Polish government to the delegation of Orthodox Rabbis who visited Poland during the past two weeks as the representatives of the Rabbinical Committee for the Preservation of Jewish Cemeteries in Poland. This committee is composed of major American Orthodox Rabbinic organizations including the Chassidic Rabbinate.

Because of our experiences during the Holocaust, the cause of protecting Jewish cemeteries is important to both my husband and myself. Here is a letter from a committee of prominent rabbis that he headed, which worked with the Polish government to protect Jewish cemeteries there.

The public is largely unaware that the heroism and self-sacrifice of Torah Jewry during the Holocaust have been largely ignored both in museums such as Yad VaShem and the Holocaust museums in Washington and New York, as well as in films, literature and the like. R' Rubin is trying very hard to awaken the public to this issue. Pictured here, following a recent meeting on this subject are: R' Rubin (seated center), flanked by New York State Senator Seymour Lachman (r.), and orthodox community activist George Klein(l.). Standing are Dr. Michael Birnbaum, director of the Shoah Foundation and Dr. Mays, director of the New York Holocaust Museum.

painful discovery. In those days, it was cause for mourning if one tradesman desecrated the holy Shabbos. Here today we have reached the low point where we actually gather to celebrate and honor one who is *Shomer Shabbos*!

"It is thus better to mourn one grocer who sells on the holy Sabbath than to celebrate one who is *shomer Shabbos*."

With the A-mighty's help, the Chassidic community in Flatbush continued to grow. Today Flatbush is home to approximately seventy *shtieblach*, as well as to many well- known yeshivos, and large Orthodox shuls with prominent rabbis.

How different Flatbush is today from the first Shabbos that we officially opened our doors for *davening*! Back then, over thirty very fine *mispallelim* attended our *shtiebel*.

The current honorary president of our congregation, Mr. Mordechai Friedman, told us that when he was considering whether or not to move to Flatbush from Crown Heights, he sought the opinion of our worthy friend, R' Sholom Brod, *a"h*. Mr. Brod gave Mr. Friedman sterling advice, saying, "The Muzsayer Rebbe's *shalosh seudos* in Flatbush is nicer than the one I had in Crown Heights." R' Mordechai Friedman is very active in our *beis midrash*. He makes it his business to be responsible for covering the budget, giving *shiurim*, and quickly extending an

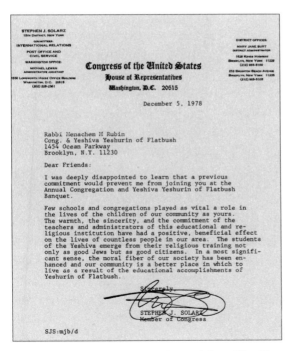

A letter from then-congressman Steven Solarz of Brooklyn

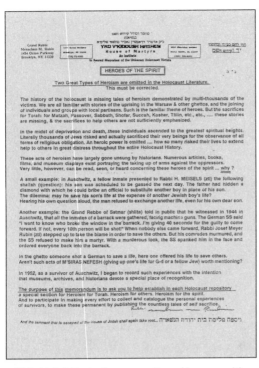

R' Rubin's letter to the community seeking recognition for the mesiras nefesh of religious Jews during the Holocaust

open hand on behalf of worthy charities.

The *berachach* given to my husband by the Boyaner Rebbe — that we should always be able to put together at least a kosher *minyan* in Flatbush — proved to be based on an erroneous outside impression of Flatbush. Not only did we begin with our twenty or more *shomer Shabbos* men, but we were fortunate to have quality *baalei batim* who would have been prominent *Yidden* even in the Rebbe's own East Side community. Indeed, our "ten" turned into something like thousands of souls in Flatbush and Midwood, *kein yirbu*. May Hashem watch over this community as it continues to grow, both in actual numbers of observant *Yidden* and in its overall devotion to Torah and *mitzvos*.

Continuing the Chain

YEAR AFTER YEAR WENT BY WITHOUT OUR HAVING A CHILD. I SAW ONE specialist after another, but the results were frustrating. Then, one beautiful spring day, as I sat in the office of a specialist at Brooklyn Jewish Hospital, I received the most unexpected, incredible news. The doctor told me that not only was I expecting — I was already four months along! I stared at the doctor in stunned amazement. Why, only that

R' Rubin helps to honor the Rosh HaYeshivah of Yeshivah Torah Vodaath,
HaRav Avraham Pam, shlita

R' Rubin (seated second from left) with the Belzer Rebbe (seated left), shlita, in our home

morning I had been moving some heavy ceramic flowerpots
around the porch of our apartment and painting them, totally
unaware of my condition!

I must have appeared pale or dazed when I returned home,
because my husband quickly brought me a chair and insisted that I
sit down. He asked whether it was time to express praise and gratitude

A simchah at Khal Yeshurin

R' Rubin, visiting the Ponoviezer Rosh HaYeshivah,
R' Elazar Menachem Man Schach, shlita

to Hashem. Stammering, I imparted to him the wonderful news we had yearned for so long. He, too, was full of amazement.

Five months later our dear son, Chaim, was born and was named after my holy father, the Ranziver *tzaddik, zt"l, H"yd*. Today, he is the Rebbe of the Ropshitz Congregation in Boro Park. He and his wife have been blessed with an outstanding family — our grandchildren.

The very devoted Satmar *Chassidim* claim that on the Rosh Hashanah prior to my son's birth, the Satmar Rebbe gave a very special *berachah* before the blowing of the *shofar*. He said that he fervently hoped that women who had been married for several years without having been granted the gift of children, should be blessed with children that year.

The night our son was born, the Satmar Rebbe, who usually did not speak on the telephone, made an exception on our behalf. At four o'clock in the morning the *gabbai* called my husband, then the Satmar Rebbe himself took the receiver and wished my husband a heartfelt "*mazel tov.*" The Rebbe indicated that he felt as if a huge responsibility had been lifted from his shoulders. Over the years, he had worried about us and taken it upon himself to look out for our welfare. Now that we were finally blessed with parenthood, my dear uncle felt relieved and happy for us.

After we had our son, we were blessed with two exceptionally fine daughters, who are now married to *rabbanim*, descendents of the great *tzaddikim*, with dear children of their own. When I gaze at

Congregation Yeshurun plays an important role in the religious, civic, and political life in Flatbush and beyond

my family as we sit around the *seder* table, I always remind myself that the very final solution is dictated by Heaven.

Over the years, our house has been filled with the laughter of children and grandchildren, shining links in the golden chain of our Chassidic lineage. This is our greatest vengeance against the Germans and their collaborators, who sought to liquidate the Jewish population in every corner of the world, starting with European Jewry. In spite of their intense and cruel efforts to break our bodies and spirits, the Germans failed miserably in their efforts. My husband and I, together with all the other survivors, are living proof of that. We were uprooted from our old lives and set down in foreign soil, where we grew new roots and began to sprout more branches on our family tree. We are alive and well, and are seeing our future generations enter this world. Now, half a century after the end of the war and the fall — in shame and disgrace — of the supposedly invincible Third Reich, Hitler and his collaborators are gone, while we, both individual Jews and the Jewish people as a whole, continue to thrive and grow.

Hitler thought he had his Final Solution — but we know the truth. When my husband, R' Rubin, visited the bunker in which Hitler *ym"sh* stayed, he scrawled on the wall: It is Heaven which has Its own "Final Solution."

Epilogue

"Write it in the book, it shall be remembered."

WITH THESE WORDS, MY VENERABLE RELATIVE, THE GRAND Rabbi of Altshtut, Rabbi Aron Yeruchem, *zt"l*, began his emotion-packed book, *"Lo Tishkach,"* "Do Not Forget." He declares that he cannot find suitable wording to fully describe the scope and the depth of the Jewish suffering, or of the Nazi-German brutality and inhumanity to other human beings. Indeed, one could say that we would have to invent a whole new vocabulary to properly catalogue and describe the enormity and the sheer, unrestrained viciousness of the campaign of torture and mass murder, begun by the German and Austrian Nazis against the helpless Jews, and eagerly carried on by their many willing collaborators from many nations. And even then, words might still fail us in trying to fully detail to those fortunate enough not to have experienced firsthand, what actually happened.

The book *"Lo Tishkach"* was published in 1949, in Yiddish, but Rabbi Yeruchem requested that its powerful message be expressed in English, as well. In this memoir, I have followed his advice never to forget that which was so cruelly done to us, and through us to all of humanity. But more than half a century has now passed. Our emphasis today is to look ahead, as well as backward, and to see the sun which now shines upon us, rather than the hurricane through which we have come.

Let us quote from the Book of *Exodus* (3:2): *"v'hasneh einenu ukal —* and the bush is not consumed."* What does this phrase symbolize?

During the time of Israel's greatest suffering, the Egyptian ruler Pharaoh slaughtered Jewish babies and bathed in their blood. An angel, meanwhile, appeared to Moses in the deep burning flame of a bush. The fire was furious, but the bush remained intact. Moses wondered in amazement: I observe here a Higher Power. Why does the fire not consume the bush?

The Divine Presence proclaimed, "I am the G–d of Abraham, Isaac and Jacob. I have come to rescue My people." The A–mighty further told Moses that He would bring them to the Land of Israel.

Why did this promise come by way of a raging, burning fire? And why by way of a *sneh*, a bush? It is most likely that the meaning and essence of this amazing happening is the promise of the Eternal One for Israel! Even when a ruler destroys innocent Jewish babies, even when a fire burns with all its might, the eternal existence of the bush remains: *"V'HASNEH EINENU UKAL!* And the bush is not consumed."* But what is the meaning and the symbolism of the *sneh*?

This we will discuss in a moment. But before we proceed, let us indicate that gentile thinkers have always pondered the mystique of Jewish survival. Allow me to paraphrase what Mark Twain wrote about the Jews in 1897.[1]

---

1. This widely-known quotation is taken from his essay, "Concerning the Jews," which appeared in the September, 1898 issue of *Harper's New Monthly Magazine*.

He said that although Jews constitute only one percent of the human race, their prominence and importance is out of proportion to the smallness of their numbers. The Jew has contributed greatly in literature, science, art and music, "also way out of proportion to the weakness of his numbers." All of this has come in the midst of pogroms and Holocausts — while their opponents, including the Babylonians and the Romans, have been brought down and defeated. These other peoples, the writer said, "made a vast noise, and they are gone," while the Jew "saw them all, beat them all, and is now what he always was, exhibiting no decadence, no infirmities of age, no weakening of his parts, no slowing of his energies, no dulling of his alert and aggressive mind. All things are mortal, but the Jew; all other forces pass, but he remains. What is the secret of his immortality?"

The answer is: the promise of He Who created you and me, as well as the great, humane nation in which we live, that our bush will never be consumed! This answers that ringing question. Coming back to the question, "Why a bush?" let us note that this is the only place in all the Scriptures where the word *hasneh* appears. Let me repeat this last statement for emphasis — only in *Exodus* 3:2 do we find *"hasneh."* Just here — when the A–mighty promises Moses that the Children of Israel will not be consumed and that He will bring them to the Land of Israel.

It is explained among Chassidic Rebbes that according to *Gematria,* teachings derived from the numerical value of each letter, the Hebrew word *hasneh* has the same numerical value as the last letters of the verse, *Shema Yisrael!* The *Shema,* of course, was the very last verse that the martyrs of the Roman Empire heroically sang out, as well as the verse that millions of Holocaust victims called out before dying, while they still lived as Jews.

Let me relate one such frightening episode. When one group of *kedoshim* said aloud *"Shema Yisrael"* before stepping into the Zyklon B shower, a monstrous Nazi-German SS creature decorated with a medal, probably given to him for "great achievement in barbaric cruelty," stopped one Polish Jewish victim and barked at him, "What does that mean, that I hear so many of you repeating it?" The victim told him that the *Shema*, of course, means "Hear O Israel, the L–rd our G–d, the L–rd is One" — the age-old "pledge of allegiance" to G–d's unity and unchallenged authority. "Go on," the German scoffed. "This will not help you. We will rule Europe for the next one thousand years."

This episode allows us to thoroughly understand the meaning of the prayer, "*Asei l'maan sh'mecho*, A–mighty, help us for the honor of Your own Name." That subhuman German echoed the crazed belief that millions of Germans and Austrians clung to with almost religious fervor — that theirs was supposedly destined to be the "Thousand Year Reich" and that they had the "right to rule over other people whom they thought were their inferiors."

However, the eternal promise of the burning bush says otherwise! You, Mr. Nazi Barbarian, are dead. Your murderous, subhuman "Fuhrer" died like a wild animal even while denouncing his old Nazi Party comrade, Himmler, and your generals as traitors. My own captor in Selish, the mass murderer Eichmann, was hanged in Jerusalem. The name "Nuremberg" became the symbol of the indictment and verdict of German guilt for the most horrific event in the history of humankind. I quote former German Chancellor Helmut Kohl, who declared in 1996 at the opening of a Holocaust-related exhibition in Wansee,[2] "The Wansee results is a crime whose immensity overwhelms the capacity for human comprehension." The German nation has even now just barely recovered from the unprecedented shameful inhumanity of the cruel murder of innocent humans.

But we — the intended Jewish victims — are here. The bush was not consumed, nor were we. We are rebuilding our ruins, reestablishing our families and reconstructing the Jewish Nation, may it please the A–mighty.

Our Sages explain the meaning of the A–mighty's promise to Abraham: "Your children will be like the dust of the earth," meaning

---

2. A Berlin suburb which was the site of the notorious conference in January, 1942, at which officials of the German government drew up plans for "The Final Solution."

everyone will step on that dust, but the dust will outlive them all. Mr. Twain, the answer to your logical question lies in the promise of G–d to Moses, "… and the bush will not be consumed." Hence, this book, *The "Final Solution" is Life: A Chassidic Dynasty's Story of Survival and Rebuilding.*

A SPEAKER ONCE DISCUSSED THE SYMBOLISM OF THE WORD *HASNEH*, the bush. In Kabbalah, the sacred Jewish texts seeking deep mysti-

Hasneh cal meanings, *Gematria*, which we have already defined as the finding of meanings in words and phrases through the numerical value of Hebrew letters, is a very important component. A venerable, noted Rebbe has taught that if we examine the lines that King David wrote in *Psalms* (44:7), "*ki olecho horagnu kol hayom,* for You, [the A–mighty,] we were killed every day," we find that the first letters add up to 120 [*kaf*=20; *ayin*=70; *hei*=5; *kof*=20; *hei*=5].

The four letters of *hasneh* also add up to 120 [*hei*=5; *samech*=60; *nun*=50 *hei*=5]. Likewise, the final letters of the verse, *Shema,* as previously indicated, add up to 120 [*ayin*=70; *lamed*=30; *hei*=5; *vav*=6; *hei*=5; *daled*=4]. The number 120, of course, has further significance in that it is the exact number of years that Moses lived. So, by appearing in the form of a burning bush when He gave the great prophet the promise for the rescue of His people, the A–mighty signaled all of this to Moses — that like the bush, Jews would be burned; that victims would die with the *Shema* on their lips; but ultimately, the Jewish nation would not be consumed.

The word *"Shoah,"* the commonly used name for the Holocaust, means utter and catastrophic destruction, and certainly, Hitler meant it to be such for all of us. But now, some 50 years later, the tide has turned. The sun is shining again and the Jewish people are blooming, please G–d, *kein yirbu,* may it come to be so and may there be more to come. Without keeping this fact in mind, the history of the Holocaust is an incomplete story, like a body without a soul.

The moral of the Holocaust focuses on this centrally important theme. I have often told my children, grandchildren and other close relatives that, in spite of everything, I have survived. I am here to bear witness to what I saw and personally experienced during those horrific years: being interned with my husband and mother in the Selish ghetto just weeks after our wedding; the ghastly trip in the cattle car to Birkenau; the death march to Stutthof; the Ukrainian guards smashing my husband's leg in Ebensee; being trapped in a burning barn; the struggle to overcome typhus after liberation; the frustrating search for my husband and other surviving relatives.

Yet, out of all that suffering and the brushes with death, a glimmer of sunlight broke through the dark storm clouds. I was reunited with my husband. My esteemed uncle, the Satmar Rebbe and his Rebbetzin miraculously survived, as did several of my husband's siblings and other relatives. We began a new life in America, rebuilding our shattered family and establishing a Chassidic *kehillah* in Flatbush.

A *bachur* once approached us and said, "Seeing you here, in front of me — after all the horrors you experienced — has made me realize that the A–mighty G–d does, indeed, rule the universe!"

The *bachur's* insight and words were wise. In one short statement, he explained why we, *Am Yisrael*, managed to rise out of the ashes and rebuild our roots while those who sought to destroy us are gone.

Rebbetzin Chana Rubin
Muzsayer Rebbetzin